Forum for Linguistics and Translation Studies

ISSN 2836-645X

Forum for Linguistics and Translation Studies (FLTS) is an international, peer-reviewed journal. FLTS welcomes submissions originating in translation studies and linguistic research, specifically in the fields of translation and interpretation, syntax, semantics, pragmatics, cognitive-functional linguistic topics, language teaching and language policy, philosophy of language. FLTS caters to a comprehensive audience, ranging from language researchers, linguists, teachers, educationalists, interpreters, translators and those with a general interest in language and linguistics. The journal aims to encourage the free exchange of information between researchers by being a forum for the constructive discussion and debate of issues in both theoretical and applied research. The journal welcomes all types of paper from traditional 'full' research articles, review articles and book reviews. Papers based on the findings of corpus or experiment-oriented research are particularly welcomed.

Editor-in-Chief: Prof. Feng Duan (Sichuan University)

Executive Editor: Dr. Guocai Zeng (Sichuan University)

Editorial Board

Prof. Bingjun Yang (Shanghai Jiao Tong University)

Dr. David Porter (Hunan Normal University)

Prof. Deming Mei (Shanghai International Studies University)

Prof. Emma Borg (Reading University)

Prof. Gang He (East China Normal University)

Prof. Hans Boas (The University of Texas at Austin)

Prof. Hongru Li (Heilongjiang University)

Prof. Ian Mason (Heriot Watt University)

Prof. Jordan Zlatev (Lund University)

Prof. Kasia Jaszczolt (University of Cambridge)

Prof. Limin Liu (Sichuan University)

Prof. Longgen Liu (Shanghai Jiao Tong University)

Prof. Najar Robyn (Flinders University)

Prof. Petra Broomans (University of Groningen)

Prof. Philippe Humblé (Vrije Universiteit Brussel)

Prof. Shihong Du (Southwest University)

Prof. Yin Wang (Sichuan International Studies University)

Prof. Yuhai Peng (Sichuan University)

Prof. Zaijiang Wei (Guangdong International Studies University)

Forum for Linguistics and Translation Studies is published biannually by Colorado Academic Press, USA.

ADD: 1758 Emerson St, Denver, CO 80218

Website: www.capjournals.com

Forum for Linguistics and Translation Studies

ISSN 2836-645X

Volume 1, Issue 1, June 2023

Contents

Framing in Political Translation and Interpretation: A Comparable Corpus-based Analysis into Cross-lingual Narratives
Minxia Hu and Shuangming Huang..1

A Study on Default Subjects in Chinese
Xiaoxia Pan...22

Mind Modeling of Bodily Motion-Emotion Expressions
Hongbo Li...32

Investigating the Unexplored Dimension: Instrumentalizing the Domain-Specific Manifestation of Foreign Language Tolerance of Ambiguity
Shijie Wang...46

A Contrastive Study of Food Metaphors in Chinese and English under Extended Conceptual Metaphor Theory
Zhongzhong Zhang...61

A Contrastive Study of Chinese Learners' Implicit Semantic Learning of Shape Classifiers in English and Chinese Contexts
Yaoyu Hu..75

A Study on Vowel Acoustic Phonetics of Elementary English Learners in Chengdu and Chongqing Sub-Cluster in Southwest Mandarin
Mengxing Fu...91

Foreign Language Learners' Emotions in China (2012-2022): A Review and the Prospect
Xilin Xu..102

On the English Existential and Presentational Constructions: An Interactive Construction Grammar Perspective
Ziyan Li and Xia Guo...118

A Cognitive Approach to the Syntactic Features and Semantic Functions of Chinese Noun Classifier *Tiao*
Qiuyi Huang...129

Framing in Political Translation and Interpretation: A Comparable Corpus-based Analysis into Cross-lingual Narratives

Minxia Hu[1], Shuangming Huang[2]
[1]Sichuan University
[2]Utrecht University

Abstract

Based on two comparable parallel corpora since the COVID outbreak, this article examined self-framing in the political translation and interpretation of the Communist Party of China (CPC) by Chinese state actors and other-framing by the journalists of the *New York Times* (*NYT*). Results from analyses of keywords, exposures, collocates, synonyms, and semantic networks showed that: (1) "CPC" was the dominant self-label while the "Chinese Communist Party" ("CCP") was the common translation used by critical other-framers. Such disparity seemed to be motivated by ideology-based framing beyond the tradition of usage. (2) The mention of CPC/CCP became increasingly frequent in 2020 and 2021, with self-framing interest peaking in 2021 for the CPC centenary and other-framing interest peaking in 2020 for accountability over the initial COVID-19 response, Hong Kong and Xinjiang issues and the US's travel ban of party members and families. (3) An image of good governance and moral legitimacy self-constructed in Chinese official discourse stood in sharp contrast with that of an authoritarian dictatorship in conflicts with its own people and external powers in the other-constructed *NYT* discourse. The modernity of Chinese characteristics was reviewed to explain the disparity between China's development-oriented framing and the human rights-based framing of Western media presented by *NYT*. This study of the cross-lingual frames for the largest and longest ruling party in the world shed light on the great ideological and power rivalry in the post-COVID era.

Keywords

political translation and interpretation; self-frame; other-frame; ideological and power rivalry; COVID-19; corpus-based analysis

---

Corresponding author: Shuangming Huang, Institute for Language Sciences, Department of Languages, Literature and Communication, Utrecht University, Utrecht, Netherlands. E-mail address: s.huang2@uu.nl.

1. Introduction

With China's growing economic integration into the world and with the evolving turbulences of COVID-19, top leaders of China have repeatedly called for improving the narratives around the Chinese nation and its ruling party (Xi, 2013, 2019, 2021). The Communist Party of China (CPC) was born in 1921 after the Chinese people, intellectuals in particular, underwent a great awakening amidst foreign invasions and humiliations and after Marxism-Leninism became the guiding ideology rallying the Chinese workers' movement (Xi, 2021-7-1). In the early days, the party was named the Chinese Communist Party (CCP), indicating the strong influence and support of the Communist International. A young Mao Zedong himself wrote down "C. C. P." on a blackboard as he explained the party to the poor peasant members in a village (Sun & Li, 2021). Five generations of communist leaders, i.e. Mao Zedong (1949–1976), Deng Xiaoping (1978–1992), Jiang Zemin (1993–2003), Hu Jintao (2003–2013), and Xi Jinping (2013–now), have ruled China since they won the civil war against the Nationalist Party (or Kuomintang, KMT) led by Jiang Jieshi (or Chiang Kai-shek), who fled to Taiwan from the mainland after the defeat. There are currently over 95 million formal Chinese Communist members in China (Ministry of Organization, CPC, 2021). This large membership is not a result of rapid non-selective recruitment today. The minimum wait time from submitting an application to becoming a formal member is three years and three months, according to the CPC Charter.

The end of 2019 saw the sudden outbreak of a novel coronavirus (COVID-19) in the Chinese city of Wuhan. As the number of cases increased rapidly worldwide, the epidemic was declared a global pandemic by the World Health Organization (WHO, 2020). Since then, the pandemic response by different actors has been presented in ideologically influenced narratives (Harper & Rhodes, 2022). In the studies on the US public's adoption of the COVID-19 mitigation measures, such as social distancing, liberals were found to be more likely to practice mitigation, while conservatives less so (Christensen et al., 2020; Hart et al., 2020). The main motive behind China's COVID narrative was believed to court favor and support for the government both at home and abroad, through a centralized and positive responsibility-solution frame (Lemus-Delgado, 2022; Zhang, 2022), or for pragmatic reasons, with the state working as a "salesman" to promote economic interests (Ji & Liu, 2022).

The pandemic has posed discursive challenges and opportunities for political leaders, who recruited various strategies to enact authority and win public support (Jaworska & Vásquez, 2022). For instance, both US President Donald Trump and UK prime minister Boris Johnson adopted a masculinist "strong leader" frame to hide their recklessness-led infection and incoherent pandemic response (Jones, 2021). The German chancellor Angela Merkel leveraged a "national unity" frame to explain why the COVID restrictions were necessary while sympathizing with personal freedom being limited (Jaworska, 2021). Cyril Ramaphosa, President of South Africa, constructed a metaphor of the nation as a "family" and the national addresses as "family meetings" to invoke trust and compliance (Hunt, 2021). Indian prime minister Narendra Modi developed a "duty" frame to convince his countrymen that compliance was expected service (Sambaraju, 2022). New Zealand's prime minister Jacinda Ardern employed a "team" frame to resonate with the country's sporting culture (Hafner, C. A., & Sun, T. (2021). New York governor Andrew Cuomo exploited affective, relational family stories as evidence to support the stay-at-home policy (Vásquez, 2021). In China, the CPC general secretary Xi Jinping led a "people's war against

COVID," achieving admirable results at the expense of personal and economic freedom. The country only had 25,491 deaths and 7,026,344 confirmed cases of COVID-19 from January 3, 2020, to September 16, 2022, in a population of more than 1.4 billion (WHO Dashboard-China, 2022). In India, a country with a comparable population, the same period saw 528,273 deaths and 44,522,777 cases (WHO Dashboard–India, 2022). The Indian economy, however, did become the fifth largest in the world during this period.

In general, politicians favor the war metaphor, and the media try to "reframe" the COVID response (e.g. Bates, 2020; Semino, 2021). War metaphors used in the COVID context might prepare the population for hard times, convey compassion and empathy, facilitate behavioral change and acceptance of extraordinary sacrifices and boost national resilience (Seixas, 2021). However, war metaphors were not found to significantly affect decision-making in empirical studies (Panzeri, Di Paola & Domaneschi, 2021).

The mediatization of politics has increased the importance of the media on political processes and actors (Strömbäck, 2008). Consistent growth was found in the percentage of articles with a media-centric focus in political communication research over the past decade (Bucy & Evans, 2021). However, recent research investigating political party leadership in the COVID response seemed to exclusively focus on either the state or the media as the dominant actors, rather than offering cross-sectoral self-vs.-other comparison. To fill this gap, this article adopts an ideological dichotomy of *self vs. other* (Van Dijk, 1998) to compare the interpretive frames of the CPC constructed by the party state itself and a critical other, the *New York Times*. Four specific questions on the framing of the CPC since the COVID outbreak are addressed through analyses of large-scale comparable corpora:

Q1. How is the party labeled in the Chinese and *NYT* discourse?
Q2. How prominently is the CPC framed in the Chinese and *NYT* discourse?
Q3. What are the key topics related to the CPC in the self and other frames?
Q4. What are the framing strategies used by the Chinese and *NYT* framers?

2. Literature review

2.1. Conceptual roots of framing

The theoretical roots of framing can be traced to psychology and sociology (Pan & Kosicki, 1993). The psychological and cognitive origins of framing lie in the experiments by Kahneman and Tversky (1979, 1984). They examined how different framing of essentially identical scenarios could lead people to different decisions and value judgments. With only bounded rationality, people often rely on their fast, intuitive and emotional thinking system, rather than the slow, deliberative and logical system for decision-making (Simon, 1982; Kahneman, 2003, 2011). Such psychological tendency points to the necessity of frames in a complex environment as "persistent patterns of cognition, interpretation, and presentation, of selection, emphasis, and exclusion" (Gitlin, 1980: 7). Framing assigns narratives to a *schema*, which is a scheme, pattern or template made up by a multitude of phrases, sentences or arguments, to be used for inference and definition of truth (Corcoran & Hamid, 2016). Framing involves the cognitive processes of "moral evaluations, causal reasoning, appeals to principles, and recommendations for treatment of problems" (Weaver, 2007:146).

Meanwhile, the sociological and communicative constructs of framing assume that people construct realities based on salient yet incomplete information. Individuals activate certain frameworks to process information, organize experience and make judgments (Goffman, 1974, 1981). Framing does not necessarily mean that communicators would try to deceive their audiences, but simply to reduce issue complexity given the constraints of communication (Gans, 1979). Framing can be understood as a more refined version of agenda setting (McCombs, 2004). When communicators cannot tell people "what to think" but "what to think about" (Cohen, 1963: 13), agenda setters try to get time and attention from the audience to an issue while framers construct "the label and interpretive schema" for the issue (Scheufele & Tewksbury, 2007: 14).

To frame in a communicative context is to select some aspects of a perceived reality and make them more salient in such a way as to promote a specific (a) problem definition, (b) causal interpretation, (c) moral evaluation, and/or (d) treatment recommendation (Entman, 1993: 52). First, a frame is defined only in relation to a specific issue, event or political actor (Entman, 2004: 23-24). Second, in causal attribution, frames are classified as either *episodic* (a one-time event) or *thematic* (a broader trend). More responsibility was attributed to agents for thematic than for episodic frames (Iyengar, 1991). Third, a set of "culturally available frames" in elite discourse can be utilized for moral support of a specific stance (Gamson & Modigliani 1987: 144). Framers make meaning by embedding their frames in larger socio-cognitive systems (Gamson, 1992). Lastly, treatment recommendation is validated or invalidated through different framing. Positive or negative attributes of frames often lead to corresponding evaluations (Wanta & Tarasevich, 2019: 4). For instance, under the frame of "free speech," 85% of respondents would favor allowing a hate group to hold a political rally, whereas only 45% would if the frame was "given the risk of violence" (Sniderman & Bullock, 2004).

2.2. Framing actors, processes and effects

The media are the major primary sources of political information (McCombs & Shaw, 1972). The political elite use speeches, posters, press conferences, debates, letters and articles to communicate their agenda and frames to the public through traditional and social media (Gonçalves, 2018). Such framing is branded with different terminologies such as *propaganda* (Lasswell, 1927), *political advertising* (Kaid & Holtz-Bacha, 2006), *political communication management* (Johnson, 2008), *political public relations* (Strömbäck & Kiousis, 2011), *political marketing* (Lees-Marshment, 2012) and *political reputation management* (Schnee, 2015). Political or media frames turn fluid reality into meaning structures through "a chain of signification" (Reese, 2001: 15; Sieff, 2003). Political and media actors can frame the situations, attributes, choices, actions, issues, responsibility and news (Hallahan, 1999). This process involves "sources, journalists, and audience members functioning in a shared culture" (Kosicki, 1993: 55). Hence, the frame effects are influenced by the credibility of sources, strength and frequency of competitive journalistic coverage and the ideological leanings and knowledge of the audience.

Min & Luqiu (2021) found that the perceived credibility of sources played a significant role in mediating the persuasive effects of Chinese international propaganda among US and South Korean audiences. Shehata & Strömbäck (2021) only confirmed positive learning effects on political attitudes from traditional and online news websites. Lau, Rogers & Love (2021) found that although explicit attention to issue stories was associated with greater perceived importance, random exposure had no causal effect. Edy and Meirick (2007) found that audiences combined elements of a war frame and a crime frame in their understanding of September 11 and the Afghanistan War, meaning that the persuasive effects might be a function of competing frames.

The ideological divide and knowledge disparity of the audience play an important role in modulating the framing effects. Ideology has a "group-based and self-serving nature" (van Dijk, 1998: 129). This often causes the polarization of in-groups and out-groups, or us and them (ibid: 69), forming an ideological square that (a) expresses/emphasizes information that is positive about us; (b) expresses/emphasizes information that is negative about them; (c) suppresses/de-emphasizes information that is positive about them; and (d) suppresses/de-emphasizes information that is negative about us (ibid: 267). That is why campaigns are more likely to use conservative frames in Republican-leaning districts and liberal frames in Democratic-leaning districts (Arbour, 2014). Ideology about the fundamental right and wrong plays an important role in public opinion (Ciuk & Rottman, 2021). As for knowledge disparity, repetition of frames might have a greater effect on less knowledgeable individuals, whereas more knowledgeable individuals are more likely to compare the relative strength of alternative frames (Chong & Druckman, 2007). People who have a heterogeneous knowledge base are more resistant to fake stories than those who only know treatment recommendations congruent with their ideology (Rhodes, 2021).

Power and ideology are exercised through discourse (Fowler et al., 1979; Wodak, 1998). Uncovering hidden features in discursive practices makes explicit how social practices are shaped and the subsequent effects on power and ideological structure (Fairclough, 1992). Therefore, this study combines framing and discourse analysis to examine the narratives on the Communist Party of China produced by the self (the Chinese state actors) and the other (the *New York Times*).

3. Materials and methods

3.1. Corpus design

In order to address the research questions, a comparable parallel corpus was built (fig. 1). According to Baker (1995: 234), comparable corpora "should cover a similar domain, variety of language and time span, and be of comparable length." In terms of parallel corpora, McEnery et al. (2000: 179) define it as corpora that consist of paired source texts (ST) and target texts (TT). The corpus used in this study consists of four separate sub-corpora, made up of the source texts drawn from Chinese official discourse (hereafter ST-CODC), its English target texts (hereafter TT-CODC), and the source texts drawn from the *New York Times* (hereafter ST-*NYTC*) and its Chinese target texts (hereafter TT-*NYTC*). Both ST-CODC and TT-*NYTC*, and TT-CODC and ST-*NYTC* are in the same language and similar in size, and cover contents on the same subject matter (i.e., the CPC) and over the same time span (2020-2021), which makes them comparable. The CODC contains paired original Chinese and translated English texts, and the *NYTC* contains paired original English and translated Chinese, which makes them parallel. The information of the corpus is summarized as follows (also in table 1):

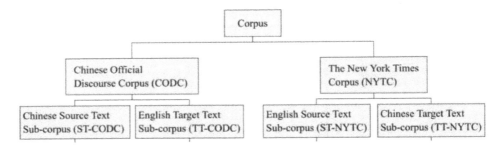

Figure 1. Corpus structure

3.1.1. The Chinese official discourse corpus (Hereafter CODC)

The CODC includes 664 parallel texts, which consist of (a) 112 speeches, addresses and remarks by Chinese leaders; (b) 504 transcribed state-level regular press conferences held by the Ministry of Foreign Affairs of the People's Republic of China; and (c) 48 official documents, including statements, declarations, resolutions, white papers and government work reports. Data can be accessed on their official websites, www.fmprc.gov.cn and www.gov.cn. The corresponding English translations were completed by China's institutional translators and interpreters and uploaded on the websites. In total, CODC contains 3,979,098 tokens.

3.1.2. The New York Times corpus (hereafter NYTC)

The *New York Times* (hereafter *NYT*) is among the top three most popular US daily newspapers. The *NYT* might have a special interest in China and its ruling party, given the fact that it was banned in China due to its report on a CPC leadership corruption scandal in 2012. The image represented by the *NYT* may be representative of its conflict with the Chinese official discourse. When collecting data on the *NYT*, first, "zhongguo gongchangdang" and its abbreviation "zhonggong" was used as two search words on the official website (Chinese edition www.cn.NYTimes.com) to extract news reports relevant to the CPC. The search results generated 3,515 news reports. Second, all articles were revisited and checked by a self-written Python script to ensure only those English/Chinese parallel texts published during 2020–2021 remained. As a result, there are 2,075 parallel articles collected with 5,878,280 tokens in total.

Table 1. Corpus profile

Sub-corpus	Corpus size	Materials
CODC	664 parallel texts	2020: 259 press conferences & 62 speeches
ST-CODC	1,932,084 Chinese tokens	21 official documents
TT-CODC	2,047,014 English tokens	2021: 245 press conferences & 50 speeches
Total	3,979,098 tokens	27 official documents
NYTC	2075 parallel news reports	2020: 1108 articles about China from the *NYT*
ST-*NYTC*	2,914,340 English tokens	
TT-*NYTC*	2,963,940 Chinese tokens	2021: 967 articles about China from the *NYT*
Total	5,878,280 tokens	

3.2 Corpus analytical tools

This research adopted the approach of corpus-based analysis, including keyword lists, concordances and semantic network analysis. The main tools included Python for data collection and cleaning, Sketch Engine (Kilgarriff et al., 2014) for corpus analysis, and KH coder (https://khcoder.net/en/), an open-source tool for semantic network analysis. For the first step, the frequency function was utilized to examine the distribution of "CPC" and "CCP" occurrences in CODC and *NYTC*. The second step involved generating keyword lists from the concordance corpora to investigate the salient topics around the critical event. Next, the frames formed in the discourses were compared through the Word Sketch collocations of "CPC" and "CCP." Finally, a semantic network analysis was conducted to compare the functional clusters of the self-frame and other-frame (Segev, 2022).

4. Results and discussion

4.1 Self-label vs. other-label

An apparent discrepancy between the lexical choices of the party name was revealed in the self-discourse and other-discourse (table 2). Specifically, in the self-narrated TT-CODC, in over 70% of the cases, "the Communist Party of China" (171 times) or its acronym, "CPC," (730 times) were adopted. All other expressions occurred less than fifty times. The retrieval of the concordance lines of these other expressions revealed that they were predominantly used by foreign journalists in press conferences' Q&A sessions. Based on the data, it can be concluded that in China's self-presentation, "the Communist Party of China" or "CPC" was the commonly accepted translation. In comparison, in other-framed ST-*NYTC*, there were 12 different English expressions for the party, without one being used more than 40%. Among them, the top 3 expressions were "Chinese Communist Party" (424 times), "the Communist Party" (340 times) and "the Party" (326 times). The "Communist Party of China/CPC," the standard expression adopted by the Chinese state, occurred less than 1%.

The uniform self-label of CPC and the rejection of such self-label by critical other-framers have several interpretations. Complex linguistic and non-linguistic dynamics may be at play. China's self-label highlights "of" in "the Communist Party of China." The official translators said that this preposition was important to expressing the relationship of a part of something to its whole (Li, 2021). In other words, it was emphasized that the party belongs to China and Chinese people. From the perspective of other-framers, it could be argued that CCP and similar expressions have a much longer linguistic history of use than the CPC expressions. The hard-core CPC members used the CCP label in the early days. Hence, the traditional name was preferred over the will of the named. However, the CPC case was distinguishable from the recent "Belt and Road" (B&R) expression. B&R was widely denounced as a misnomer but nevertheless adopted by native English media (Wang, 2021). Is it possible for the linguistic discrepancies to have deep sociopolitical roots? It might have reflected the power struggle between China and international society (Buzan & Lawson, 2020). The difference between adoption and non-adoption underscores efforts for stance-taking and meaning-making.

Table 2. Different English expressions of the CPC in TT-CODC & ST-NYTC

Chinese	TT-CODC			ST-NYTC		
	English	Freq.	Percent	English	Freq.	Percent
zhongguo gongchandang	CPC	730	72.21	Chinese/China's Communist Party	424	34.67
	Communist Party of China	171	16.91	the Communist Party	340	27.80
	Chinese Communist Party	48	4.75	the Party	326	26.66
	the Party	38	3.76	CCP	42	3.43
	it	15	1.48	(China's) ruling Communist Party	30	2.45
	CCP	6	0.59	Communist Party of China	21	1.72
	the Communist Party	3	0.30	it	14	1.14
				Chinese Communist	11	0.90
				Chinese/China	6	0.49
				Communist regime	4	0.33
				Chinese /China's Party	3	0.25
				Communist China	2	0.16

4.2 Exposure made by the self and other

This section examines the exposure that the CPC received in 2020–2021. As shown in Figure 2, CPC was mentioned 492 times in TT-CODC in 2020, concerning topics such as the CPC's role in COVID-19, its track record of governance and China-US relations. As 2021 marked the centenary of the founding of the CPC, the subject was brought up more often in the year, occurring 633 times, up by 28.66%. Common topics included the history and evolution of the CPC, the importance of the CPC's leadership to China and the Party's goals and resolutions. A series of special white papers and resolutions were published to reintroduce the CPC to the world. (e.g., "Resolution of the Central Committee of the Communist Party of China on the Major Achievements and Historical Experience of the Party Over the Past Century," Central Committee of the Communist Party of China, 2021-11-11).

Intriguingly, considerable prominence was also given to CPC in the other-discourse. In ST-NYTC, CPC was mentioned 821 and 627 times in 2021 and 2022. The high exposure of CPC indicates that NYT kept close track of the Party. The year 2020 saw an interest peak in CPC concerning the COVID-19 situation, protests in Hong Kong, and the US travel ban on CPC members (e.g., "US Wants to Bar Members of China's Communist Party. Who Are They?" Mozur, 2020). In 2021, apart from the aforementioned topics, the newspaper covered CPC's centenary celebrations, with reports ranging from its "centennial history" and current policymaking, to speculation on the "next generation of Communist leaders" (e.g., "Follow the Party Forever: China Plans a Communist Birthday Bash." Hernández, 2021).

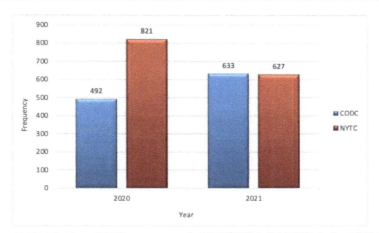

Figure 2. Distribution of CPC occurrences in TT-CODC & ST-*NYTC* during 2020-2021

4.3 Key topics related to the party

This section analyzes topics that are frequently mentioned with the CPC through keyword lists generated by Sketch Engine. *Keywords* refer to the words that are statistically significant in one corpus ("nodes") compared to another corpus ("references") (Scott and Tribble, 2006: 55). They reflect the "focus of the text" (Baker, 2004: 348). Concordance keywords were employed to get a clearer picture of the immediate lexical context around the word of interest (e.g., Marchi, 2010; Taylor, 2010). The CPC node corpus was created with concordance lines of CPC, with 500 characters left and right of the keywords in context (KWIC). The reference corpus was British National Corpus. The top 30 keywords related to CPC in TT-CODC and ST-*NYTC* were extracted and listed in the order of the keyness value (table 3). A close observation of them shows that there are similarities and differences (fig. 3).

In terms of the similarities, there are 10 shared keywords among the top 30 keywords of the two sub-corpora, concerning three main topics: (1) CPC leadership ("China," "Chinese," "Xi," "Jinping," "CPC"). (2) The COVID-19 pandemic ("COVID-19," "Wuhan," "pandemic"). (3) human rights issues (Xinjiang). This indicates that, be it its self-presented image or the other-represented image, Covid-19 and China's leadership were the two main topics by which the CPC's image was constructed.

As for the differences, the CPC was self-framed around three topics in TT-CODC that were uninteresting to the other framer. (1) China's political system. The system features the leadership of CPC ("CPC-led") and the participation of other "non-affiliate" and "non-CPC" parties in China's political life (Chinese People's Political Consultative Conference, "CPPCC"). (2) CPC achievements and legitimacy. The "centenary" celebrations focused on the success in poverty "alleviation" and meeting the goal of building a moderately prosperous society ("xiaokang"). The primary goal of its "people-centered" "endeavors" is to achieve national "rejuvenation." (3) Foreign policy. CPC attaches great importance to boosting "China-US" relations through the "win-win" and "cooperation" approach. The key figures guiding China's US policy are mentioned (state councilor "Jiechi Yang," who was also known as "Tiger Yang" and foreign minister "Yi Wang").

In ST-*NYTC*, the CPC image was deconstructed and reconstructed mainly in the following three other-frames: (1) Critics of CPC. *NYT* pays special attention to high-profile dissidents and whistle-blowers (former high-ranking

CPC members) who openly criticize the CPC ("Zhang," "Ren," "Xu," "Guo"). (2) CPC presence in Chinese tech companies and social media. The focus is on the CPC presence and political tool-making of China's tech companies ("Huawei," "Alibaba") and various social media platforms ("Weibo," "TikTok," "WeChat," "Twitter"). (3) Democracy and human rights issues. A cruel and undemocratic image of CPC was presented in the reports of the human rights abuses of "Uighurs" in "Xinjiang" and the dissent-quashing of "pro-democracy lawmakers" in "Hong Kong."

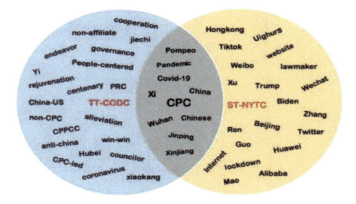

Figure 3. Different and shared keywords related to the CPC in TT-CODC & ST-*NYTC*

Table 3. Top 30 keywords related to the CPC in TT-CODC & ST-*NYTC*

No.	TT-CODC Keyword	Keyness	Freq.	ST-*NYTC* Keyword	Keyness	Freq.
1	CPC	4834.5	1766	CPC	4746	1,752
2	Jinping	1115.3	283	COVID-19	1839.9	491
3	COVID-19	855.4	217	Jinping	1030.9	275
4	Pompeo	719.6	189	Xi	711.2	903
5	alleviation	363	142	Wuhan	705.9	205
6	rejuvenation	352.8	138	Beijing	508.5	787
7	non-affiliate	351.4	89	Xinjiang	453.2	166
8	China-US	351.4	89	Biden	448.4	128
9	CPC-led	349	232	Trump	293.1	280
10	Xinjiang	344.6	120	Internet	237.7	118
11	Wuhan	315.5	87	lockdown	232.8	63
12	Xi	281.7	340	Zhang	229.2	80
13	pandemic	275.8	81	Pompeo	221.6	61
14	Chinese	236	2,276	China	203.2	2,703
15	people-centered	233.3	59	Ren	190.8	62
16	coronavirus	227.3	58	website	184.5	49
17	endeavor	225.1	62	Weibo	180.8	48
18	win-win	216.1	60	TikTok	177	47

19	Hubei	215.9	58	Huawei	173.6	70
20	councilor	207.8	53	Alibaba	169.5	45
21	anti-China	204.2	53	Xu	159.8	61
22	Yi	194.1	78	Guo	154.6	48
23	non-CPC	193.9	49	WeChat	150.8	40
24	PRC	189.5	62	Hong Kong	149.5	1,040
25	CPPCC	183.5	48	Chinese	146.8	1,488
26	cooperation	181.3	576	Twitter	145.4	70
27	China	175.8	2,224	lawmaker	138	51
28	Jiechi	174.2	44	pandemic	135.8	76
29	centenary	166.7	241	Mao	135.3	140
30	xiaokang	161.9	195	Uighurs	134.8	37

4.4 Framing strategies

4.4.1. Collocate analysis —leadership vs. authoritarianism

As reflected in Table 4, TT-CODC and ST-*NYTC* only share a few verbs that collocate with "CPC," including "celebrate," "have," "lead" and "pursue." "Celebrate" ranks high, as the Party was celebrating its 100th birthday in 2021. "Lead" and "pursue" reflect the CPC's status in China and its goals. However, the use of other verbs suggests the two sides hold different judgments on the CPC.

In TT-CODC, the CPC was presented in a leadership frame that represented Chinese people and strove for their good. Its leading role and significant status were highlighted through the repeated use of verbs such as "unite," "remain" and "represent." "Put," "uphold," "strive" and "set" occurred in similar complementary contexts where the CPC "puts people first" "upholds peace, development, equity" and "strives for the well-being of the Chinese people." Another set of verbs underscored the achievements made by the CPC, including how the economy has "grown" stronger with carefully "formulated" plans and how it "succeeded" in lifting people out of poverty and "won" their support (see narrations in example 1).

Example 1:

(1) The CPC united and led the people to rely on themselves and strive to build their homeland with strong determination and concerted effort (white paper, 2021).

(2) CPC has **grown** into the world's largest Marxist governing party with over 98 million members (vice FM Xie Feng, 2021).

(3) CPC has **succeeded** in **leading** the Chinese people to free their minds, seek truth from facts, and advance with the times (white paper, 2021).

(4) Over the past 70-plus years, CPC has **led** the Chinese people in **formulating** and implementing 13 five-year plans (white paper, 2021).

In ST-*NYTC*, the CPC was represented with a focus on its control and authoritarian rule. The most significant verb collocation with CPC was "control," stressing the Party's "absolute" and "hardline" governance. "Seek," "keep," "try" and "want" were repeatedly used to reinforce the stereotypes the West holds toward the Communist

Party. For instance, the CPC "keeps an iron grip on China's political system" and "seeks to expand its ideology and authoritarian vision." Another set of verbs were employed to list the CPC's aggressive actions, including the threat it "poses," restrictions it "imposes," actions it "pushes," policies it "announces" and criticisms it "rejects" (Example 2).

Example 2:

(1) In China, CPC **controls** the courts and heavily **censors** the media. (Bradsher & Lee, 2021-12-08)

(2) CPC is **pushing** through **hardline** actions, including mass surveillance efforts in the mainland and a **crackdown** on pro-democracy activists in Hongkong. (Hernández, 2020-04-22)

(3) China has come under heavy fire from Western countries, especially the United States, Britain and Australia, for its new constrictions on Hong Kong. CPC has aggressively **rejected** those criticisms. (Wang & Buckley, 2020-12-11)

(4) ... to remind people just how much of a danger CPC **poses** to our shared democratic values. (May, 2020-12-22)

(5) CPC **imposes** strict constraints on dissent and public debate. (Chen, 2021-07-21)

Table 4. Top 20 verbs with "CPC" as subject in TT-CODC & ST-*NYTC*

No.	TT-CODC			ST-*NYTC*		
	Lemma	Score	Co-occurrences	Lemma	Score	Co-occurrences
1	lead	10.6	32	control	10.9	35
2	celebrate	8.6	6	celebrate	8.3	5
3	put	8.4	8	seek	8	7
4	uphold	8.4	6	pose	7.8	4
5	remain	8.3	7	impose	7.8	5
6	have	8.2	120	pursue	7.7	3
7	represent	8.1	5	carry	7.7	4
8	unite	8	4	regard	7.6	3
9	strive	8	4	keep	7.6	4
10	formulate	7.9	4	reject	7.5	3
11	create	7.8	4	own	7.4	3
12	take	7.8	8	try	7.4	6
13	come	7.7	5	push	7.2	3
14	set	7.7	4	have	7.2	95
15	grow	7.6	4	want	6.9	3
16	succeed	7.6	3	make	6.8	6
17	exercise	7.5	3	lead	6.8	3
18	win	7.5	3	announce	6.6	3
19	pursue	7.4	3	work	6.6	3
20	consider	7.4	3	use	6.5	3

4.4.2. Semantic network analysis – national unity and development vs excessive control

Figures 4 and 5 display the semantic clusters of the CPC node corpus in TT-CODC and ST-*NYTC* respectively, which group nodes into several clusters of words that tend to appear together in the same sentence using modularity. These words often construct common meanings, and thus enable us to reveal the various themes and frames in the text (Segev, 2022: 26). The size of a node suggests its centrality. The width of the ties indicates the number of sentences in the corpus that mentioned each pair of words (ibid: 29).

There are six clusters in the CPC self-discourse (fig. 4). The largest cluster, "Subgraph 01," centers on two themes: nation-building accomplishments and China-US relations. The CPC has implemented "national" "policies" and "measures" to alleviate "poverty" in China and made contributions to "world peace." It is concerned with diplomatic relations with the US, especially Secretary of State Pompeo's alarming call for the Free World to stand up against Beijing.

"Subgraph 02" introduces the Chinese socialism system and its successful application in China. The word "people" holds a prominent position in this cluster, which corresponds to CPC's governance philosophy of representing the "fundamental interests" of the people. Under the leadership of "CPC Central Committee" with comrade "Xi Jinping" at the core, CPC blazed the "path of socialism with Chinese characteristics" and has won "strong support" from the people. In the fight against the COVID pandemic, it "makes all-out efforts" and always puts the "life and health" of the people first.

"Subgraph 03" highlights "development" under the CPC rule. Politically, it has established a "new socialist model" ratified by the "National Congress." Economically, it's committed to "building a moderately prosperous society" and achieving "common development." Socially, it "continues" to "promote progress" and "protect basic human rights."

"Subgraph 04" emphasizes the two "centenary" goals. The first centenary goal had been reached by 2021: with the "founding" and "leadership" of the "party," China not only won independence and victory against "foreign" aggressions and invasions for the "first time" in modern "history," but also made "great achievements" in socioeconomic undertakings. Objectives for the second "centenary" (in 2049) were listed. "Subgraph 05" focuses on China's "political system," "governance," rule of "law" and principles" of "cooperation with other parties or states." "Subgraph 06" stresses China's efforts in promoting "democracy" and "upholding" the rules and norms of the "international/global community" as a major developing "country/power."

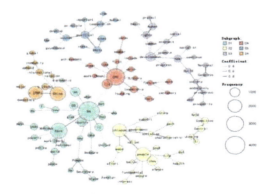

Figure 4. CPC's Semantic Clusters in TT-CODC

In comparison, semantic clusters are more scattered in ST-*NYTC*, with a total of 11 subgraphs. Before the functional analysis of these clusters, "Subgraph 05/09/11" are excluded because they only contain commonly-used non-ideological words ("you" "she" "do" "not" "last week/month."

The largest cluster, "Subgraph 01," discusses the rule of "CPC" on diverse issues. For CPC's domestic relations with state and non-state actors (the Chinese "government," "state," "officials," the "people," "party members"), the newspaper recognizes CPC's capacity to mobilize ("call"), but its oppressive "control" and "rule" over non-governmental "groups" appear more frequently in the context. In addition, it is concerned about CPC's "political" campaign around the "world" through state media such as "(global) times." It reports opinions from CPC's key personalities ("who," "former").

"Subgraph 02/07/10" includes similar ideology-loaded terms for CPC's controversial handling of Taiwan, Hong Kong and Xinjiang affairs. Cluster "Subgraph 02" includes "authority," "system," "police" and "Taiwan," stressing the undemocratic system, police enforcement and CPC's authoritarian ruling in Taiwan. Cluster "Subgraph 07" contains "Xinjiang" and "rights," concerning the human rights violation in Xinjiang. Cluster "Subgraph 10" contains "Hong (Kong)," "protest," "national" "security" and "law," referring to the implementation of national security law and crackdown on protests in Hong Kong.

"Subgraph 03" deals with the CPC's response during the "COVID-19" "outbreak." The Chinese city of "Wuhan" "became" the first in the world to undergo city-wide lockdown to reduce "cases." CPC's "campaigns" to advocate the superiority of its governance model and mute "public" dissatisfaction were criticized severely. "Subgraph 04" reflects the new developments in "China"-"US" relations and the pivot of the "foreign" policy of the "Trump administration." Limiting the impact of the US-China trade war on the "global economy" was considered a priority. "Subgraph 06" focuses on Chinese media and companies. This cluster echoes one of the findings found in key topics that *NYT* is concerned that Chinese "companies/businesses" and "social networks/news media" are turned into CPC tools for political campaigns. "Subgraph 08" focuses on the power of Xi Jinping as the supreme CPC leader.

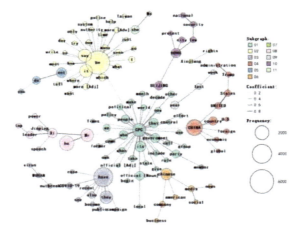

Figure 5. CPC's Semantic Clusters in ST-*NYTC*

4.4.3. Thesaurus analysis—legitimacy vs. dictatorship

With Sketch Engine's Thesaurus function, word clouds of CPC's synonym lists in TT-CODC and ST-*NYTC* were generated (figs. 6 and 7). The circle size refers to frequency, and the distance from the center indicates the similarity score.

In TT-CODC, the top 10 words that are highly synonymous to CPC include "Party," "Committee," "UN," "government," "States," "Jinping," "Xinjiang," "US," "side" and "politician." The CPC is self-represented as a "party" led by its Central "Committee," with Xi "Jinping" at its core, fulfilling its duty just as other legitimate "government" "administration" does, such as those in the "US" and "Russia." It represented "China" in international relations, both bilateral and multi-lateral ("Australia," "Japan," "ROK," "Pakistan," "Africa" "ASEAN," "EU"), and in international "organizations" such as the "UN." A lot of state or institutional actors were presented.

In ST-*NYT*C, the top 10 words associated with the CPC include "party," "Xi," "government," "administration," "Beijing," "authority," "Taliban," "US," "Jinping" and "state." These synonyms indicate that similar to that in TT-CODC, the CPC was regarded as the "party" led by President "Xi" "Jinping." It represented the "official" "government" and "authority" in "Beijing," with the "Trump"/"Biden" "administration" as its political counterparts. Interestingly, "Taliban" ranked seventh in the CPC synonym network. A closer examination of the two words through Word Sketch Difference reveals that common words that CPC and Taliban shared include "topple," "take," "control," "rule," "leader" and "sanction." This might suggest the *NYT* associated the CPC's image with an extremist "military" organization in Afghanistan.

The most conspicuous difference between the self-constructed and other-constructed cognitive associations is that, in TT-CODC, the CPC is synonymous with the collective term of "people," whereas in ST-*NYT*C, the CCP is associated with very specific actors such as "university," "students," "family," "women" and "parents."

Figure 6. The word cloud of CPC's top 30 synonyms in TT-CODC

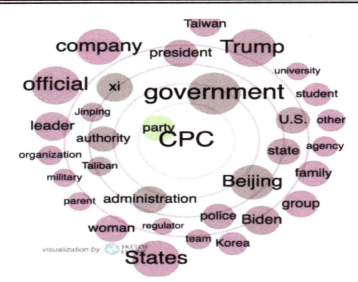

Figure 7. The word cloud of CPC's top 30 synonyms in ST-*NYTC*

5. Conclusion

Through a comparable parallel corpus-based analysis, this article compared the competing frames of the Communist Party of China in the discourses produced by the party state and by the *New York Times* in 2020 and 2021 since the COVID outbreak. Results from analyses of keywords, exposures, collocates, synonyms and semantic networks showed that: (1) "CPC" was the dominant self-label while the "Chinese Communist Party" ("CCP") was the common label used by critical other-framers. Such disparity seemed to be motivated by ideology-based framing beyond the tradition of usage. (2) The mention of CPC/CCP became increasingly frequent in 2020 and 2021, with the self-framing interest peaking in 2021 for the CPC centenary and the other-framing interest peaking in 2020 for the accountability over the initial COVID-19 response, Hong Kong and Xinjiang issues and US travel ban of party members and families. (3) An image of good governance and moral legitimacy self-constructed in the Chinese official discourse stood in sharp contrast with that of an authoritarian dictatorship in conflict with its own people and external powers in the other-constructed *NYT* discourse. (4). The CPC's positive self-framing approach favored development and unity for the people, while the negative other-framing strategy of *NYT* focused on the infringement of personal and economic freedom by the party state.

This study of the competing frames for the largest and longest ruling party in the world shed initial light on the increased ideological and power rivalry between the state and the media across national borders in the post-COVID era. The findings elucidate how competitive framing could contribute to strategic meaning making. The current research was oriented toward quantitative mapping. Future studies could expand on theorization and offer more in-depth qualitative analysis of the on-going CPC narratives in China and around the world as a window to understanding a complicated party running an ancient civilization state.

References

Baker, Mona. 1995. "Corpora in Translation Studies: An Overview and Some Suggestions for Future Research". *Target*, 7(2):223-243.

Baker, Paul. 2004. "Querying Keywords: Questions of Difference, Frequency, and Sense in Keywords Analysis". *Journal of English Linguistics*, 32(4):346-359.

Baker, Paul & McEnery, Tony. 2005. A Corpus-Based Approach to Discourses of Refugees and Asylum Seekers in UN and Newspaper Texts". *Journal of Language and Politics*, 4(2):197-226.

Bates, Benjamin R. 2020. "The (In)appropriateness of the WAR Metaphor in Response to SARS-CoV-2: A Rapid Analysis of Donald J. Trump's Rhetoric". *Frontiers in Communication*, 5(50). https://doi.org/10.3389/fcomm.2020.0005012.

Bauer, Paul C. & von Hohenberg, Bruno C. 2021. "Believing and Sharing Information by Fake Sources: An Experiment". *Political Communication*, 38(6):647-671.

Bradsher, Keith & Lee, Min-Hee. 2021, December 7. "Ahead of Biden's Democracy Summit, China Says: We're Also a Democracy". *New York Times*, https://www.NYTimes.com/2021/12/07/world/asia/china-biden-democracy-summit.html.

Bucy, Erik P. & Evans, Heather K. 2021. "Media-Centric and Politics-Centric Views of Media and Democracy: A Longitudinal Analysis of Political Communication and the International Journal of Press/Politics". *Political Communication*, 39(2):254-265. https://doi.org/10.1080/10584609.2021.1966595.

Buzan, Barry & Lawson, George. 2020. "China Through the Lens of Modernity". *The Chinese Journal of International Politics*, 13(2):187-217.

Chen, Eva. 2021, July 20. "One of China's Biggest Stars Faces a #MeToo Storm". *New York Times*. https://www.NYTimes.com/2021/07/20/world/asia/kris-wu-china-metoo.html.

Chong, Dennis & Druckman, James N. 2007. "A Theory of Framing and Opinion Formation in Competitive Elite Environments". *Journal of Communication*, 57(1): 99-118.

Christensen, Steven R., Pilling, Emily B., Eyring, Jolyn B., Dickerson, Geoffrey, Sloan, Cory D. & Magnusson, Brian M. 2020. "Political and Personal Reactions to COVID-19 During Initial Weeks of Social Distancing in the United States". *PloS One*, 15(9), e0239693.

Ciuk, David J. & Rottman, Joshua. 2021. "Moral Conviction, Emotion, and the Influence of Episodic Versus Thematic Frames". *Political Communication*, 38(5): 519-538.

Cohen, Bernard C. 1963. *The Press and Foreign Policy*. NJ: Princeton University Press.

Corcoran, John & Hamid, Idris S. 2016. "Schema". In E. N. Zalta & U. Nodelman (eds.), *The Stanford Encyclopedia of Philosophy*. https://plato.stanford.edu/archives/fall2016/entries/schema.

Edy, Jaesub A. & Meirick, Patrick C. 2007. "Wanted, Dead or Alive: Media Frames, Frame Adoption, and Support for the War in Afghanistan". *Journal of Communication*, 57(1): 119-141.

Entman, Robert M. 1993. "Framing: Toward Clarification of a Fractured Paradigm". *Journal of Communication*, 43(4): 51-58.

Entman, Robert M. 2004. *Projections of Power: Framing News, Public Opinion, and US Foreign Policy*. Chicago: University of Chicago Press.

Fairclough, Norman. 1992. "Discourse and Social Change". NY: Polity Press.

Firth, John. R. 1957. "A Synopsis of Linguistic Theory, 1930-1955". In J. R. Firth (eds.), *Studies in Linguistic Analysis* (pp.1-32). London: Philological Society.

Fowler, Roger, Bob Hodge, Gunther Kress & Tony Trew. 1979. *Language and Control*. London: Routledge and Kegan Pau.

Gamson, William A. 1992. *Talking Politics*. Cambridge: Cambridge University Press.

Gamson, William A. & Andre Modigliani. 1987. The changing culture of affirmative action. In R. D. Braungart (eds.), *Research in Political Sociology* (pp.137-177). London: JAI.

Gans, Herbert. 1979. *Deciding What's News*. NY: Pantheon Books.

Gitlin, Todd. 1980. *The Whole World Is Watching: Mass Media in the Making and Unmaking of the New Left*. California: University of California Press.

Goffman, Erving. 1974. *Frame Analysis: An Essay on the Organization of Experience*. NY: Harper & Row.

Goffman, Erving. 1981. "Frame Analysis: An Essay on the Organization of Experience." Gamson, William". *Contemporary Sociology*, 4(6): 1093-a-1094.

Gonçalves, Gisela. 2018. "Political Cmmunication". In R. Heath & J. Winni (eds.), *The International Encyclopedia of Strategic Communication*(pp.1-6). NJ: Wiley. https://doi.org/10.1002/9781119010722.iesc0129.

Hafner, Christoph A. & Sun, Tongle. 2021. "The 'Team of 5 million': The Joint Construction of Leadership Discourse During the COVID-19 Pandemic in New Zealand". *Discourse, Context & Media*, 43:100523. https://doi.org/10.1016/j.dcm.2021.100523.

Hallahan, Kirk. 1999. "Seven Models of Framing: Implications for Public Relations". *Journal of Public Relations Research*, 11(3): 205-242. https://doi.org/10.1207/ s1532754xjprr1103_02.

Hallahan, Kirk, Holtzhausen, Derina, van Ruler, Betteke, Verčič, Dejan & Sriramesh, Krishnamurthy. 2007. "Defining Strategic Communication". *International Journal of Strategic Communication*, 1(1): 3-35.

Hameleers, Michael & Natascha Fawzi. 2020. "Widening the Divide Between Them and Us? The Effects of Populist Communication on Cognitive and Affective Stereotyping in a Comparative European Setting". *Political Communication*, 37(5): 612-634.

Harper, Craig A. & Rhodes, Darren. 2022. "Ideological Responses to the Breaking of COVID-19 Social Distancing Recommendations". *Group Processes & Intergroup Relations*. https://doi.org/10.1177/13684302221074546.

Hart, Peter S., Chinn, Sedona & Soroka, Stuart. 2020. "Politicization and Polarization in COVID-19 News Coverage". *Science Communication*, 42(5): 679-697.

Hatzir, Noa A, Segev, Elad, Watanabe, Kohei & Tago, Atsushi. 2022. "The News Coverage of Threats". In E. Segev (ed.), Semantic Network Analysis in Social Sciences (pp. 32-52). NY: Routledge.

Hernández, Javier & Horton, Chris. 2020, April 22. "Coronavirus Crisis Offers Taiwan a Chance to Push Back Against China". *New York Times*. https://www.NYTimes.com/2020/04/22/world/asia/coronavirus-china-taiwan.html.

Hernández, Javier. 2021, April 19. "Follow the Party Forever: China Plans a Communist Birthday Bash". *New York Times*. https://www.NYTimes.com/2021/04/19/world/asia/china-communist-party-anniversary.html.

Hunt, Sally. 2021. "Covid and the South African Family: Cyril Ramaphosa, President or Father"? *Discourse, Context & Media*, 44:100541. https://doi.org/10.1016/j.dcm.2021.100541.

Iyengar, Shanto. 1991. "Is Anyone Responsible? How Television Frames Political Issues". Chicago: University of Chicago Press.

Jaworska, Sylvia. 2021. "Competence and collectivity: The Discourse of Angela Merkel's Media Communications During the First Wave of the Pandemic". *Discourse, Context & Media*, 42:100506. https://doi.org/10.1016/j.dcm.2021.100506.

Jaworska, Sylvia & Vásquez, Camilla. 2022. "Covid-19 and the Discursive Practices of Political Leadership: Introduction". *Discourse, Context & Media*, 47:100605. https://doi.org/10.1016/j.dcm.2022.100605.

Ji, Chengdong & Liu, Hanzhang. 2022. "State as Salesman: International Economic Engagement and Foreign News Coverage in China". *Political Communication*, 39:1, 122-145.

Johnson, Dennis (Ed.). 2008. "The Handbook of Political Management". NY: Routledge.

Jones, Rodney H. 2021. "The Wounded Leader: The Illness Narratives of Boris Johnson and Donald Trump". *Discourse, Context & Media*, 41:100499. https://doi.org/10.1016/j.dcm.2021.100499.

Kahneman, Daniel. 2003. "Maps of Bounded Rationality: A Perspective on Intuitive Judgment and Choice". In T. Frängsmyr (ed.), *Les Prix Nobel: The Nobel Prizes 2002*, (pp. 449-489). Stockholm: Nobel Foundation.

Kahneman, Daniel. 2011. *Thinking, Fast and Slow*. NY: Farrar, Straus and Giroux.

Kahneman, Daniel & Tversky, Amos. 1979. "Prospect Theory—Analysis of Decision Under Risk". *Econometrica*, 47(2):263-291.

Kahneman, Daniel, & Tversky, Amos. 1984. "Choices, Values, and Frames". *American Psychologist*, 39(4):341-350.

Kaid, Lynda Lee & Holtz-Bacha, Christina (Eds.). 2006. *The Sage Handbook Of Political Advertising*. California: Sage.

Kilgarriff, Adam, Baisa, Vít, Bušta, Jan, Jakubíček, Miloš, Kovář, Vojtěch, Michelfeit, Jan, Rychlý, Pavel, & Suchomel, Vít. 2014. "The Sketch Engine: Ten Years On". *Lexicography: Journal of ASIALEX*, 1(1):7-36.

Kosicki, Gerald M. 1993. "Problems and Opportunities in Agenda-Setting Research". *Journal of Communication*, 43(2):100-127.

Lasswell, Harold D. 1927. *Propaganda Techniques in the World War*. NY: Knopf.

Lau, Richard R., Rogers, Kathleen & Love, Jamel. 2021. "Media Effects in the Viewer's Choice Era: Testing Revised Agenda-Setting and Priming Hypotheses". *Political Communication*, 38(3):199-221.

Lees-Marshment, Jennifer (Ed.). 2012. *The Routledge Handbook of Political Marketing*. NY: Routledge.

Lemus-Delgado, Daniel. 2022. "COVID-19, the Chinese Communist Party, and the Search for Legitimacy in the International Arena". *Chinese Journal of Communication*. DOI: 10.1080/17544750.2022.2052131.

Li, Jingze. 2021, July 26. "Meeting the 'National Translation Team' of the Communist Party of China: How to Build a Bridge Between China and the West". China News Agency. https://www.chinanews.com.cn/gn/2021/07-26/9528760.shtml.

Marchi, Anna. 2010. "The Moral in the Story: A Diachronic Investigation of Lexicalised Morality in the UK Press". *Corpora*, 5(2):161-190.

McCombs, Maxwell E. 2004. "Setting the Agenda: The Mass Media and Public Opinion". NJ: Blackwell.

McCombs, Maxwell E. & Shaw, Donald L. 1972. "The Agenda-Setting Function of Mass Media". *The Public Opinion Quarterly*, 36(2):176-187.

May, Tiffany. 2020, December 22. "A Hong Kong Activist, Nathan Law, Seeks Political Asylum in Britain". *New York Times*. https://www.NYTimes.com/2020/12/21/world/asia/nathan-law-hong-kong-uk-political-asylum.html.

Min, Bumgi & Luqiu, Luwei Rose. 2021. "How Propaganda Techniques Leverage Their Advantages: A Cross-National Study of the Effects of Chinese International Propaganda on the US and South Korean Audiences". *Political Communication*, 38(3):305-325.

Mozur, Paul. 2020, July 17. "US Wants to Bar Members of China's Communist Party. Who Are They?". *New York Times*. https://www.NYTimes.com/2020/07/16/world/asia/china-communist-party-travel-ban-explain.html.

Pan, Zhongdang & Kosicki, Gerald M. 1993. "Framing Analysis: An Approach to News Discourse". *Political Communication*, 10(1):55-75.

Panzeri, Francesca, Di Paola, Simona & Domaneschi, Filippo. 2021. "Does the COVID-19 War Metaphor Influence Reasoning?" *PLoS ONE*, 16(4), e0250651. https://doi.org/10.1371/journal.pone.0250651.

Partington, Alon. 1998. "Patterns and Meanings: Using Corpora for English Language Research and Teaching". Amsterdam: John Benjamins.

Qin, Yaqing. 2018. *A Relational Theory of World Politics*. Cambridge: Cambridge University Press.

Reese, Stephen D., Gandy, Oscar. H. Jr. & Grant, August E. 2001. "Framing Public Life: Perspectives on Media and Our Understanding of the Social World". NJ: Lawrence Erlbaum.

Rhodes, Samuel C. 2021. "Filter Bubbles, Echo Chambers, and Fake News: How Social Media Conditions Individuals to be Less Critical of Political Misinformation". *Political Communication*, 39(1):1-22.

Rosenberg, Justin. 2021. "Results and prospects: An Introduction to the CRIA Special Issue on UCD". *Cambridge Review of International Affairs*, 34(2):146-163.

Rosenberg, Justin, & Boyle, Chris. 2019. "Understanding 2016: China, Brexit and Trump in the History of Uneven and Combined Development". *Journal of Historical Sociology*, 32(1):e32–e58.

Sambaraju, Rahul. 2022. "My Countrymen Have Never Disappointed Me: Politics of Service in Modi's Speeches During Covid-19". *Discourse, Context & Media*, 100594. https://doi.org/10.1016/j.dcm.2022.100594.

Scheufele, Dietram A. & Tewksbury, David. 2007. "Framing, Agenda Setting, and Priming: The Evolution of Three Media Effects Models". *Journal of Communication*, 57(1):9-20.

Schnee, Christian. 2015. *Political Reputation Management: The Strategy Myth*. NY: Routledge.

Segev, Elad. 2022. "How to Conduct Semantic Network Analysis". In Segev, E. (Ed.), *Semantic Network Analysis in Social Sciences* (pp. 16-31). NY: Routledge.

Seixas, Eunice C. 2021. "War Metaphors in Political Communication on Covid-19". *Frontiers in Sociology*, 5:583680. doi: 10.3389/fsoc.2020.583680.

Semino, Elena. 2021. "Not Soldiers But Fire-Fighters—Metaphors and Covid-19". *Health Communication*, 36(1):50-58.

Shehata, Adam & Strömbäck, Jesper. 2021. "Learning Political News from Social Media: Network Media Logic and Current Affairs News Learning in a High-Choice Media Environment". *Communication Research*, 48(1):125-147.

Sieff, Elaine. 2003. "Media Frames of Mental Illnesses: The Potential Impact of Negative Frames". *Journal of Mental Health*, 12(3):259-269.

Simon, Herbert A. 1982. *Models of Bounded Rationality: Volume 3: Empirically Grounded Economic Reason*. Massachusetts: MIT Press.

Sinclair, John. 1991. *Corpus, concordance, collocation*. Oxford University Press.

Sniderman, Paul M. & Bullock, John. 2004. "A Consistency Theory of Public Opinion and Political Choice". In W. E. Saris & P. M. Sniderman (eds.), *Studies in Public Opinion* (pp. 337-358). NJ: Princeton University Press.

State Council Information Office of the People's Republic of China. 2021. "Poverty Alleviation: China's Experience and Contribution" [White Paper]. Xinhuanet. http://www.xinhuanet.com/english/download/2021-4-6/FullText.pdf.

----2021. "China's Epic Journey from Poverty to Prosperity" [White Paper]. Gov. https://english.www.gov.cn/archive/whitepaper/202109/28/content_WS61528550c6d0df57f98e0ffa.html.

---- 2021. "Resolution of the CPC Central Committee on the Major Achievements And Historical Experience of the Party Over the Past Century" [White Paper]. Gov. https://english.www.gov.cn/policies/latestreleases/202111/16/content_WS6193a935c6d0df57f98e50b0.html.

Strömbäck, Jesper. 2008. "Four Phases of Mediatization: An Analysis of the Mediatization of Politics". *The International Journal of Press/Politics*, 13(3):228-246.

Strömbäck, Jesper & Kiousis, Spiro (Ed.). 2011. *Political Public Relations: Principles And Applications*. NY: Routledge.

Sun, Wei & Li, Haihua. 2021, February 2. "Mao Zedong Led New Members to Join the Party and Take the Oath During the Jinggangshan Period". qstheory.cn. http://www.qstheory.cn/laigao/ycjx/2021-02/02/c_1127055975.htm.

Taylor, Charlotte. 2010. "Science in the News: A Diachronic Perspective". *Corpora*, 5(2):221-250.

van Dijk, Teun A. 1998. "Ideology: A Multidisciplinary Approach". California: Sage.

Vásquez, Camilla. 2021. Leading with Stories: Andrew Cuomo, Family Narratives and Authentic Leadership". *Discourse, Context & Media*, 41:100507. https://doi.org/10.1016/j.dcm.2021.100507.

Walter, Dror & Ophir, Yotam. 2021. "Strategy Framing in News Coverage and Electoral Success: An Analysis of Topic Model Networks Approach". *Political Communication*, 38(6):707-730.

Wang, Binhua. 2021. "Presentation, Re-presentation and Perception of China's Political Discourse. An Analysis About Core Concepts on the 'Belt and Road' Based on a Comparable Corpus". In B. Wang and J. Munday (eds.), *Advances in Discourse Analysis of Translation and Interpreting* (pp. 9-23). NY: Routledge.

Wang, Vivian & Buckley, Chris. 2020, December 11. "Jimmy Lai, Media Mogul, Is Charged Under Hong Kong's Security Law". *New York Times*. https://www.NYTimes.com/2020/12/11/world/asia/china-hong-kong-jimmy-lai.html.

Wanta, Wayne & Tarasevich, Sofiya. 2019. "Agenda-Setting and Priming Theories". In T. P. Vos, F. Hanusch, A. Sehl, D. Dimitrakopoulou & M. Geertsema-Sligh (eds.), *The International Encyclopedia of Journalism Studies* (pp. 1-6). NJ: Wiley.

Weaver, David H. 2007. "Thoughts on Agenda Setting, Framing, and Priming". *Journal of Communication*, 57(1):142-147.

WHO. 2020, March 11. "WHO Director-General's Opening Remarks at the Media Briefing on COVID-19."https://www.who.int/director-general/speeches/detail/who-director-general-s-opening-remarks-at-the-media-briefing-on-covid-19---11-march-2020.

WHO. 2022, September 16. "WHO Health Emergency Dashboard." https://covid19.who.int/region/searo/country/cn.

WHO. 2022, September 16. "WHO Health Emergency Dashboard." https://covid19.who.int/region/searo/country/in.

Widdowson, Henry G. 1995. "Discourse Analysis: A Critical View". *Language and Literature*, 4(3):157-172.

Wodak, Ruth. 1998. "Language, Power and Ideology". Amsterdam: John Benjamins.

Xi, Jinping. 2013, December 30. "Speech at the 12th Collective Study Session of the Political Bureau of the 18th CPC Central Committee". http://cpc.people.com.cn/n1/2022/0516/c443712-32422207.html.

---- 2019, January 25. "Speech at the 12th Collective Study Session of the Political Bureau of the 19th CPC Central Committee". http://cpc.people.com.cn/n1/2019/0125/c64094-30590946.html.

---- 2021, May 31. "Speech at the 30th Collective Study Session of the Political Bureau of the 19th CPC Central Committee". http://cpc.people.com.cn/n1/2021/0602/c64093-32120102.html.

----2021, July 1. "Speech at the Ceremony Marking the Centenary of the Communist Party of China." Xinhuanet. http://www.xinhuanet.com/english/special/2021-07/01/c_1310038244.htm.

Xie, Feng. 2021, June 13. "Speech at an Exchange with Diplomatic Envoys from North America, Oceania, Latin America and the Caribbean before the CPC's 100th Anniversary".

https://www.fmprc.gov.cn/web/ziliao_674904/zyjh_674906/202106/t20210613_9180805.shtml.

Zhang, Zhan. 2022. "Contesting Legitimacy in China's Crisis Communication: A Framing Analysis of Reported Social Actors Engaging in SARS and COVID-19". *Chinese Journal of Communication*, DOI: 10.1080/17544750.2022.2049835.

Zhu, Yifan & Kim, Kyung Hye. 2020. "The Individual on the Move: Redefining Individualism in China". *Translation and Interpreting Studies*, 15(2):161-182.

Zimmermann, Fabian & Kohring, Matthias. 2020. "Mistrust, Disinforming News, and Vote Choice: A Panel Survey on the Origins and Consequences of Believing Disinformation in the 2017 German Parliamentary Election". *Political Communication*, 37(2):215-237.

A Study on Default Subjects in Chinese

Xiaoxia Pan
Sichuan University

Abstract

This paper examines the meaning generation of default subjects (syntactically absent subjects) in Chinese based on meaning holism and logical reasoning. *Meaning holism* holds that the meaning of an expression depends on its relationship to other expressions in language. *Logical reasoning* refers to the logical thinking and analysis that helps to unravel the underlying patterns, causes and effects within a specific context or scenario. The study argues that logic is universal to languages, and Chinese differs from European languages in that it follows logical reasoning rather than formal reasoning. The typological characteristics of Chinese together with its preference for logical reasoning result in its flexibility in form, which is shown in default subjects in Chinese sentences. The study holds that meaning holism and logical reasoning are powerful in explaining the meanings of sentences with default subjects.

Keywords

default subject; meaning holism; logical reasoning

1. Introduction

As far as European languages are concerned, complexity of language form is obviously linked to precision. Words change their forms according to function, which is a manifestation of vitality. As Humboldt (2001:125) put it, the longer and more complex the sentence, the richer and more varied the relations between words; it is clear that the need to distinguish grammatical categories in detail is first and foremost determined by the tendency to construct complex and long compound sentences. Unlike inflectional European languages, Chinese is an isolated language, with no changes in word forms. It relies on word order and particles to convey meaning. It lacks grammatical marks. Particles or auxiliary words are sometimes used, yet they are not indispensable. In addition to these auxiliary words, Chinese expresses all grammatical forms via word order, words whose established forms never change and the connection between meanings.

There are a large number of sentences in Chinese that have no subjects or agents of action and seem to be incomplete syntactically. However, the omission or absence of such a subject or agent does not hinder the

---

Xiaoxia Pan, College of Foreign Languages and Cultures, Sichuan University, Chengdu, China. E-mail address: panxx@scu.edu.cn.

understanding of the sentence meaning, for it is not difficult for a reader or listener to figure out the supposed subject or agent. This paper names these formally or syntactically absent subjects or agents *default subjects* and aims to explore the meaning-generation mechanism underlying them.

2. Default subjects in Chinese

Based on the related research conducted by some scholars, such as Shen Xiaolong (2019), this study will focus roughly on four main types of default subjects, with some of the examples quoted from the above-mentioned study.

2.1. Default subjects in an inter-text

It is very common to read the following sentences in Chinese:

(1) *fàn zuò hǎo, sǎosao   dì, zhāi xià chuānglián wàngwang   tiān.*
    meal cook done sweep sweep floor take down curtain   watch watch sky
    "Cook, sweep the floor, take down the curtains and look up at the sky."

The above example is a statement, not an imperative sentence. *Fàn* (meal) is seemingly a subject of the first section, yet it cannot serve as the subject of the following two sections. The subject can only be pinned down according to its preceding text. The preceding sentence states that this morning, Aunt Yao, as usual, got up before dawn and lit the lamp to cook. Example 1 is simply a description of what she did next. That is, after the breakfast was cooked, she swept the floor, took down the curtains and looked up at the sky. Aunt Yao in the preceding text is the default subject of the following one.

Take one more example:

(2) *yì shǐ   you shuì bù zháo, xīn lǐ   zhí   dǎ   zhǔ yì.*
    a while Aux. sleep not Aux. heart inside continuously make idea
    "(Subject) was unable to fall asleep for a while, and kept thinking of ideas in (subject's) mind."

The subject of the sentence is obviously absent. It can only be made clear by the preceding context.

In addition to the above cases in which the default subjects are closely related to the subjects of the preceding text, there are sentences where the default subject of a certain part can be the implied agent of another part within the sentence. For instance:

(3) *jiàbuzhù   yáo dàshěn tiāntiān   luōsuō,   dào dǐ   bǎ   nǚér*
    cannot stand Yao aunt   every day talk endlessly to the end BA daughter
nǚxu   shuō   huó   xīn le, biàn zédìng shíyīyuè qīhào jiéhūn.
son-in-law persuade active heart PFV then choose November seven   marry
"Not standing Aunt Yao's daily verbosity, they were in the end persuaded and chose November 7 as their wedding day."

Example 3 consists of three clauses, and there is no subject in each of them. Interestingly, they have different default subjects. The subject of the first section is actually Aunt Yao's daughter and her son-in-law, who are the object of the BA clause in the second section, while Aunt Yao is the default subject of the BA clause. The subject of the third clause might be ambiguous. It is probably Aunt Yao's daughter and her son-in-law. It also might be all three of them who jointly scheduled the marriage for November 7.

Such phenomena have been explained in terms of "intertextuality." "Aunt Yao" in the first section is intertextual with the implied agent in the second section, and "daughter and son-in-law" in the second section is intertextual with the implied agent in the first section.

Intertextuality was first proposed by Kristeva (1969), a French post-structuralist critic aiming to emphasize that any single text is not self-contained and its meaning is generated through cross-reference with other texts. Kristeva (2016:12) admits that her theory of intertextuality has been inspired by the Chinese way of thinking. Intertext, also known as *intertextual rhetoric*, is a rhetoric method commonly used in ancient Chinese poetry and prose. Intertextuality is often used in modern Chinese sentences to reflect on each other, resulting in concise and musical expressions (Shen Xiaolong, 2019; Shen Jiaxuan, 2019).

2.2. Default subjects in existential sentences

Subjects are often omitted in existential sentences. For example, take the following sentences:

(4) *jiào tang li   zhǐ   shèng xia   yī-gè   mó mó, yòu   lǎo yòu lóng.*
     church inside only remain   one-CLF mother Aux. old Aux. deaf
"There was only one mother left in the church, old and deaf."

(5) *yáo dòng   duì guò gài   le   sān-jiān   fang,   shì pútáo hé   tiěnǎo*
     dwelling cave opposite build PFV three-CLF room   be Putao and Tienao
de   xīn fang.
Aux. new house
"Across the dwelling cave, three rooms were built, a new house for Putao and Tienao."

(6) *ménkǒu jǐ   zhe   duī   rén,   diǎn   zhe   jiǎojiān kàn   rènao.*
     doorway crowd Aux. CLF people   tiptoe Aux. tiptoe   watch bustle
"A crowd of people crowded at the door, standing on tiptoe to watch the bustling scene."

(7) *nánbian lái   le   gè   lǎobó,   tí   zhe   yī-miàn tóngluó.*
     south   come PFV CLF   uncle   carry Aux.   one-CLF gong
"There's an old man from the south, carrying a gong."

In examples 4 and 5, the new information in the existential sentence serves as the theme of the second section. The only mother in the church was old and deaf. The three rooms built across the dwelling cave were a new house for the couple. In example 6, the new information in the first half, namely the existential sentence, is the default subject of the second half. People stood on tiptoe to watch something. In example 7, the old man in the existential sentence is the default agent of the second section. That is, the old man was carrying a gong.

2.3. Default subjects in multi-line narrative

In a multi-line narrative, agents of different parts jointly and tacitly function as the subject of the later part. For example:

(8) *dōngxǐ mā   hé   shén pó   zài wàimiàn,   shàoyǒng   zài   lǐmiàn,*
     Dongxi mother and sorceress stay the outside   Shaoyong   stay the inside

  gé zhe yī-shàn mén shuōhuà.
  separate Aux. one-CLF door talk

"Dongxi's mother and the sorceress stayed on the outside, (and) Shaoyong was on the inside, talking through a door."

The first two clauses describe the states of the different agents, Dongxi's mother and the sorceress on the one hand and Shaoyong on the other. The following third section has no subject in it, yet the agents in the previous two sections jointly serve as its subject. That is, the three of them talked through the door.

Here is one more example:

(9) *pútáo jià niú, sūn huáiqīng fú lí, zhòng xià shí duō*
  Putao harness cattle Sun Huaiqing hold plough plant down ten odd
  mǔ xiǎomài.
  CLF wheat

"Putao harnessed cattle, Sun Huaiqing held up the plough, (and they) planted more than ten acres of wheat."

The first two clauses are about what each agent did, yet there is no subject in the third one. The default subject of "plant" is actually both Putao and Sun Huaiqing.

2.4. Default subjects in the first modifiers

In Chinese, the first modifier of a sentence is often tacitly taken as the subject of the later section. Such default subjects can be seen in the following example sentences.

(10) *sūn shàoyǒng dào shǐ tún shí tiān gāng hēi,*
   Sun Shaoyong arrive Shi village Aux. sky just dark
   ràng yī-cháng yǔ jiāo de lǐwài   tòushī
   let one-CLF rain pour Aux. inside and out wet through

"It was just dark when Sun Shaoyong arrived in the Shi village, soaked to the skin in a rain."

"Sun Shaoyong" is a part of the adverbial clause, which is just a modifier of the whole sentence, yet it becomes the default subject of the second half.

Another example:

(11) *nà tiān tā liǎng-gè zhí dǎ xū de jiǎo*
   that day he two-CLF continuously turn weak Aux foot
   cǎi zài jiǎodēng shàng jué de yīzhèn wànniànjùhuī.
   tread on pedal on feel Aux. a burst of despair

"That day, his two weak feet stepped on the pedal (and he) felt a burst of despair."

Obviously, the subject of "feel" cannot be his feet. It is he who feels that all hopes are dashed. However, "he" is not the subject of the first half of the sentence. It is just a modifier, yet it functions as the default subject of the second half.

Default subject sentences are abundant in Chinese, which is closely related to its language type and characteristics.

3. Characteristics of the Chinese language

Chinese is a typical isolated language with no morphological changes. The characteristic of this kind of language is that it does not generally express the role of grammar through inflection, that is, the internal morphological change of the word, but expresses the grammatical meaning through independent function words and fixed word order. Unlike European languages, which use linguistic formal means to display syntactic relations and realize the connection of words or sentences, Chinese depends on the connection between words or sentences by means of the meaning connection between units.

Chinese does not attach phonics to grammatical modifiers as external markers, but leaves it to the reader to identify grammatical modifiers from word order and deduce their meaning from context. It emphasizes the understanding of meaning rather than the grammar of morphological coordination. As Humboldt (2001:105) put it, Chinese is almost completely different from all known languages in its grammatical construction. There is always a part of the grammar of any language that is explicit, shown by means of signs or grammatical rules; the other part is hidden, which can be assumed without the aid of markers and grammatical rules, yet in Chinese, the proportion of explicit grammar is very small compared with hidden grammar. Sapir (1921:108) maintains a similar view by stating, "Chinese, with its unmodified words and rigid sequences, has a compactness of phrase, a terse parallelism, and a silent suggestiveness that would be too tart, too mathematical, for the English genius."

There is a lot to be assumed in Chinese. Without the aid of markers and grammatical rules, the logical connection of context is required. It follows that Chinese is a paratactic language. Then how are linguistic units logically and semantically connected in Chinese?

4. Meaning holism and logical reasoning

The Chinese way of thinking is often referred to as *graphic*. The characteristic of graphic thinking is that the understanding of a thing is confirmed by its relation to other things (Shen Xiaolong, 2019). Thus, this way of thinking requires a more holistic view on meaning.

The idea of meaning holism has been embodied in Saussure's structuralism and Frege's contextualism, but Quine (1951) was the first to introduce this topic into the philosophy of language. He argued that "our statements about the external world face the tribunal of sense experience not individually but only as a corporate body" and "the unit of empirical significance is the whole of science" (Quine, 1951:42). *Meaning holism* was then developed by philosophers such as Wittgenstein (1953) and Davidson (1967, 2001). Wittgenstein says, "To understand a sentence is to understand a language" (1953: 199); Davidson (1967) states in *Truth and Meaning* that sentences (and thus words) have meaning only in the context of language. In general, meaning holism holds that the meaning of an expression (linguistic or mental) is determined by its relationship with other expressions in the same system (Wang, 2016).

However, meaning holism has been refuted by some scholars. Dummett (1991) argues that meaning holism must lead to various linguistic difficulties, one of which is that if meaning holism is correct, communication between speakers will be impossible. J. Fodor and E. Lepore (1992) indicate that meaning holism is mistaken since it faces the problems of instability, compositionality and objectivity. These problems can be dealt with by Sellars's (2003) defense and development of meaning holism. According to Sellars, the meaning of a word is its referential roles, and only in a logical space can a word or sentence have any referential roles.

Sellars (2003) describes a systematic *logical space*, or *conceptual space*, composed of concepts. In this space, any word is connected with other words, and there is no meaningful word independent of logical space. The web of meaning can spread throughout the language system. The function of a word or sentence depends on its position in the logical space, that is, with which words or sentences it has reasoning relations; different words are also distinguished from each other by their different functions (Zhang, 2018). In the logical space, the meanings of words constitute a systematic network and are interdependent. A logical space is similar to a model in which the determination of the meanings of words and sentences in the model depends on the reasoning relationships between other words and sentences in the model.

Chinese expressions, such as "*zǒu guòqù kāimén*" (walk to open the door) and "*kāimén zǒu guòqù*" (open the door to walk through), are understood and treated as a continuous process consistent with the state of affairs. They are in different order, and the primary and secondary are different, corresponding to two different events respectively. They follow the logic of reasoning, which is viewed as close as possible to the original state of affairs.

The logic of reasoning, or logical reasoning, refers to the logical thinking and reasoning that helps to unravel the underlying patterns, causes, and effects within a specific context or scenario. It involves examining the relationships and connections between different elements to draw logical conclusions and make informed decisions.

Zhang (2020) states that logic derives from language; thus, different languages have different logic. The view that different languages have different logic is accepted by some scholars, such as Shen Jiaxuan (2019), Shen Xiaolong (2019) and Wang (2020). As for what is the logic of language, different scholars may have different views, yet it can be generally defined as the science of studying the reasoning in natural language through the analysis of the form, semantics and pragmatics of natural language; it aims to study logical problems in natural language (Zhou, 1994; Wang, et. al., 1989). Traditional logic and classical logic mainly study morphological or semantic reasoning, while linguistic logic mainly studies pragmatic reasoning, the reasoning that needs to supplement or add some omitted or missing premises according to specific contextual factors in order to reach a real conclusion (Hu, 2003). In essence, logic is the science of reasoning.

If it is true that different languages have different logic, then arises the question of whether the principles of logic and logical thoughts embedded in the natural language vary from language to language? If so, there will be no universal logic. If the principles of logic vary from language to language and from people to people, then there will be no effective and successful communication. Grammar is not logic, although in fact it is inseparable from logic (Lv & Zhu, 1979:179). This paper holds that logic is universal to all languages and all people around the world and that Chinese is different from most European languages in its preference for logical reasoning rather than formal reasoning.

5. Discussion

The formal expression of language is a linear sequence. We can only use finite linear sequences to express the richness of thoughts. The semantic minimalists insist that a sentence has cross-context semantic content, formed according to the compositionality principle. The meaning of a word or a sentence can be given and ascertained while remaining compatible with meaning holism (Liu & Pan, 2018). The meaning generation of a sentence is based on the conceptual or logical space triggered by its words and logical reasoning. Meaning holism and logical reasoning are more capable of explaining how the meaning of a sentence is generated, especially some peculiar linguistic phenomena, such as default subject sentences in Chinese.

5.1. Default subjects

Default subjects, such as the ones in examples 1 and 2 in section 2, are common in Chinese. They can be easily traced back to the preceding text to make clear what they are. Thus, such a Chinese sentence or text needs to be placed in a broader text to be understood, for it is usually composed of a chain of actions or events in chronological order. Aunt Yao got up, lit the lamp, cooked the breakfast, swept the floor, took down the curtains, and looked up at the sky. Aunt Yao did those deeds one by one. Chinese tends to use short sentences to report a sequence of actions or events rather than using long, complex sentences organized with a verb as the center. While run-on sentences are more likely to be used to narrate the events, it is also normal to use choppy sentences to give a narrative, which are usually avoided in English writing. The disconnection of run-on sentences is one of the most important characteristics of Chinese flexibility (Shen Jiaxuan, 2019: 37). Default subjects are quite common in run-on sentences and choppy sentences. For example:

(12) *lǎo wáng ne? yòu shēngìng-le ba. yě gāi qǐng-gè jià ya.*

old Wang Aux. again fall ill -PFV Aux. Aux. should ask for-CLF leave Aux.

"What about Lao Wang? (He's) sick again. (He) should ask for a leave" (Shen Jiaxuan, 2019:36)

The subject in the first run-on sentence becomes the default subject for the second and the third in example 12. The flexibility of Chinese renders it more necessary to take a holistic view of context for the understanding of the meaning. Meanwhile, logical reasoning helps to analyze and examine the relationships and connections between elements, such as the relationship between Lao Wang and the actions like getting sick and asking for a leave.

Meaning holism and logical reasoning are the theoretical basis for understanding the meaning of sentences with intertextual default subjects, such as example 3 in section 2. All of the three clauses in this sentence have no subjects. It requires more logical thinking and reasoning to unravel the underlying relationships within this specific scenario. The first clause, "*jiàbuzhù yáo dàshēn tiāntiān luōsuō*" (cannot stand Aunt Yao's daily verbosity) lacks the logical subject of "stand." In the second clause "*dàodǐ bǎ nǚér nǚxu shuō huó xīn le*" (in the end persuade daughter and son-in-law), the agent of "persuade" is absent. It is not syntactically stated who chooses the date in the third clause, "*biàn zédìng shíyīyuè qīhào jiéhūn*" (choose November 7 for marriage). Three events and two parties are involved. It is not difficult to figure out the relationship between the two parties, namely Aunt Yao versus daughter and son-in-law. However, we need more logical reasoning to examine the connection between the events. The meaning of one clause is closely related to and is somehow determined by the other clauses in the sentence, or even a broader context sometimes. When put in a holistic view and given sufficient reasoning, it can be understood as follows: It is Aunt Yao's daughter and son-in-law (their names are Yao Zhilan and Wu Tianbao according to a larger context) who cannot stand Aunt Yao's endless talking every day (her daily nagging theme is to get them married quickly); they are finally persuaded by their mother into getting married; then they choose a date for their wedding.

Logical reasoning also plays a very important role in deciding the logical subject of the second half in existential sentences with default subjects. Take example 4 in section 2.2 for instance, *"yòu lǎo yòu lóng"* (old and deaf) must be a description of someone or an animal. In the conceptual or logical space triggered by the words in the sentence, the only animate being is the *"mó mó"* (mother), who thus is tacitly taken as the subject of the later part. It should be noted that the second part of example 4, *"yòu lǎo yòu lóng"* (old and deaf), is not just an attributive in Chinese. Instead, it is a predicate, and its thematic subject is hidden in the first clause.

In example 5, the default subject is also a theme for the second part. Unlike 4, this one requires more logical reasoning to determine the default subject. Both *"yáo dòng"* (dwelling cave) and the newly-built *"sān-jiān fang"* (three rooms) can function as the thematic subject of the second clause, yet within the given situation, it is more reasonable that the three newly built rooms become the new house (or bridal chamber) for the young couple. The meaning of the sentence can be better understood in connection with other sentences or in a wider context.

In examples 6 and 7, the absent subject is the agent of the action verb in the second clause. There is no difficulty in examining the connections between the different elements to get the default subject to realize a semantic gestalt. Syntactically speaking, the existential sentence in 6 is followed by a serial verb construction, *"diǎn zhe jiǎojiān kàn rènao"* (stand on tiptoe and watch the bustling scene); the existential sentence in 7 is followed by a verb-object construction, *"tí zhe yī-miàn tóngluó"* (carry a gong). They are supposed to be adverbials in English to indicate a concomitant state.

Default subjects in multi-line narratives comparatively rely more heavily on reasoning to be pinned down. There are three people involved in example 8. Two of them, namely *"dōngxǐ mā"* (Dongxi's mom) and the *"shénpó"* (sorceress), form a narrative line, while the third one, *"shàoyǒng"* (Shaoyong) forms another line. The first two clauses, complete in syntactic form, provide a narrative about them respectively. However, there is no subject in the third clause. The logical space or conceptual space triggered by the verbs *"gé"* (separate) and *"shuōhuà"* (talk) requires that there are people separated by a door and they talk together. So the default subject of the third clause should be three of them, two of them on this side of the door and one of them on the other side, talking through the door. The meaning of the third clause is dependent on the previous ones and generated by a holistic view and much logical reasoning.

The linguistic phenomenon that an element in the first modifier of a sentence functions as the default subject of a later part of that sentence is common in Chinese but unacceptable in English and most other European languages. To understand the meaning of such a sentence, we need to do much logical reasoning within a specific scenario. For instance, in example 11, the subject of the first half or, to be more specific, the agent of the action verb *"cǎi"* (tread/step), is modified by a quite complicated modifier, that is, *"tā liǎng-gè zhí dǎxū de jiǎo"* (his two continuously weakening feet). This treading action is closely followed by the perception event of feeling, with no grammatical markers such as a comma. Much logical thinking and reasoning should be conducted to examine the relationships and connections between different elements and to unravel the underlying cause and effect in that specific context. It is the man rather than his two feet who feels a burst of despair. The reason why he feels desperate is that his feet are becoming increasingly weak. The person involved in the first modifier becomes the default subject of the second event in the sentence.

5.2. Other controversial cases

Some verb-object collocations, such as *"dǎsǎo wèishēng"* (do cleaning) were once thought to be illogical. However, they are widely accepted and used. Wang (2020) clarifies its motivation from the perspective of salience and the special characteristics of Chinese verb-object structures. Unlike some languages, in which only a typical patient can be an object of a verb, in Chinese the object position of a verb can be filled by many other elements than a typical patient. When people engage in a "cleaning" activity, the result they want to see is a "state of hygiene." Therefore, "hygiene" is a very prominent argument in this particular context, and if it needs to be represented, its preferred representation is *"dǎsǎo wèishēng"* (do cleaning) (Wang, 2020). Wang maintains that this does not seem logical, but it is logical in language, and this logic of language is absent in English, because English verbs are not as open as Chinese verbs in taking objects.

This expression can also be well understood via meaning holism and logical reasoning. The verb *"dǎsǎo"* (sweep away/ clean up) triggers a logical space or conceptual space in which many elements are logically involved and connected, such as the agent of the action, the patient, the location, the tools, and even the purpose. Any elements related to this event can be triggered. Only when it is logically reasonable can it be acceptable and meaningful. In fact, in English expressions, such as "clean the orange powder off the bathtub" and "clean the room", it is hard to tell which is a typical patient of the verb. There are similar expressions like *"zuò wèishēng"* (do some cleaning) and *"zuò qīngjié"* (do some cleaning), which are difficult to explain from the perspective of arguments but can be explained via meaning holism and logical reasoning.

Expressions such as *"chī shítáng"* (eat in a canteen) are quite common but special in Chinese. Their meaning generation mechanism can also be expounded by meaning holism accompanied by logical reasoning. The logical space triggered by the verb *"chī"* (eat) involves the eater, the stuff to be eaten, the location where the eating event takes place, the dinnerware, and so on. The meaning of the expression can be logically reasoned out, although *"shítáng"* (canteen) is formally an object of the verb and there is no grammatical marker to indicate it is a location where the event takes place. Other locations can be used, such as *"chī dàfàndiàn"* (eat in a big restaurant) *"chī cāngying guǎnzi"* (eat in a small restaurant). There are other expressions like *"chī dàwǎn"* (eat a large bowl of something). Chinese is quite flexible and tolerant in form, yet there are logical connections between them.

The expressions "the sun is rising" and "the sun is setting" are considered against logical reasoning if we follow Copernican heliocentric theory. According to this theory, the sun is actually not moving, but the earth is moving. However, the expressions are similar and acceptable in Chinese and other languages. Thus, the logical reasoning we resort to is not necessarily the hard science. How the external objective world appears in the linguistic world of human beings depends on our feelings and cognition of the world, and it might not be completely consistent with the objective world (Wang, 2020).

6. Conclusion

The current study examines four types of Chinese sentences with syntactically or formally absent subjects, which are named default subjects in this paper. It is argued that this linguistic phenomenon is closely related to the typological characteristics of Chinese. By arguing that logic is supposed to be universal to languages and people around the world, the study then refutes the view that different languages have different logic, and holds that Chinese differs from European languages in that it has a different way of thinking and it follows logical reasoning rather than formal reasoning. Thus, meaning holism and logical reasoning will be effective and powerful in the semantic studies on Chinese, especially on its peculiar linguistic phenomena, such as default subjects. Meaning holism holds that the meaning of an expression depends compositionally on its relationship to other expressions in language. Logical reasoning refers to the logical analysis and deduction of principles and patterns within a given situation or context, which involves examining the relationships and connections between different elements to draw logical conclusions. Based on meaning holism and logical reasoning, the study analyzes the meaning generation of default subject sentences and a few other cases. It turns out to be effective. However, more evidence and further studies are needed for a more definitive conclusion regarding the effectiveness of the above theories.

References

Davidson, D. 1967. "Truth and Meaning". *Synthese*, 17(3): 304–323.

Davidson, D. 2001. "A Coherence Theory of Truth and Knowledge". In Davidson, D. (ed.), *Subjective, Intersubjective, Objective*, Oxford: Oxford University Press.

Fodor, J. and Lepore, E. 1992. *Holism: A Shopper's Guide*, Oxford: Blackwell.

Hu, Zehong. 2003. "Linguistic Logic and Pragmatic Reasoning". *Academic Research*, 12: 69-71.

Humboldt, W. von. 2001. *Essays on Humboldt's Philosophy of Language*, Trans. by Yao Xiaoping. Shangshao: Hunan Education Press.

Kristeva, Julia. 1969. *Séméiôtiké: recherches pour une sémanalyse*, Paris: Edition du Seuil.

Kristeva, Julia. 2016. *Subject, Intertextuality, Psychoanalysis—Collection of Lectures by Kristeva at Fudan University*, Shanghai: Sanlian Bookstore Publishing.

Liu, Limin & Pan, Xiaoxia. 2018. "On Compatibility of Minimal Semantic Content of Sentence with Meaning Holism: Inspiration from Gongsun Long's Proposition that Horse Is What We Use to Name a Form". *Journal of Sichuan University (Philosophy and Social Science Edition)*, 219(6): 100-106.

Lv, Shuxiang, & Zhu, Dexi. 1979. *Lectures on Grammatical Rhetoric* (2nd edition). Beijing: China Youth Publishing House.

Quine, W. V. 1951. "Two Dogmas of Empiricism". *Philosophical Review*, 60: 20–43.

Sapir, Edward. 1921. *Language: An Introduction to the Study of Speech*. New York: Harcourt, Brace.

Sellars, W. 2003. *Empiricism and the Philosophy of Mind: Introduction and Study Guide*. Cambridge: Harvard University Press.

Shen, Jiaxuan. 2019. *Beyond Subject and Predicate – Dui-speech Grammar and Dui-speech Format*. Beijing: The Commercial Press.

Shen, Xiaolong. 2019. *The Study of Chinese Characteristics*. Shanghai: Fudan University Press.

Wang, Aihua. 2016. "Meaning Holism and the Puzzle of Utterance Understanding". *Foreign Language Research*, 188(1):7-14.

Wang, Canlong. 2020. "Logical Logic and Linguistic Logic — Start with 'Today in History'". *Research on Chinese as a Second Language*, 1:1-13.

Wang, Weixian, & Li, Xiankun, & Chen Zongming. 1989. *Introduction to Linguistic Logic*. Wuhan: Hubei Education Press.

Wittgenstein, L. 1953. *Philosophical Investigations*. Oxford: Basil Blackwell.

Zhang, Mengwen. 2018. Sellars' Logical Space—A Defense for Meaning Holism. *Studies in Philosophy of Science and Technology*, 35(6): 14-19.

Zhang, Shilu. 2020. *Lecture Notes on Chinese History*. Shanghai: Oriental Publishing Center.

Zhou, Liquan (ed.). 1994. *Logic—The Theory of Correct Thinking and Effective Communication*. Beijing: People's Publishing House.

Mind Modeling of Bodily Motion-Emotion Expressions

Hongbo Li
Sichuan University

Abstract

This paper aims to construct a mental mode for bodily motion-emotion expressions and the consciousness process. Based on the Theoretical Model of Doublet Structure of Consciousness for Speech, the Doublet Structure of Consciousness for bodily motion-emotion expressions exemplifies the interaction of linguistic expression and consciousness and also emphasizes national and cultural traits in itself, focusing on the mental-physical supervenience of emotions on the bodily motions. These traits are found to be closely tied to the consciousness via which the possible world is reflected in nature by linguistic expressions. Thus the causal analysis of bodily motion-emotion expressions, as a causal implication based on a causal relationship, take both intentionality and context into consideration as well. Consequently, the mental modeling of bodily motion-emotion expressions from the perspective of the mental-physical supervenience, and viewing such supervenience as a core theory, should construe the bodily motion-emotion expressions in the following three aspects: the identity as the cause, the invariance of the variation as the guarantee of the cultural implication, and the further causal analysis of expressions.

Keywords

bodily motion-emotion expressions; Doublet Structure of Consciousness; mental-physical supervenience; identity; causal implication

1. Introduction

Linguistic expression is always an expression within a certain national cultural atmosphere, the essence of linguistic expression is a linguistic representation of the dual structure of consciousness, and the main content of its expression is how the mind reflects the possible world. The *reflection in the mind of the possible world* refers to the subjective response of a person to the possible world under conditioned stimuli. Subjective responses include the person's subjective reaction to the concrete stimuli of reality, such as the subjective reaction to sound,

---

Hongbo Li, Ph.D, College of Foreign Languages and Cultures, Sichuan University, Chengdu, China. E-mail address: 715123410@qq.com.

light, electricity, taste, etc., in the first signaling system[①]. The motions result from the concrete stimuli of reality. They also include the subjective reactions to the abstract stimuli of reality by human beings in the second signaling system, such as the subjective reaction to the verbal text and phonetic symbols, etc., and the expressions of motions result from the abstract stimuli of reality. In addition, the reaction itself is a kind of feeling, emotion, or sensation. And emotions could be regarded as the sum of all responses to external stimuli. For the subject, such feelings, emotions, and sensations are the experience of his sense of satisfaction, and thus emotions are essentially the sum of cognitive judgments and psychological evaluations of changes in physical conditions. So it is argued that linguistic expressions are the expressions of emotions, considering the linguistic expressions of motions as the expressions of emotions, and it is under such motivation that bodily motion-emotion expressions are generated and interpreted.

As a linguistic expression describing how consciousness reflects the external possible world, the bodily motion-emotion expression is just a linguistic facsimile structure (Xu, 2015a), which, once it gives us a stimulus in the form of linguistic words or sound symbols, will produce mental feelings about the physical content embedded in such linguistic expressions, i.e., physical properties trigger mental properties, and mental properties are supervenient upon physical properties: the cause of mental physical supervenience is the identity between motions and emotions; the process of such a supervenience is a process of mental-physical isomorphism in which a metaphor is generated and a gestalt transformation occurs from the source to the target, maintaining the identity of the two; and the result of mental physical supervenience is the construction of bodily motion-emotion expressions. The interpretation of bodily motion-emotion expressions must elevate to the level of causal implication, taking into account the specific, historical, cultural, and national connections between motions and emotions and the constraints of environment and intentionality as well, so as to realize the causal implication of bodily motion-emotion expressions.

Therefore, in the following discussion, we will try to construct a mind model for the analysis of bodily motion-emotion expressions from the perspective of mental-physical supervenience, in three aspects: the dual structure of consciousness (Ibid), the ethnicity and cultural properties, and the mental-physical supervenience. The relationship between the three is as follows: First, the dual structure of consciousness is a mental description of the process of consciousness reflected in bodily motion-emotion expressions, which mainly solves the problem of "what." Second, the ethnicity and cultural properties of bodily motion-emotion expressions is a research paradigm, which mainly solves the problems of "why" and "how"; and because of the universality of bodily motion-emotion expressions in the daily discourse within a certain national cultural circle and the relative specificity of understanding it, we have to put special emphasis on its ethnicity and cultural properties when analyzing this kind of emotional expression, so we can explain ourselves within the national cultural circle in which we are located, and at the same time, we can make the "outsiders" of a certain culture understand the speech with the characteristics of a certain culture. Third, mental-physical supervenience is the core theory that can solve the problem of "how to interpret" bodily motion-emotion expressions.

2. Dual Structure of Consciousness

To apply the dual structure of consciousness to the study of bodily motion-emotion expressions is to analyze how the cognitive subject notices and recognizes the "motion," which is based on the noticing and recognizing of the motion in the possible world, and the content of the noticing and recognizing includes both the physical and psychological properties of the motion. The content of attention and awareness includes both the physical and psychological properties of the motion, that is, the properties of the motion that can cause the subject of awareness to think that it is "like something," and the psychological properties are supervenient to the physical properties. Discourse expression is the reflection of consciousness to the possible world, and consciousness is the sum of human response to external stimuli, which is manifested as the unity of emotions, feelings and sensations, so the discourse expression of "motion" will develop from senses to feelings, from the feeling to the metaphor or the metonymy of emotions with the same feelings, producing the psychological feeling of expressing emotions metaphorically or metonymically. Once such mental feelings are generated, they produce imagery in consciousness, the feeling of the entity in the world of energy, and in another aspect, the feeling of one thing in the world of possibilities "like" another. The metaphors are about the former like framework, while the metaphors are about the entity framework.

The bodily motion-emotion expressions take only the form of motion expressions in everyday discourse and written language, and the stimuli we get from such signals belong to the real abstract stimuli, so we could possibly feel them as real motions happen. But there still exist two situations: some of the motions described actually take place, such as "fluttering eyebrows, dancing, baring teeth, grinning," and so on; while others do not happen, such as "turning the stomach, raising the heart in the throat, exploding the lungs, laughing at the liver, pulling down the face," and so on.

The development of the feeling of the expression of "bodily behavior" into psychological feeling is an inevitable process of consciousness because linguistic expression is the reflection of consciousness on the possible world, and this reflection will inevitably develop from feeling into psychological feeling, and the content of psychological feeling is the causal relationship between bodily behavior and emotion, which is the process of supervenience of mind and matter; meanwhile, the generation and construction of linguistic expression is also the process of supervenience of mind and matter; at the same time, the generation and construction of language is also the process of supervenience of mind and matter. At the same time, the generation and construction of linguistic expression is also the result of the supervenience of mind and matter: motion is "matter," the mental feeling of motion is "mind," and the mental feeling of motion is supervenient to the attributes and characteristics of motion. Because of the connection between motion and emotion in physiology and in a certain national culture circle, the real motion that we feel due to emotion is the "body," which is adjacent to the emotion in the mental feeling, and thus can produce a metaphorical construction in the mental feeling. For example, "mei fei se wu" （眉飞色舞） and "shou wu zu dao" (手舞足蹈) are adjacent to "happy," and "ci ya lie zui" (呲牙咧嘴) is adjacent to "pain, anger," and "chui xiong dun zu" is adjacent to "anxious, angry". The inauthentic motions that we feel have also gone through a history in the cultural circle of the Chinese language. The inauthentic motion that we feel is also historically and culturally precipitated in the Chinese language culture circle, and because of certain cultural origins, it has become a state of existence that "resembles a certain kind of emotion," which can produce a metaphorical construction in the psychological feeling. For example, "dao wei kou" (倒胃口) is similar to "disgust," "xin ti dao sangzi yan" (心提到嗓子眼) is similar to "nervousness," "fei zha" (肺炸) is similar to "disgust," "gan dan xiang zhao" (肝胆相照) is similar to "brotherly concern." "la xia lian" (拉下脸) is similar to "angry."

The discourse expression of "mei fei se wu" (眉飞色舞) obtained through the above process of the supervenience of mind and matter is a kind of facsimile structure, describing a person's pleased and excited appearance; at the same time, it also reflects people's psychological feelings toward "mei fei se wu" because of the adjacency between the act of "mei fei se wu" and the emotion of "happy," "mei fei se wu" can be used as a metaphor for "happy." Because the behavior of "mei fei" and the emotion of "happy" are adjacent to each other, "fluttering" can be used as a metaphor to refer to the emotion of "happy," and the metaphor and the ontology can be realized. The metaphor and the ontology can be transformed into a gestalt, and finally, the motion-emotional metaphorical expression of "dancing in a flurry of colors and being happy" can be constructed in our mental feelings, which is reflected in the linguistic expression of "mei fei se wu." At the same time, this kind of mimetic structure follows the causal relationship between the mimetic structure and the ontological structure in the possible world: the causal relationship between the ontological structure and the mimetic structure is based on the same relationship between the two things, including the relationship of adjacency and similarity, etc.; the feeling of the causal relationship is the process of generating the metaphorical "bodily behaviors," and the bodily behaviors and the emotions are the same as those in the metaphorical "bodily behaviors," which are the same as the emotion. The process from generating the body behavior to the state of the metaphorical "body behavior is transformed into a gestalt in the mental feeling, and a facsimile structure describing such a process is obtained. The facsimile structure superficially describes the physical relationship between things, but in fact it reflects the psychological feeling of the cognition subject on the causal relationship between things. Therefore, we say that the facsimile structure is a linguistic representation of the mental feeling of causal relationship, and its generation process is the reflective activity of consciousness on the possible world, which is reflected as a dual structure of consciousness, as shown in the following figure:

Figure 1. Schematic of the dual structure of consciousness

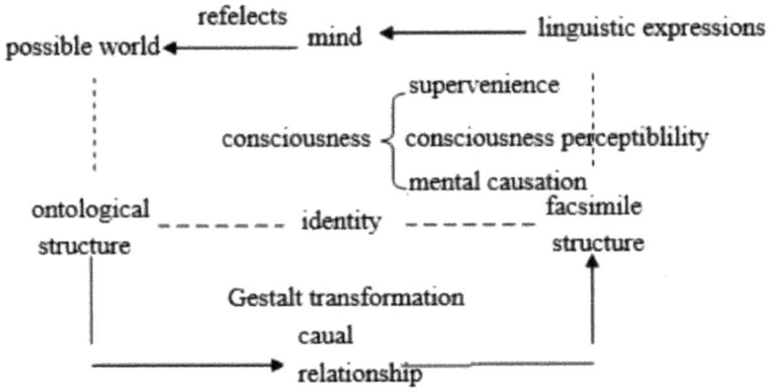

The above "dual structure of consciousness" demonstrates the process of interaction between linguistic expression and consciousness: linguistic expression is essentially the reflection of the mind on the possible world, which is a representation of the dual structure of consciousness; the reflection of the mind on the possible world is mainly carried out by conscious activity. The conscious activity from linguistic expression to the possible world and from the possible world to linguistic expression is a dynamic process, which involves the gestalt transformation of the facsimile structure and the ontological structure on the basis of sameness, and this process reflects the causal relationship between the ontological structure and the facsimile structure. The description of the feeling of such a causal relationship is indispensable for a clear account of the cause, generation, construction, and production of linguistic expression.

In terms of cognitive science, consciousness is a subjective response to the outside world, including the response of the first signaling system to stimuli from objectively existing external objects, and also the response of the second signaling system to stimuli from abstract things such as verbal words and speech symbols. For example, if the wind blows and a tree moves, it will respond to the stimulus. Psychologically, consciousness is complex, and analyzing linguistic expressions from the perspective of the philosophy of mind is that they may be related to the following three aspects of consciousness: mental-physical supervenience, conscious sensibility, and psychological causality. In a nutshell, mental-physical supervenience means that the feelings produced by the mind are supervenient to the objects; the mind feels the objects, and how it manifests itself is the content of conscious sensibility; the supervenience between the mind and the objects is depicted as psychological causality. Mental-physical supervenience, conscious sensibility and psychological causality are all the consciousness activities closely related to language expression in language research, among which, mental-physical supervenience is in the core position; but mental-physical supervenience is definitely not isolated, and it has to be subjected to the constraints of conscious sensibility and psychological causality in order to ensure that the mental-physical supervenience can realize the construction and generation of linguistic expressions under the premise of following the basis of mind-object homogeneity and the law of mind-object isomorphism; the heart and object attached by the mental-physical supervenience can be used as the basis of language expression. Generation; the linguistic expression obtained by the mental-physical supervenience is essentially a kind of conscious feeling of people for the possible world, and all conscious feelings are related to national and cultural accumulation, so the causal implication process of analyzing and interpreting the linguistic expression must take into account the intentionality and context constraints.

3. Ethnicity and cultural properties

Motion-emotion expressions refer to the use of bodily behavior as a metaphor for some kind of emotion, which may be embodied in metaphorical or metonymic expressions, and often appear separately in everyday discourse in the form of "bodily behavior." Similar expressions have been studied in the "motion-emotion metaphor" in four languages: English, Swedish, Bulgarian and Thai (Zlatev, 2012). The most accepted research paradigm for the study of such national and cultural expressions is the research paradigm of "ethnopragmatics."

The term "ethnopragmatics" refers to "the interpretation of language use in terms of culture-internal concepts, i.e., interpretation in terms of speakers common values, standards, priorities, and settings, rather than in terms of commonalities set by pragmatics; *ethnopragmatics* (also referred to as *ethnopragmatics*) is a term used to describe the use of language in the context of a particular language. Ethnopragmatics (also known as *cross-cultural pragmatics*) is characterized by cultural features and a very specialized and nuanced portrayal of cultures."[2]

The theory of natural semantic meta-language is a theory proposed by Wierzbicka (1996) to analyze semantics, in which "natural semantics" refers to a set of semantic primitives, which are universal to all peoples. The words corresponding to these semantic primitives can be found in any natural language of mankind, and their meanings are corresponding and equivalent in each natural language; the number of these words is not large in a language, and their meanings are relatively stable, and the use of words is understood on the basis of the concepts of dignity, values, beliefs and attitudes, social categories, emotions and so on, so that the use of words by different peoples is different because they have different ideas and feelings. Therefore, the use of speech is different among different peoples, because they have different ideas and feelings. Cultural values construct the "hidden" meaning behind the structure of discourse (Liao, 2007), and we must take into account the constraints of intentionality and context on the generation and understanding of discourse when we study the discourse expression of people in a certain cultural circle; this is the cultural value of discourse expression. So it is not easy to understand and elucidate another culture's use of language, or to make "outsiders" of a certain culture understand the use of language with a certain culture's characteristics, because these concepts are embedded in the language of the respective cultures, and some of them may not be clear even to the native speakers.

To sum up, the use of "natural semantic metalanguage" for description and characterization, i.e., the use of concise, culturally shared "semantic primes" as vocabulary, is not an easy task— that is to say, the use of concise, culturally shared "semantic primes" (primes) as vocabulary for semantic-pragmatic depiction, constituting "cultural scripts" (Wierzbicka, 1996), which is very useful in cross-cultural comparisons and in the cultural characterization of linguistic expressions. Such semantic elements, if they have a fixed pattern, can become a schema of a logical model. Prof. Jordan Zlatev borrowed this "naturalistic meta-language" approach in his cross-cultural comparative study of "motion-emotion metaphor" in eight languages, including English, Chinese, Spanish and Thai and provided 116 "motion-emotion metaphor meta types" using English as the meta-language, such as: Fall Into, Sink Into, Throw X Down In, Soar, Pull X Down, Break Down, Ripple X, Swell, Press X, Shoulder X, and so on. Among them, there are 50 "motion-emotion metaphor type schemata" corresponding (correlating) to them in English, 46 in Chinese, and 23 in Thai (Li, 2015). Taking Chinese as an example, the body-emotion metaphor type schemata in English as a meta-language appear separately as "body behavior" in Chinese, and we select the more specific "schema" in Chinese for English-Chinese comparative understanding, as shown in the following table:

Table 1. Unique motion-emotion metaphor schema in Chinese.
(F = self is figure, FP = part of self is figure, LM = landmark, A = agent.)

	Self-caused		English gloss	Caused	English gloss
+translocative/+bound	(5)	F chu LM (fengtou)	F goes beyond fengtou	(23) A chui F shang LM	A blows F up to LM
	(6)	F xia LM tai	F steps down tai	(24) A peng F dao LM	A carries F to LM
	(7)	F guo LM (kan)	F crosses threshold	(25) A mao-HUO	A sends out HUO
	(9)	FP (xin) luo di	heart falls to ground	(26) A sa-QI	A lets out QI
				(27) A xie-QI	A lets out QI
+translocative/-bound	(13)	FP (QI) lai	QI comes	(30) A chui-peng F	A inflate F
	(16)	FP (xin) feizou	heart flies away	(35) A la xia FP (lian)	A pulls down face
-translocative/+bound				(38) A an-xin	A stabilizes heart
				(40) A fen-xin	A divides heart
				(41) A fang-xin	A puts aside heart
				(43) A jing-xin	A stabilizes heart
				(45) A pian-xin	A tilts heart
				(48) A fan-lian	A turns over face
				(50) A sao-xing	A clears away interest
				(51) A jie-QI	A removes QI
-translocative/-bound	(21)	FP (xin) piao	heart floats	(54) A dan-xin	A shoulders heart
	(22)	FP (xin) dang	heart swings		

The cultural scripts[3] of bodily behavior-emotional expression involved in this paper will be different from those appearing in the table above, which are mainly cultural scripts about physical depictions of bodily behaviors and depictions of inauthentic bodily behaviors, which are mainly visceral behaviors. Integrating this empirical evidence into an explanatory and predictive model, we obtain a mental-physical supervenience model of body behavior-emotion expression in Chinese: the process of mental-physical supervenience is the process of recognizing the subject's conscious feeling of body behavior, which reflects the dual structure of consciousness, emphasizing both the ethnicity and cultural nature of linguistic expression, and taking mental-physical supervenience as the core process, the result of mental-physical supervenience. The result of mental-physical supervenience is the construction of bodily motion-emotion expressions, and the interpretation of the expression is based on causal implication, which is based on a "cause and effect relationship" and subject to the constraints of intentionality and context.

4. The basic model of the two-way relationship of mind-body supervenience

The study of entailment begins with entailment as a relational category. Causality is the classic example of what we call the *relation of determination* or *dependence*. Causes determine their effects, and the existence and properties of the effects are determined by their causes." (Kim, 1994) Supervenience is a relation inside the series of dependence or decision relations, including causality. The philosophical importance of such a series of dependence or determination relations lies in the fact that it provides a way or means by which entities, properties, events, etc. enter into a dependence or determination relation of one to the other, creating a system in which internal things interact. Viewing entailment as a relational category is a new perspective and paradigm for us to examine the complex relations in the world (Yin, 1998), and causality, which includes dependence and determination relations, appears to be particularly salient.

Second, related research on entailment in the field of philosophy of mind is also closely related to the mind-body problem, which involves the relationship between mind and body: whether the mind depends on the body or whether the body determines the mind. One of the research focuses in the philosophy of mind is to study the relationship between human mental properties and external things, so the study of entailment in the philosophy of mind mainly focuses on mental-psycho supervenience, which holds that human mental properties are entailed with the physical properties of the things concerned. However, mind-body causation is not causation in general, because the mind does not fully obey physical causation, but has a degree of autonomy, nondeterminism or nonphysicality, which is commonly called *freedom of will*. This freedom of will may enable me not to retract my hand when I feel pain, thus violating the usual laws of causation. In this way, the mental is both dependent and independent of physical relations, unlike fully deterministic causal relations. Davidson calls this mental-physical relationship "supervenience." Therefore, the study of supervenience in the context of mind-body issues is also a study of causality; this causality also emphasizes the joint role of free will and environment (Chen, 2010:71-79).

Third, causal entailment research focusing on mind-body issues also follows a basic belief of philosophers of science: everything in nature can evolve and evolve from lower-level things to higher-level things according to its evolutionary program, forming a class hierarchy from lower-level things to higher-level things. In this structure, things at higher levels are based on things at lower levels and are supervenient to things at lower levels. This is in line with the concept of "downward causation" proposed by Kim Jae-kwon (1994), which states that causation in macro-events follows causation in micro-events; similarly, a mental event can be deduced from a physical event as a cause because it follows the physical event that caused it, which in this case is "causation," based on the "bottom-to-top deterministic relation." Therefore, we regard the mental event (the perceived motion) as the trigger for causal derivation, based on the above-mentioned derivation of the entailment relation. In summary, we can draw a basic schema of the two-way relationship between the mind and the object (Figure 2):

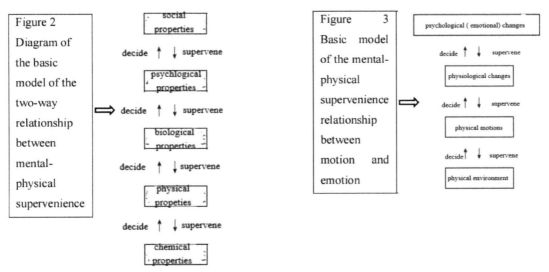

From this, it can be seen that the core issue in the study of entourage is as follows: In the causal relationship of mind-object entourage, under the guidance of this two-way model of causality, we try to combine mind-object entourage with the study of language, what specifically can be investigated in the linguistic phenomenon, and how to construct an explanatory model of linguistic expression with the two-way model of causality of mind-object entourage; this is the next problem we want to solve.

5. Mental-physical supervenience motion-emotion expressions

5.1. The mind-body supervenience relationship of motions and emotions

We choose body behavior-expression as a research object combining mental-physical supervenience and language research because body behavior-emotion expression is a kind of language expression that intuitively embodies mental-physical supervenience: body behavior directly or indirectly embodies emotional changes, and emotion is supervenient to body behavior, and the two are causal to each other. The basic schema of mind-body supervenience is shown in Figure 3:

From the Figure 3, the motion that directly reflects the emotional changes is purely physiological behavior. The expression of this behavior can be directly analyzed through the relationship between emotion and behavior, such as "mian hong er chi" (面红耳赤) behavior expression is supervenient to the emotion of shame or indignation; "lian hong bo zi cu" (脸红脖子粗) is supervenient to the emotion of excitement; "mu deng kou dai" (目瞪口呆) is supervenient to shock, "chi zhi yi bi" (嗤之以鼻) is supervenient to contempt, "yao ya qie chi" (yao ya qie chi) is supervenient to hatred, "zhang kou jie she" (张口结舌) is associated with confusion or fear, "fan bai yan" (翻白眼) is associated with resentment or dissatisfaction, and "mian mian xiang qu (面面相觑)is associated with fear or helplessness. The expression of these types of motions should be understood in relation to the mechanism of metonymy.

Motions that indirectly reflect emotional changes are also literally motions, only that these behaviors do not really happen in the physical world, e.g., broken heart, sinking heart, exploding lungs, collapsing appetite, etc.; unlike the behaviors described in the above physical-emotional metaphors, the behaviors here are not directly supervenient to the emotions, but rather to psychological feelings based on the behavioral changes. These psychological feelings have a deep cultural origin and are similar to people's core emotions, which makes the behavior in this type of expression indirectly supervenient to the emotion based on similar psychological feelings. For example, "xin sui" (心碎)is indirectly supervenient to the emotion of sadness and despair; "fei zha" (肺炸)is indirectly supervenient to anger; "gan dan xiang zhao" (肝胆相照) is indirectly supervenient to concern; and so on. Expressions of this type of motion should be understood in the context of metaphorical mechanisms.

5.2. The mental-physical supervenience of metaphorical and metonymic expressions

Metaphors and metonymies, as a way of thinking, are inherently mind-physical in their mental properties: metaphorical thinking and metonymic thinking are both based on low-level physical events. And the construction of both metaphor and metonymy in linguistic expression has to be based on the direct access of perception: People rely on the direct access of perception to directly feel the similarity or adjacency of two things and realize the mental construction of metaphor or metonymy from one thing to another through the activity of similarity or adjacency of Gestalt mental conversion: What springs up in linguistic expression is "A is B" (A is B). Such expressions may be metaphors or metaphors.

"The study of metaphor involves two theories of mental-physical supervenience: the theory of mental-physical supervenience and The Transparent Thesis (The Transparent Thesis), both of which are scholarly claims of scholars holding a physiologist (physicalism) view in the philosophy of mind. In principle, the direct access of sensation also implies the idea that 'mind' follows 'matter.'"(Xu , 2015c: 4) And Fan Dongping (2010) argues that "in the study of philosophy of mind one can use 'mental-physical supervenience' to illustrate the relationship between high-level conscious phenomena and low-level physical facts." Metaphorical studies involve direct access to sense perception as much as metaphorical studies, and metaphors even behave more directly. Metaphors and metonymies as a mental activity belong to our higher level of conscious phenomena, and the basis for the combination of mental-physical supervenience and metaphorical and metonymic studies lies in the mental-physical supervenience of metaphors and metonymies themselves.

In bodily motion-emotion expressions, if the depiction of behavior is not real behavior, and, at the same time, it has similarity with a certain emotion in terms of psychological feelings, for example, the similarity between "xin sui" (心碎) and sadness in terms of psychological feelings, and the similarity between "la xia lian" (拉下脸) and anger, it could be supposed that "zhui ru ai he"(坠入爱河) is similar to two people falling in love, "zhui ru shen yuan"(坠入深渊) is similar to despair, and so on. Therefor it constitutes a physical-behavioral-emotional metaphor, where the behavior is the metaphor and the emotion is the ontology, and where the ontology (the emotion) doesn't show up, so we have "xin sui" to indirectly metaphorically express sadness, "la xia lian" to metaphorically express anger, "zhui ru ai he" to metaphorically express falling in love, "zhui ru shen yuan" metaphorically expresses despair, and so on.

If A and B are adjacent to each other in the expression, for example, if A is used in place of B, A can be a part of B, or a cause or a consequence of B, and so on, such an expression is a *metonymy*. In the bodily motion-emotion expressions of the behavior the depiction of the behavior is the real behavior, but is also due to some kind of emotional change induced by the behavior, such as happy induced by the "smile," angry induced by the "cross eyes," stunned induced by the "jaw dropping," etc. The direct access of perception makes it possible for us to directly understand the above behavioral descriptions as the emotions that triggered them. The direct access of perception allows us to interpret the above behavioral descriptions as the emotions that evoke them, thus constructing a motion-emotion metaphor.

The motion-emotion metaphor uses the unreal behavioral changes of the body or viscera as a metaphor for emotion, and the motion-emotion metaphor uses one of the behavioral changes of the body when the emotion changes as a metaphor for emotion. Both belong to the same motion-emotion expression, and they both embody the mental-physical supervenience nature of motion and emotion: emotion follows motion, and the core relationship between the two is causality: emotion is the cause of triggering behavior, and behavior is the effect caused by emotion. The core relationship between the two is causality: emotion is the cause of behavior, and behavior is the result of emotion.

6. Causal derivation of bodily behavior-emotion expression

The core of the mind-body entailment of behavior and emotion in bodily behavior-emotion expression is causality, so we can use causal derivation to explain the construction and generation of bodily behavior-emotion metaphor and bodily behavior-emotion metonymy. Below we use the example of the physical-behavior-emotion metaphor to illustrate how the theory of mind-body entailment, when combined with the study of metaphors, can be used to make causal inferences on the basis of mind-body entailment.

It is important to note that there is a causal relationship between the high-level conscious phenomena involved in the metaphor and the low-level physical events that act as ontologies, yet it is not a general causal relationship because the mind is not fully subordinated to physical causality but has a degree of autonomy or nondeterminism or nonphysicality, which is commonly referred to as free will. Chen Xiaoping says that this this is what Davidson calls the "principle of causal interaction": "The relationship of the psyche to the physical is both dependent on and independent of the physical, unlike a fully deterministic causal relationship. Davidson calls this relation of the mental to the physical 'entailment.'" (Chen, 2010:71-79) So the ultimate understanding in the above example will vary from person to person, from time to time, and from place to place, and this is where the constraints of context and intentionality come into play. Why do we have a more general consensus on the behavioral expression of "pulling down the face" as an expression of anger, "getting angry, getting mad"? This is the "mind" on the "object" subjective mobility in the role, the degree of mobility by the subject's intentionality and context constraints, thus affecting the degree of consensus, should be directly proportional. That's why we have a lot of such metaphors in Chinese, and we can also find similar phenomena in other languages. For example, in English, "I was downcast by the whole situation," "I broke down under the pressure."

The study of the mind-body supervenience of physical-behavioral-emotional metaphors is to "illustrate how the use of metaphors follows the mind-body supervenience — on the one hand, how 'things' (behavior) constrain 'mind' (emotion), and at the same time, how 'things' (behavior) constrain 'mind' (emotion) on the one hand, and how 'mind' exercises its own autonomous will at the same time, and to use this idea to explain some of the important features of metaphors." (Xu, 2015b:3) The process of the "heart" exercising its own autonomous will here is the process of causal derivation in conjunction with context and intentionality. Here we cite Xu Shenghuan (2015b) as a visual illustration of the mental-physical supervenience dimension of the above metaphor study:

Figure 4. Schematic diagram of the mind-object entourage of source and target

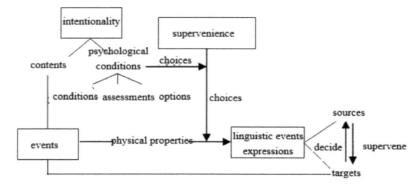

The process of mental-physical supervenience in physical-emotional mytonyms and that of physical-emotional metaphors is more or less the same, which can also be illustrated by the above diagram. The "motions" depicted in bodily motion-emotion expressions are "events" that have a supervenience relationship with "emotions," such as "dian tou," (点头) "wei xiao," (微笑) "qiao qi" (翘企) and so on. "Events" such as "点头," "微笑," 挥手," "crossing one's fingers," and so on, which actually happen, while those in "xin luo di" (心落地) and "fei zha,"(肺炸) "gan dan xiang zhao,"(肝胆相照) "rou chang cun duan," (柔肠寸断) etc., do not happen. They have in common that they are "events" that are supervenient to "emotions" in the consciousness. This process of supervenience of mind and matter is roughly like this: behavioral expressions are felt as "events" at the beginning, or they really happen, or they don't really happen; the real behavior is the behavioral entity triggered by emotion, and the non-real behavior is also the result of the cultural precipitation and "emotion" in the cultural circle of the Han Chinese people in terms of discourse expression. In the Han Chinese cultural circle, because of the close connection between cultural sedimentation and "emotion" in discourse expression, the sensation of these "events" develops into feelings: either adjacent to the emotion and existing in the consciousness as a "depository" or related to the emotion because of the cultural origin of the emotion. The emotion is similar to the motion because of its cultural origin and exists in the consciousness as a "state."

Why is it possible to produce such neighboring or similar feelings? For example, why can "dian tou" be a subsitition or metaphor for "appreciation," and why can "wei xiao" be "happy"? Why is "hui shou" be "welcome," and why can "xin luo di" be "being relieved"? All these "why" questions can be answered by the constraints of intentionality on the supervenience of mind and matter. It is people's intentionality, including imagery content and imagery attitude, that chooses what kind of feeling to give to the "event" in the process of mental-object supervenience and thus arrives at the "use case event" that has a causal relationship with the "event." The "use case event" that has a causal relationship with the "event" can be derived from the "use case event". The expression of "motion" is perceived as a "use case event" that has a physiological and cultural connection with "emotion," i.e., "motion-emotion" expression, and this is the "motion-emotion" expression. The expression of "emotion" is the process of following the mind and object under the constraints of intentionality, so that a certain kind of motion is fixed in a specific cultural circle to express the expression of emotion, i.e., the expression of motion-emotion. When people see or hear the expression of "body behavior," they will immediately have a feeling, and this feeling is the process of generating the reflective consciousness of "body behavior," which is expressed by certain body behaviors or characteristics of body behaviors (such as). The linguistic expression of emotion in terms of a certain physical act or a characteristic of a physical act (e.g., the characteristic of being "like a certain emotion") is thus constructed in consciousness, and metonymy is related to the "body" of the physical act, and metaphor is related to the "state" of the physical act. Metonymy is related to the real body motions, and metaphor is related to the supposed body motions in our consciousness.

7. Conclusion

The physical act as an "event" is selected as a metaphor or metonymy for "emotion" in the process of causally attached consciousness, and the resulting "physical-emotional" expression is the "use case event." The resulting "body-act-emotion" expression is a "use-case event," a discourse expression that conforms to the "dual structure of consciousness" and reflects the conscious process of the subject of cognition's mental feelings about the "body-act," which is essentially a process of causal supervenience. It is essentially the process of the supervenience of mind and matter. We have to analyze the bodily motion-emotion expressions in order to further explain the question of "why it can be expressed in this way," which is also the purpose of our mental modeling.

The study of the mind-body supervenience of bodily motion-emotion expressions should start from three aspects. The first aspect is the identity of "motion" and "emotion," which is the basis for the mind-body supervenience of "motion-emotional" expressions. This is the cause of the mental-physical supervenience process of "physical act-emotion" expression. The second aspect is the mind-object isomorphism on the basis of homogeneity, which is the process of generating the physical act-emotion expression, that is, the process of the "physical act" becoming a metaphor through intentional selection, and the Gestalt transformation to the ontology "emotion." This is the process of generating the body-emotion expression, i.e., the process of "body behavior" becoming a metaphor through intentional selection and transforming to the ontology "emotion" through the process of gestalt transformation, which embodies the "invariance of transformation". The third is to further analyze the linguistic expression obtained through the supervenience of mind-objects and to emphasize the cause and effect of the body-emotion expression through the analysis of the causal connotation. This causality is constrained by intentionality and context, reflecting the national culture.

Notes

① http://baike.baidu.com/link?ur.

② Goddard(2004) [Goddard in The ethnopragmatics and semantics of "active metaphors," Goddard points out the ethnopragmatics point of view, and points out that the research methodology is to use "natural semantic meta-language" and "semantics" as meta-language to make semantics. "as a meta-language to make semantic descriptions and provide 'cultural scripts" (Liao, 2007: 479).

③ "Cultural script" is a key technique in the ethnopragmatics paradigm, which refers to the use of the meta-language of semantic elements to describe certain attitudes, evaluations, assumptions shared by people in a certain language area and to make statements. Depending on the level of generalization of cultural scripts, they can be divided into different "levels," mainly involving thoughts, words and behaviors. (Liao Qiaoyun, 2007).

References

Chen, Xiaoping. 2010. "A Discussion of the Concept of Supervenience". *Philosophical Studies*, (4): 71-79.

Goddard, C. 2004. "The Ethnopragmatics and Semantics of 'Active Metaphors'". *Journal of Pragmatics*, 36(7):1211-1230.

Kim, Jae-kwon. 1994. "Concepts of Supervenience". *Philosophy and Phenomenological Research*, (12): 153.

Li, Hongbo. 2015. "Study on Chinese Motion-Emotion Metaphor from a Perspective of Social Cognition, Proceedings of the Fourth Northeast Asia International Symposium on Language". *Literature and Translation*, July 24-26, Tongliao, China, pp. 82-87.

---- 2016. "A Study on the Bodily Motion-Emotion Expressions from a Perspective of Supervenience," Doctoral dissertation, Sichuan University, China.

Liao, Qiaoyun. 2007. "A New Paradigm for Pragmatics Research—A Review of Ethnopragmatics", *Foreign Language Teaching and Research*, (3): 477-479.

Wierzbicka. 1996. *Semantics: Primes and Universals*, Oxford: OUP.

Xu, Shenghuan. 2015a. "Dual Structure of Language Use and Consciousness," *Foreign Language Studies*, (2): 3-11.

---- 2015b. "The Mind-Object-Following Dimension of Metaphor Research". *Foreign Languages*, (4): 2-11.

Yin, Xiao, 1998. "A Primer on J. King's Theory of Attachment", *Journal of Central China Normal University (Humanities and Social Sciences Edition)*, (3): 12-17.

Zlatev, Jordan. 2012. "Metaphor and Subjective Experience: A Study of Motion-Emotion Metaphors in English, Swedish, Bulgarian, and Thai". In Ad Foolen, ed., *Moving Ourselves, Moving Others: Motion and Emotion in Intersubjectivity, Consciousness and Language*, Amsterdam: Philadelphia: John Benjamins Publishing House, p. 434.

Investigating the Unexplored Dimension: Instrumentalizing the Domain-Specific Manifestation of Foreign Language Tolerance of Ambiguity

Shijie Wang
University of Cambridge

Abstract

This study examines the underexplored relationship between tolerance of ambiguity (TA) and second language (L2) learning, specifically addressing the intricate aspects of TA within language typology. We have instrumentalized and validated the Foreign Language TA (FLTA) scale, a novel 20-item instrument assessing tolerance towards typological differences across five linguistic domains (semantic, phonological, morphosyntactic, thematic, pragmatic) and four ambiguity subtypes (novelty, complexity, insolubility, incomprehension). Tested on 795 Chinese L2 English learners, the study reveals that domain-general TA has minimal correlation with L2 proficiency, contradicting existing hypotheses in applied linguistics research. To compare, the two domain-specific scales, showing distinct discriminant validity, enhance predictive power by accounting for 8.7% of proficiency variability, with 3.7% being unique to the new FLTA scale. This finding challenges the blind use of the generic TA scale(s), highlighting instead the importance of recognizing the complexities inherent to specific language pairs. Such malleability thus allows for application across a varied range of languages and learner profiles. We posit that this broadening of the learner experience space marks a pioneering step towards the development of tailored models to assess the influence of the FLTA on L2 learning, hence setting a baseline for future explorations.

Keywords

tolerance of ambiguity; instrument development and validation; domain-specificity; typological differences; multivariate analysis

1. Introduction

Tolerance of ambiguity (TA) is a psychological construct that has garnered considerable interest in the field of applied linguistics due to its potential implications for second language (L2) learning. Defined as "the tendency

---

Shijie Wang, University of Cambridge. E-mail address: sw985@cantab.ac.uk.

to perceive ambiguous situations as desirable" (Budner, 1962, p. 29), TA is believed to influence an individual's ability to navigate the inherent complexity and unfamiliarity of L2 learning processes. As such, it is postulated that learners possessing a higher TA level would display a greater affinity for language acquisition, which may eventually culminate in enhanced L2 proficiency.

Existing research into the application of TA within applied linguistics reveals two distinct categories. The first strand highlights TA as a sociopsychological variable, emphasizing its relevance in relation to tolerance for divergent values, social orientations, and novel environments (Dewaele & Li, 2013; Herman et al., 2010). In contrast, the second perspective positions TA as a domain-specific variable, with a specific focus on the uncertainties associated with L2 processing (Ely, 1995). Both approaches share empirical support for the connection between TA and linguistic phenomena such as multilingualism (Dewaele & Li, 2013), vocabulary knowledge (Başöz, 2015), and foreign language proficiency (Wang, 2020).

To extend this discourse, the present study endeavors to investigate a hitherto unexplored aspect of TA—its domain-specific manifestation in relation to typological differences between languages. We begin by synthesizing key findings from prior studies, paying particular attention to the varied operationalizations of TA and their respective conceptual underpinnings. Subsequently, we propose a novel foreign language TA (FLTA) scale, designed specifically to assess tolerance of ambiguity surrounding typological discrepancies. Details on scale development and validation are provided, alongside comparisons with existing instruments. Finally, utilizing the newly developed FLTA scale, we re-examine the relationship between foreign language achievement and TA in an effort to advance our understanding of their interplay.

2. Literature review

This section provides an overview of the two types of operationalizations of TA in the field of applied linguistics, encompassing both the domain-general sociopsychological aspect and the domain-specific language learning aspect.

2.1. Domain-general sociopsychological aspect of TA

Within applied linguistics, several studies have focused on the sociopsychological aspect of TA, drawing on operationalizations employed in psychological research (e.g., Budner, 1962). A notable study conducted by Dewaele and Li (2013) adopted Herman et al.'s (2010) domain-general TA scale and uncovered a small yet significant effect between multilingualism and TA (N = 2,158). Subsequent replications (e.g., Wei & Hu, 2019) and follow-up studies (e.g., Liu et al., 2017) have also predominantly utilized Herman et al.'s (2010) scale. This 12-item instrument evaluates tolerance for differing values, social orientations, and unfamiliar environments. For instance, participants are asked to rate their level of comfort when interacting with individuals who possess vastly dissimilar values.

In this regard, the TA-achievement relationship indicates how an open-mindedness-like TA trait could help enhance foreign language proficiency. Unfortunately, previous studies have yielded inconsistent results in various contexts. While van Compernolle's (2016) replication study revealed a positive correlation between TA and multilingualism (Spearman rho = .19), it contradicted prior findings reported by Dewaele and Li (2013) (eta^2

=.008). This huge discrepancy requires (1) further corroborations based on similar instruments and (2) a close investigation into the applicability of the instruments in different contexts. To compare, Liu et al.'s (2017) replication failed to identify any statistically significant "correlation between global proficiency on TA" ($p = .196$). The third replication effort by Wei and Hu (2019) revisited previous findings with more methodologically rigorous methods, producing an R^2 of .014. As such, the present study aims to act as a partial replication to further substantiate the link between TA and achievement.

In terms of this line of research, one limitation is the inadequate critical examination of the instrument employed. In Herman et al.'s (2010) original study, though the overall 12-item scale is reliable (Cronbach's α = .73), the four subdimensions of TA reported inadequate reliability (Cronbach's α < .6) for analysis. Given that Cronbach's α will increase systematically with more items (Ferketich, 1991), the overall instrument's reliability remains disputable without evaluating interitem correlations.

Wei and Hu's (2019) study provided information on validity and reliability, but also with a key limitation arising from the data-driven modification of the scale. This study utilized principal component analysis (PCA) to explore the factorial structure of TA in the Chinese EFL context. Within the three dimensions they detected, it is found that only a 3-item factor corresponds to the factorial structure in the original study, which was then named the "TA core" (*ibid.*, p. 1214). This three-item factor was hypothesized to be stable in different cultural contexts and then used to represent the whole TA construct. Although the existence of a cross-culturally valid factor is interesting, this purely data-driven approach cannot afford the operationalization of TA as this 3-item dimension. If evaluating these three items (items 3, 7, and 8), it could be found that the content centers on "willingness to visit a foreign country," which fails to represent the complicated concept of TA. Additionally, this procedure is methodologically problematic because PCA ignores the structure of the factors (Fabrigar & Wegener, 2011) but only extracts the factors which could explain as many variances as possible (Thompson, 2004). In terms of factorial structure, the researchers should employ "a 'proper' factor analysis model such as the maximum likelihood factor model" (Basilevsky, 2009, p. 98).

2.2. Domain-specific language learning aspect

The other line of research operationalizes TA in a domain-specific manner. To the best of our knowledge, Ely's (1995) Second Language Tolerance of Ambiguity (SLTA) Scale is singular in its exploration of language-related ambiguity tolerance. This instrument delves into "a broad spectrum of language activities" (p. 439) by examining learners' reactions to certain dimensions, incomprehension, inarticulateness, intricacy, and incongruency, within the second language (L2) acquisition process. Drawing a parallel between these dimensions and the three foundational components of ambiguity—novelty, complexity, and insolubility (Budner, 1962, p. 30)—lends credence to Ely's categorization. However, it should be noted that the SLTA Scale appears to measure a general construct of linguistic ambiguity tolerance rather than specific aspects exclusive to L2 learning. Consequently, high-tolerance individuals may exhibit acceptance toward various linguistic ambiguities beyond the L2 domain. This consequently introduces potential noise in the data analysis process.

To mitigate this issue and hone in on the tolerance exclusively pertinent to foreign language learning, it is essential to assess an overlooked aspect unique to L2 acquisition: the unfamiliar L2 *per se*, with its inherent incongruity from speakers' L1. Inevitably, acquiring a new linguistic system renders foreign sounds, meanings, structures, discourses, and communicative styles markedly ambiguous as compared to one's mother tongue. Notably, Ely's (1995) scale includes only one item addressing this particular incongruity between L1 and L2 (item 11: "I don't like the fact that it's often impossible to find [Foreign Language] words that mean exactly the same as some English words."). Henceforth, our study proposes refining existing instruments to measure this underexplored dimension of typological differences between languages. Subsequent analysis in our study will encompass the comparison of the newly developed Foreign Language Tolerance of Ambiguity (FLTA) with other existing measures, elucidating their psychometric similarities and disparities. Furthermore, this study aspires to examine the distinct ways in which varying aspects of ambiguity tolerance may differentially impact foreign language learning.

3. Instrument development

3.1. Overall structure

Based on the above review of previous instruments, this section will elaborate on the conceptual structure of the FLTA scale. The FLTA scale comprises two primary dimensions—micro-linguistic and macro-linguistic—reflecting both the cerebral locales involved in language processing and their distinctive roles therein. Drawing from neuroscientific literature, the micro-linguistic dimension is engaged with the left temporal-parietal regions of the brain, which facilitate intricate language processing (e.g., Blumstein, 1981). In contrast, Alzheimer's disease studies (e.g., Kempler et al., 1987; Nebes et al., 1984) suggest that an as yet undetermined area is responsible for macro-linguistic processing. Expanding upon this context, Glosser and Deser (1991) conducted a thorough investigation of language disorders, demonstrating that these two levels possess discrete psychological and neurological characteristics. For the micro-linguistic dimension of the FLTA scale, we designed three subdimensions: semantic, phonological, and morphosyntactic TA. The macro-linguistic dimension of the FLTA scale takes on a broader perspective, encompassing thematic and pragmatic TA. By elucidating these separate aspects within the scientific framework of neurology and language processing, the FLTA scale aims to provide a robust and adaptive tool for investigating the focal construct.

In addition to this overarching framework, the FLTA scale firstly incorporates three distinct styles of ambiguity as defined by Budner (1962): *novelty* (expressions absent in L1), *complexity* (expressions more intricate than L1), and *insolubility* (expressions conflicting with L1). Secondly, a fourth core element within the TA scale was added to capture the consequence of encountering ambiguity: *incomprehension*. To compare, the construct of *inarticulateness* – another form of ambiguity featured in Ely's (1995) scale—has not been included in the FLTA scale. This exclusion stems from the observation that the anxiety related to being misunderstood appears more relevant to the generation of ambiguity, which subsequently necessitates either tolerance or rejection by listeners, rather than invoking internal experiences of uncertainty within speakers themselves.

Consequently, the designed FLTA instrument is a 20-item Likert scale, encompassing 5 linguistic dimensions and 4 classifications of ambiguity. Echoing the structure of both the general TA scale and SLTA scale, the FLTA scale employs a 5-point rating system, with approximately 30% of its items reversely keyed for enhanced validity. To further improve validity, an introductory paragraph preceding the FLTA scale will delineate the option to select "not applicable." This addition proves particularly crucial for this instrument due to two factors: (1) certain participants' foreign languages may be minimally distinct from their native languages, reducing the likelihood that they would encounter situations depicted in certain items; and (2) the instrument requires participants to engage in meta-linguistic comparisons between two languages, which may prove challenging. With respect to this demand for meta-linguistic awareness, future adaptations of this scale could greatly benefit from researchers supplying item examples tailored to the specific populations under investigation.

3.2. Item development

Before presenting the items incapsulated within the FLTA scale, it is crucial to elucidate the rationale underpinning the specific item expressions and structure. In designing the FLTA scale, we strategically employed various linguistic techniques to capture diverse facets of learners' reactions to typological differences. An essential part of our approach was to focus on three types of subjective experiences for each item: affective, motivational, and cognitive. These dimensions were carefully chosen in order to holistically examine individuals' responses to linguistic ambiguity, while also acknowledging that various aspects of learners' dispositions may impact their learning processes differently (Dörnyei & Ryan, 2015). Affective expressions (e.g., "enjoy," "dislike") explore the affective component of learners' reactions to typological differences between languages. Motivational expressions (e.g., "feel discouraged," "don't want to encounter," "get impatient") were designed to tap into learners' drives and motivations when confronting ambiguity in foreign language learning. Cognitive expressions (e.g., "embrace," "can be comfortable") focus on learners' judgments and strategic choices in response to linguistic discrepancies. Unlike the more visceral motivational and affective reactions, cognitive items probe deeper into how learners deliberately choose to adapt or refrain from adapting based on their assessments and convictions. Notably, phrasing such as "can be comfortable" rather than "feel comfortable" underscores the proactive nature of these choices made by language learners. This aspect highlights that individuals can mold their cognition and take an active role in shaping their foreign language learning trajectories.

To further substantiate their relevance and validity, six linguists at the University of Cambridge (i.e., 2 MPhil students, 1 PhD student, 1 post-doc, and 2 professors) were invited to assess how well the draft items reflected typical typological discrepancies witnessed across different language pairs. Relying on their expertise and experience in multilingualism, these experts provided invaluable feedback and suggestions to refine each item's expression. Consequently, an iterative process was employed whereby draft items were proposed, reviewed, refined, re-evaluated, and adjusted as necessary to accurately represent real-life linguistic encounters. The most notable modification was to connect the items reliably with authentic foreign language learning experiences. As users proceed through the FLTA scale items, they will encounter nuanced scenarios that are designed to resonate with their own journey in acquiring and mastering new languages, thereby promoting a more accurate and insightful assessment of their tolerance for ambiguity within this unique domain.

3.3.3. Pilot study

The questionnaire in the piloting stage contains five main sections, including basic information, the FLTA scale (see Appendix for this initial scale), Herman et al.'s (2010) general TA (GTA) scale, Ely's (1995) SLTA scale, and a 7-item self-rated foreign language proficiency scale. The participants were asked to answer the online questionnaire (https://cambridge.eu.qualtrics.com/jfe/form/SV_cGAT03nsIvq7yJw) based on their personal foreign language learning experiences. A total of 99 participants were recruited in January 2022 through the convenience sampling method. After cleaning the invalid sample (e.g., those who rated 1 for all the items), it is confirmed that 91.9% (N = 91) of the cases are valid and therefore will be analyzed in later analysis. All the participants are competent enough in at least English or Chinese to understand the content of the questionnaire. The average age of the current sample is 25.055 (SD = 6.260), with most participants doing or having attained bachelor's degrees (48.352%, N = 44) or master's degrees (32.967%, N = 30). The majority of them speak Chinese Mandarin as their first language (97.802%, N = 89), with some speaking Chinese dialects (N = 1) and languages of ethnic minority groups in China (N = 1). The average age of onset (AoO) of foreign language learning is 7.253 (SD = 2.897), with English as the most ubiquitous L2 (94.505%, N = 86).

This pilot study reveals several pertinent observations. Firstly, the 20-item FLTA scale yields a Cronbach's α of 0.853, initially indicating strong internal consistency. However, given that α values tend to increase with more items (Ferketich, 1991), it is crucial to examine the interitem correlation (0.227) and item-to-total correlation, as they may be suboptimal for subsequent analyses. Interestingly, five items displayed weak correlations with the other components (items 5, 10, 16, 17, and 18), and all these items belong to the positively coded group (i.e., higher score represents higher tolerance). This observation suggests that response contamination might have arisen due to confusion or inattention resulting from the reverse wording strategy employed in the current scale (see Sonderen et al., 2013 for a discussion). Similar issues also reappeared when analyzing Herman et al.'s (2010) GTA scale and Ely's (1995) SLTA scale. However, we will not adopt a wholesale exclusion of reversely framed items which would be deemed "a step backwards" (Seng Kam & Meyer, 2015, p. 466), as it is equally essential to balance participants' acquiescent tendencies (Jackson & Messick, 1961). A potential solution entails assisting participants in recognizing the phrasing of items by emphasizing valence-related words, thereby fostering enhanced comprehension and more accurate responses.

Upon removal of the aforementioned 5 items, the refined 15-item FLTA scale was subject to confirmatory factor analysis (CFA) to assess the extent to which the collected data aligns with a unidimensional latent construct. The proposed model generated various model fit indices, encompassing Chi-square/df (1.739), CFI (0.828), TLI (0.800), RMSEA (0.090), and SRMR (0.081). Based on the existing interpretation guidelines (cf. Brown, 2015; Thompson, 2004), the current model is deemed only marginally acceptable for subsequent analyses, necessitating another round of item investigation. This re-evaluation utilized residual covariances among the 15 items and suggested that eliminating item 1 and item 7 could modify 30.2% (47.23) of the extant Chi-square value. Subsequently, this revised 13-item FLTA scale demonstrated superior construct validity as evidenced by improved model fit indices: Chi-square/df (1.353), CFI (0.923), TLI (0.908), RMSEA (0.062), and SRMR (0.069).

Subsequently, the 7 items marked for removal were subject to thorough re-examination, soliciting input from both the six linguists and the participants to optimize the instrument further. The alterations concentrated on addressing more prevalent and universal language learning challenges, thereby promoting the instrument's applicability across an extensive array of language pairs. Moreover, adjustments were made to the item presentation to accentuate valence-related words, with the aim of clarifying each statement's directionality. In this study, an online survey format was employed, employing distinct highlighting colors to indicate positive (green) and negative (yellow) expressions (refer to table 1 for illustration). Theoretically, this approach aids participants in distinguishing between positively or negatively coded items and mitigates response contamination risks. Researchers should embrace this perspective when utilizing this instrument in various user interfaces or modalities in future applications.

Table 1: The Finalized FLTA Scale

Item No.	Dimension	Type of Ambiguity	Type of Experience	Item
1	Semantic TA	Novelty	Affective	I enjoy encountering new words in a foreign language that don't have a direct translation in my own language
2	Semantic TA	Complexity	Motivational	I often find it discouraging when a foreign language has more complicated word meanings than my own language (R)
3	Semantic TA	Insolubility	Cognitive	I struggle to understand words that have conflicting meanings between my native and the foreign language (R)
4	Semantic TA	Incomprehension	Motivational	The feeling of not comprehending the meaning of some foreign language words makes me impatient (R)
5	Phonological TA	Novelty	Affective	I find it exciting when the sounds of a foreign language are completely different from my own language
6	Phonological TA	Complexity	Motivational	I feel disheartened when the pronunciation rules of a foreign language are more complex than my own language (R)
7	Phonological TA	Insolubility	Cognitive	I feel capable of dealing with the inconsistencies in the speaking systems between my native and the foreign language
8	Phonological TA	Incomprehension	Cognitive	It troubles me when I can't understand the foreign language due to unfamiliar sounds (R)
9	Morphosyntactic TA	Novelty	Motivational	I am invigorated by learning new sentence structures in a foreign language that don't exist in my own language
10	Morphosyntactic TA	Complexity	Motivational	It discourages me when the grammatical rules of a foreign language are more intricate than my own language (R)
11	Morphosyntactic TA	Insolubility	Affective	I find it challenging to understand sentences that have contrasting grammar rules between my native and the foreign language (R)
12	Morphosyntactic TA	Incomprehension	Affective	I feel lost when I can't comprehend the foreign language due to complex sentence structures (R)
13	Thematic TA	Novelty	Cognitive	I embrace the opportunity to learn different themes or topics that my native language usually does not talk about.
14	Thematic TA	Complexity	Affective	Complex themes or topics in the foreign language that differ from my native language often overwhelms me (R)
15	Thematic TA	Insolubility	Cognitive	I can be comfortable when the themes or topics in the foreign language contradict my native language.
16	Thematic TA	Incomprehension	Motivational	Not understanding the themes or topics in a foreign language conversation frustrates me (R)
17	Pragmatic TA	Novelty	Affective	I get excited when I encounter new social rules or customs in the foreign language that don't exist in my native language
18	Pragmatic TA	Complexity	Motivational	It demotivates me when the social norms of a foreign language are more complex than my own language (R)
19	Pragmatic TA	Insolubility	Cognitive	I find myself willing to adapt, when social rules or customs in the foreign language contradict my native

Item No.	Dimension	Type of Ambiguity	Type of Experience	Item
				language
20	Pragmatic TA	Incomprehension	Cognitive	I feel uncomfortable when I can't grasp the communication norms of the foreign language (R)

Note: R denotes reverse-coded items.

For each item, please indicate your agreement using the following scale: 1 (strongly disagree), 2 (disagree), 3 (neutral), 4 (agree), 5 (strongly agree).

4. Instrument validation

4.1. Data collection

The formal study's questionnaire also encompasses five primary sections: demographic information, the finalized FLTA scale, Herman et al.'s (2010) general TA (GTA) scale, Ely's (1995) SLTA scale, and a 7-item self-rated foreign language proficiency scale. Participants were instructed to complete the online questionnaire grounded in their personal foreign language learning experiences. Unlike the pilot study conducted in January 2022, which utilized Qualtrics with support from the University of Cambridge, the formal study employed an internal survey tool developed by The New Oriental Co. Ltd.—China's most extensive private educational company in terms of program offerings, student enrollments, and geographic presence. From October 2022 to March 2023, a total of 875 participants were recruited via convenience sampling. Upon discarding invalid responses (e.g., identical ratings for all items), 90.9% (N = 795) of the cases were deemed valid and appropriate for further analyses. All participants had proficiency in either English or Chinese to comprehend the questionnaire content.

The sample's mean age was 26.741 (SD = 4.757), with a majority pursuing or having completed bachelor's degrees (33.46%, N = 266) and master's degrees (34.34%, N = 273). The remainder held less than a high school diploma (19.75%, N = 157), were studying for or held doctoral degrees (10.31%, N = 82), or had post-doctoral qualifications (2.14%, N = 17). Most participants identified Chinese Mandarin as their primary language (94.34%, N = 750), while others spoke various Chinese dialects (2.77%, N = 22) or languages of ethnic minority groups in China (2.89%, N = 23). The AoO for foreign language learning stood at 7.35 (SD = 2.78) years, with English being the most common L2 (93.71%, N = 745). Other languages in the mix included French, German, Spanish, and Japanese.

4.2. Reliability and validity

Prior to evaluating the reliability of the instrument, the normality of the FLTA scale was established based on skewness (-0.922 to 0.860) and kurtosis (-1.464 to 0.303) indices. Subsequently, the instrument's reliability was assessed by examining scale homogeneity using Cronbach's α as a function of interitem correlation (Field, 2009). With the 20-item FLTA scale producing a strong Cronbach's α value of 0.923, internal consistency is effectively supported. In light of parsimony considerations, we opted to utilize item parceling when employing the FLTA, by using the mean scores of the five linguistic subdimensions—namely, semantic, phonological, morphosyntactic, thematic, and pragmatic—to represent the latent construct (Kline, 2015). This decision was based on a series of confirmatory factor analysis (CFA) results, which are outlined in table 2 below.

Table 2: CFA for five subdimensions of FLTA

Subdimension	Chi-square/df	CFI	TLI	RMSEA	SRMR
Semantic	2.566	.961	.955	.039	.061
Phonological	2.822	.934	.945	.056	.068
Morphosyntactic	2.496	.959	.952	.042	.062
Thematic	3.514	.919	.934	.065	.071
Pragmatic	3.956	.909	.912	.068	.076

To ensure that the FLTA scale is not "old wine in new bottle," the present study will test its discriminant validity compared with Herman et al.'s (2010) GTA scale and Ely's (1995) SLTA scale. Before the analysis, the two other scales were also validated and modified because the original versions of them were not optimal to be used (Cronbach's α = .575 and .688, respectively). In terms of the GTA scale, two subdimensions were identified, including the 3-item 'TA core' (Wei & Hu, 2019; items 3, 7, and 8; henceforth Openness to Change) and a 7-item dimension (items 1, 4, 5, 9, 10, 11, and 12; henceforth Tolerance of Uncertainty). Concerning the SLTA scale, nine items were retained to represent a unidimensional concept (items 2, 3, 4, 5, 6, 7, 9, 11, and 12; Chi-square/df = 2.965; CFI = .933; TLI = .914; RMSEA = .065; SRMR = .07).

Assessment of discriminant validity for two hypothesized constructs involves comparing the estimated correlation parameter between them when constrained to 1.0 against the values obtained from an unconstrained model (Jöreskog, 1971). Carrying out a chi-square difference test on these values (all with a $p < .05$) allows for a robust investigation of discriminant validity. According to Bagozzi and Phillips (1982), when the model exhibits a significantly lower chi-square value without enforcing trait correlations equal to unity, it implies that the constructs are not perfectly correlated, thereby achieving discriminant validity. An additional evaluation of discriminant validity can be conducted by ascertaining whether the 95% confidence interval of the correlation r between distinct factors encompasses the value of 1.0 (Anderson & Gerbing, 1988). The established correlation among the four crucial TA factors supports discriminant validity, since no exceedingly high correlation coefficients were observed (all upper bounds of r are lower than 0.65). This analysis assuages concerns about potential confounding effects, demonstrating that these constructs can indeed be treated as distinct and valid dimensions within TA assessment.

5. TA in language learning

In this section, we assess the interrelationships between the three validated TA dimensions and their collective impact on language learning outcomes. As illustrated in figure 1, a correlation matrix employing Spearman's rho showcases the associations among the trinity of TA variables and the 7-item Foreign Language Proficiency scale (FLP), which exhibits internal consistency with a Cronbach's α of 0.891.

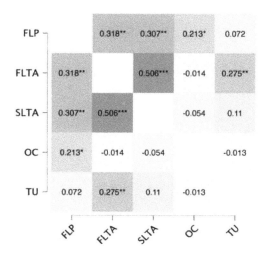

Figure 1: Spearman's rho heatmap between TA factors and foreign language proficiency

With respect to general TA, a statistically significant correlation was observed between FLP and the 3-item OC (TA core, $r = .213$, $p = .043$), whereas no such relationship was found with the 7-item TU factor ($r = 0.072$, $p = 0.497$). In comparison, Dewaele and Li (2013), using a larger sample size (N = 1,978), reported a "small but significant effect" between general TA and multilingualism ($p < 0.003$, $\eta2 = .008$ [equivalent to $r = .089$], p. 236). Similarly, in Wei and Hu's (2019) replication study, the correlation between TA core and multilingualism was marginally significant ($p = 0.059$) with a small effect size (variance-accounted-for = 1.4% to 1.9% [equivalent to $r = .118$ to $.138$]). By applying Cohen's (1988) effect size interpretation benchmarks for behavioral science, our findings tentatively confirm that general TA has a "small" ($r = .1$) or even negligible (especially for TU) influence on foreign language achievement. However, future studies employing more refined sampling methods are required to corroborate these preliminary observations.

Upon further examination of the data, a statistically significant relationship between the seemingly "negligible" TU and the new FLTA scale emerged ($r = 0.275$, $p = 0.008$), suggesting the presence of a hypothetical mediation model. In such a model (refer to fig. 2), TU may initially impact FLTA, which in turn indirectly affects foreign language learning success. Notably, the observed indirect effects were corroborated (95% confidence interval = 0.031 to 0.355 based on bias-corrected bootstrapping). This observation points to a complex interplay between influencing factors, wherein beyond its positive indirect effects via FLTA, TU might also exert negative repercussions on language achievement through alternative mediators, ultimately resulting in an ostensibly negligible correlation. For example, elevated TU levels might demotivate language learners from actively analyzing foreign social values or cultural contexts. Should this hypothesis hold true, similar concerns could arise in relation to other TA facets, as higher domain-specific TA may discourage dictionary usage or requests for clarification—both processes that could enhance accessibility to comprehensible input. To better understand this intricate dynamic, future research must incorporate a more diverse array of relevant variables for a comprehensive investigation of the TA model.

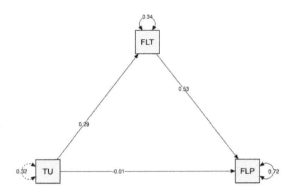

Figure 2: Mediating Path Model

Moreover, both SLTA and FLTA demonstrated statistically significant impacts on FLP ($r = .307$ and $.318$, respectively), attesting to the utility and value of domain-specific operationalization. Relative to SLTA, the newly developed FLTA scale exhibited a marginally more robust effect on language achievement. Impressively, both variables surpassed .3, classifying them as "medium" per Cohen's (1988) system and "very large" according to Wei and Hu's (2019) standards. To further comprehend the interaction between these two TA constructs, our study employed hierarchical regression to assess each variable's unique contribution. When accounting for the influence of SLTA, FLTA remains a potent predictor of the dependent variable (partial correlation $= .196$). Similarly, when controlling for FLTA's effects, SLTA's predictive power persisted notably (partial correlation $= .209$). These findings underscore the distinct nature of the two domain-specific TA constructs, which jointly contribute to foreign language proficiency prediction.

Table 2 showcases a comprehensive model, wherein GTA, SLTA, and FLTA predict FLP alongside accounting for the influence of control variables: age and education level. Prior to analysis, I examined the assumptions employed in regression analysis: multicollinearity (VIF values ranging between 1.180 and 1.745), outlier detection (Cook's distance <1 for all cases), autocorrelation (Durbin-Watson test value of 2.114, $p = .908$), normality (assessed through the P-P plot), and homoscedasticity (verified an even distribution of the residuals-vs.-predicted plot). The null model, only considering control variables, accounted for 8.0% of the total variance in FLP, with age serving as a statistically significant predictor. Subsequent to incorporating the null model, the inclusion of the four TA variables contributed to an additional 16.7% variance explanation in the dependent variable. This finding underlines the pivotal role of TA within the context of foreign language learning processes.

Table 2: Model Summary—FLP

Model	R	R^2	Adjusted R^2	R^2 Change	p
H₀	0.282	0.080	0.061	0.080	0.021
H₁	0.497	0.247	0.191	0.167	0.004

Note. Null model includes age, Education

6. Instruction for further adaptation

The adaptation of this instrument necessitates key considerations, including a thorough examination of specific linguistic contexts and language pairs relevant to a given study. The FLTA scale's development and validation were rooted in the experiences of participants proficient in English or Chinese. Consequently, researchers must account for potential cultural and linguistic variations that could emerge in different language-learning contexts. Modifying or adapting the scale may be essential to accurately address the distinct challenges and ambiguities exemplified by other language pairs. In broader applications, assessing typological distance may contribute valuable insight into results interpretation. However, determining an appropriate method for measuring such distance requires further investigation. Moreover, the relationship between the tolerance of ambiguity and the propensity to learn multiple languages, per se, warrants exploration. If a correlation does exist, the FLTA scale could potentially be employed as a predictive tool for individuals' language learning inclinations. By addressing these pivotal questions, the FLTA scale can be adapted and fine-tuned for various educational contexts, fostering a more comprehensive understanding of language learners' experiences.

Additionally, further validation and refinement steps are warranted to ascertain the reliability and validity of the FLTA scale across a range of populations. This endeavor may encompass implementing large-scale investigations that encompass diverse sets of language learners, thereby corroborating the scale's psychometric properties. It is worth noting that the current sample yielded promising results, due in part to the formal study being conducted during participants' engagement with English tutoring services. As such, they were highly attentive to the survey, given its potential impact on their learning experience. Moreover, these participants represent a distinct subset of learners who have invested resources into their English education, which inherently introduces potential selection bias. Addressing these factors in future research will contribute to a better understanding and evaluation of the applicability of the FLTA scale across various contexts and learner profiles.

Moreover, utilizing pseudorandomization for item sequencing within the survey mitigates the potential influence of contextual factors or item order on participants' responses. This strategy proves particularly critical for examining a diverse array of TA constructs, ensuring that biases arising from the placement of items are minimized. Such biases can manifest in numerous ways, such as participants choosing analogous ratings for adjacent items, particularly in cases where diverse TA constructs are assessed. Participants may consciously or unconsciously perceive the order of items as reflective of an implicit gradation or hierarchy of importance, thus shaping their responses accordingly. For example, should complexity-related questions consistently precede incomprehension-related questions, participants may start subconsciously rating these concepts similarly based on their positioning within the survey. Also, by implementing clear instructions and employing pseudorandomization throughout the survey, researchers can effectively prevent biases in evaluating the discriminant validity between distinct TA constructs.

7. Conclusion

In conclusion, this study offers a significant contribution to the field of applied linguistics by advancing our understanding of the impact and interplay of tolerance of ambiguity in the context of foreign language learning. We have successfully developed and validated an FLTA scale that examines a previously unexplored facet of TA in relation to typological distinctions. The scale addresses the domain-specific manifestation of TA in relation to typological differences between languages, filling a gap in the existing literature. By incorporating specific linguistic techniques and subjective experiences, the FLTA scale captures the affective, motivational, and cognitive dimensions of learners' reactions to linguistic ambiguity.

Evidence confirms that the FLTA instrument possesses statistical and conceptual differentiation from both the GTA scale and SLTA scale. In re-evaluating the link between TA and achievement, three critical aspects emerge. Firstly, while general TA exhibits minimal (if not trivial) effects on foreign language proficiency, the multivariate mediating model suggests a push-and-pull phenomenon warranting further exploration. Secondly, the inclusion of two domain-specific aspects of TA proves significant, as their unique contributions to predicting foreign language proficiency are substantiated in the regression model. Thirdly, after accounting for socio-biographical variables, the combined influence of all three TA aspects explains 16.7% of the variability in foreign language proficiency scores. This comprehensive analysis underscores the importance of considering multiple facets of TA when investigating its impacts on language learning outcomes.

Future studies should further investigate and refine the FLTA scale, potentially exploring its applicability and generalizability across diverse language pairs and learner populations. This could contribute to a better understanding of how the interaction between languages shapes the development of language skills and the management of ambiguity in language learning. Additionally, future research may consider exploring the longitudinal effects of TA on foreign language proficiency by tracking learners' progress over time. Such longitudinal analysis would provide valuable insights into how the role of TA changes as learners advance in their language studies.

Moreover, given the demonstrated relevance of domain-specific aspects of TA to foreign language proficiency, it is essential for future research to examine pedagogical interventions that could enhance learners' tolerance of ambiguity in linguistic contexts. Educators could benefit significantly from understanding how to incorporate activities that foster ambiguity tolerance in the classroom, ultimately contributing to more effective language instruction. In sum, by recognizing the importance of attending to the intricate nuances of TA and its impact on proficiency, we are better equipped to understand the workings of the human mind, foster meaningful learning experiences, and transcend the barriers of communication that divide us.

Appendix. FLTA instrument (initial version)

Based on your experience of learning a foreign language, please rate to what extent do you agree or disagree with the following statements:

Please select "NOT APPLICABLE" if the item is not relevant to your language learning process. For example, if you cannot recall any grammatical rule that does not exist in your mother tongue, you may select "NOT APPLICABLE" for the first item in this section.

1a. It bothers me when a grammatical rule in the foreign language does not exist in my mother tongue.

strongly disagree—somewhat disagree—neither agree nor disagree—somewhat agree—strongly agree—NOT APPLICABLE

1b. I feel discouraged when a similar sentence structure is used differently between the foreign language and my mother tongue.

1c. I can be comfortable with a sentence structure which is more complicated in the foreign language than in my mother tongue.

1d. I feel anxious when I cannot understand the function of a grammatical rule.

2a. I enjoy learning the sounds of a foreign language which do not exist in my mother tongue.

2b. I feel frustrated when a sound seems to be pronounced similarly but with subtle nuance compared with my mother tongue.

2c. It is annoying when the same letter(s) can be pronounced differently between the foreign language and my mother tongue.

2d. It worries me when I cannot recognise the word when listening to it.

3a. I don't want to encounter a meaning which does not exist in my mother tongue.

3b. I embrace words with a more sophisticated meaning compared with my mother tongue.

3c. I feel troubled when a foreign word looks like but means something different from a word in my mother tongue.

3d. I get impatient if I cannot understand the meaning of a word.

4a. It bothers me when the text is organized in a logic that I rarely saw in my mother tongue.

4b. I dislike a text which is structured in a more complicated manner compared to my mother tongue.

4c. I feel upset when the same information should be organized differently between the foreign language and my mother tongue.

4d. I like reading a foreign text for which it takes a while to understand the organizational logic.

5a. I can be comfortable with the foreign expressions which seem to be notably more/less polite than those in my mother tongue.

5b. I enjoy learning the foreign communicative style that does not exist in my mother tongue.

5c. It is sad when some aspects of communication are more complicated than those of my mother tongue.

5d. I feel shocked by some foreign approaches to communication if I cannot understand them.

References

Anderson, J. C., & Gerbing, D. W. 1988. "Structural equation Modeling In Practice: A Review And Recommended Two-Step Approach." *Psychological Bulletin, 103*(3), 411–423. https://doi.org/10.1037/0033-2909.103.3.411.

Bagozzi, R. P., & Phillips, L. W. 1982. "Representing and Testing Organizational Theories: A Holistic Construal." *Administrative Science Quarterly, 27*(3), 459–489. https://doi.org/10.2307/2392322.

Basilevsky, A. T. 2009. *Statistical factor Analysis and Related Methods: Theory and Applications* (Vol. 418). John Wiley & Sons.

Başöz, T. 2015. "Exploring the Relationship Between Tolerance of Ambiguity of EFL Learners and Their Vocabulary Knowledge." *Journal of Language and Linguistic Studies, 11*(2), 53–66.

Blumstein, S. E. 1981. "Neurolinguistic Disorders: Language-Brain Relationships." *Handbook of Clinical Neuropsychology*, 227–256. Scopus.

Brown, T. A. 2015. *Confirmatory Factor Analysis for Applied Research* (second edition),The Guilford Press.

Budner, S. 1962. "Intolerance of Ambiguity as a Personality Variable." *Journal of Personality, 30*(1), 29–50. https://doi.org/10.1111/j.1467-6494.1962.tb02303.x

Cohen, J. 1988. *Statistical Power Analysis for the Behavioral Sciences* (2nd ed.). Routledge.

Dewaele, J.-M., & Li, W. (2013). "Is Multilingualism Linked to a Higher Tolerance of Ambiguity?" *Bilingualism: Language and*

Cognition, 16(1), 231–240. https://doi.org/10.1017/S1366728912000570.

Dörnyei, Z., & Ryan, S. 2015. *The Psychology of the Language Learner Revisited*. Routledge.

Ely, C. M. 1995. Tolerance of Ambiguity and the Teaching of ESL. In J. M. Reid (Ed.), *Learning Styles in the ESL/EFL Classroom* (pp. 216–217). Heinle & Heinle.

Fabrigar, L. R., & Wegener, D. T. 2011. *Exploratory Factor Analysis*. Oxford University Press.

Ferketich, S. 1991. Focus on Psychometrics. Aspects of Item Analysis. *Research in Nursing & Health, 14*(2), 165–168. https://doi.org/10.1002/nur.4770140211.

Field, A. P. 2009. *Discovering Statistics Using SPSS: And Sex, Drugs and Rock 'N' Roll* (3rd ed). SAGE Publications.

Glosser, G., & Deser, T. 1991. "Patterns of Discourse Production Among Neurological Patients with Fluent Language Disorders." *Brain and Language, 40*(1), 67–88. https://doi.org/10.1016/0093-934X(91)90117-J.

Herman, J. L., Stevens, M. J., Bird, A., Mendenhall, M., & Oddou, G. 2010. "The Tolerance for Ambiguity Scale: Towards a More Refined Measure for International Management Research." *International Journal of Intercultural Relations, 34*(1), 58–65. https://doi.org/10.1016/j.ijintrel.2009.09.004.

Jackson, D. N., & Messick, S. 1961. "Acquiescence and Desirability as Response Determinants on the MMPI." *Educational and Psychological Measurement, 21*(4), 771–790. https://doi.org/10.1177/001316446102100402.

Jöreskog, K. G. 1971. Statistical Analysis of Sets of Congeneric Tests. *Psychometrika, 36*(2), 109–133. https://doi.org/10.1007/BF02291393.

Kempler, D., Curtiss, S., & Jackson, C. 1987. "Syntactic Preservation in Alzheimer's Disease." *Journal of Speech, Language, and Hearing Research, 30*(3), 343–350. https://doi.org/10.1044/jshr.3003.343.

Kline, R. B. 2015. *Principles and Practice of Structural Equation Modeling*. Guilford Publications.

Liu, T., Xuan, J., Lee, Y., & Ng, B. C. 2017. *What Types of Multilinguals Are More Tolerant of Ambiguity? The Role of Multilingualism and Attitudes Towards Linguistic Variation*. The 11th International Symposium on Bilingualism (ISB11), Limerick, Ireland.

Nebes, R. D., Martin, D. C., & Horn, L. C. 1984. "Sparing of Semantic Memory in Alzheimer's Disease." *Journal of Abnormal Psychology, 93*(3), 321–330. Scopus. https://doi.org/10.1037/0021-843X.93.3.321.

Seng Kam, C. C., & Meyer, J. P. 2015. "Implications of Item Keying and Item Valence for the Investigation of Construct Dimensionality." *Multivariate Behavioral Research, 50*(4), 457–469. https://doi.org/10.1080/00273171.2015.1022640

Sonderen, E. van, Sanderman, R., & Coyne, J. C. 2013. "Ineffectiveness of Reverse Wording of Questionnaire Items: Let's Learn from Cows in the Rain." *PLoS ONE, 8*(7), e68967. https://doi.org/10.1371/journal.pone.0068967.

Thompson, B. 2004. *Exploratory and confirmatory Factor Analysis: Understanding Concepts and Applications* (4th edition). APA Publications.

van Compernolle, R. A. 2016. "Are Multilingualism, Tolerance of Ambiguity, and Attitudes Toward Linguistic Variation Related?" *International Journal of Multilingualism, 13*(1), 61–73. https://doi.org/10.1080/14790718.2015.1071821.

Wang, S. 2020. *Positive Personalities and L2 Achievement: The Mediating Role of Positive Emotions* [Undergraduate Dissertation]. Xi'an Jiaotong-Liverpool University.

Wei, R., & Hu, Y. 2019. "Exploring the Relationship Between Multilingualism and Tolerance of Ambiguity: A Survey Study from an EFL Context." *Bilingualism: Language and Cognition, 22*(5), 1209–1219. https://doi.org/10.1017/S1366728918000998.

A Contrastive Study of Food Metaphors in Chinese and English under Extended Conceptual Metaphor Theory

Zhongzhong Zhang
Sichuan University

Abstract

Metaphor is no longer the research category of rhetoric, but a ubiquitous language phenomenon and way of cognition in daily life (Lakoff and Johnson 1980). After more than 40 years of development, the study of metaphor has shown an interdisciplinary, multi-level and refined development trend. This current paper uses the latest theoretical development of CMT, ECMT, to summarize the similarities and differences between Chinese and English food metaphors through the collection and analysis of metaphorical linguistic expressions in the domain of BLCU Corpus Center (BCC) and the Bank of English (BOE). In this paper, the Image Schema, the Domain, the Frame and the Mental Space, ranging from most schematic to least schematic, are used to systematically explore the cognitive representation process of the central concept metaphor ABSTRACT EMOTIONALFORMS ARE FOOD, which is presented through the diagram. The four context classifications of situational context, discourse context, conceptual-cognitive context, and bodily context in ECMT are taken to analyze and explain the reasons for the differences between Chinese and English food metaphors. The study finds that the similar usage of Chinese and English food metaphors is mainly reflected in the concept of cooking methods related to food source domain. Differences in usage focus on concepts commonly found in food metaphors, such as food preparation, cookers and flavor. This paper is a cross-language cognitive pragmatic research combined with ECMT, in order to provide a certain reference for cross-cultural communication and Chinese-English bilingual teaching.

Keywords

food metaphors; ECMT; schematic conceptual structure; multilevel context

1. Introduction

Metaphor is no longer just a category of rhetoric research, but a universal language phenomenon and way of cognition in CMT. A *conceptual metaphor* is understanding one abstract domain of experience in terms of another concrete domain (Lakoff and Johnson, 1980). Conceptual metaphors are reflected in metaphorical linguistic

---

Zhongzhong Zhang, Sichuan University. E-mail address: zungzungcheung@163.com.

expressions in practice. Taking the conceptual metaphor THEORIES ARE BUILDINGs as an example, its specific metaphorical linguistic expressions are as follows: Increasingly, scientific knowledge is constructed by small numbers of specialized workers, McCarthy demolishes the romantic myth of the Wild West, and My faith was rocked to its foundations, etc. (Zoltán, 2021). Judging from the above examples, metaphors are universal in our daily life.

The tradition of metaphor research has a long history. As early as in ancient Greece, Aristotle pointed out that metaphor was a rhetorical feature using one thing to express another thing (Aristotle, 1954). After more than 2,000 years of research on metaphor and rhetoric, Richards becomes the first scholar to study metaphor in language from a cognitive perspective (Richards, 1936). Reddy directly influences the epoch-making research on metaphor by many cognitive linguists such as Lakoff (Michael, 1979). The metaphor revolution that started in American linguistics in the 1980s was an important symbol of the birth of cognitive linguistics.

2. Brief review

After years of development, CMT is still a hot topic that scholars around the world pay close attention to. Since the beginning of the 21st century, the achievements of metaphor research have blossomed everywhere, and the research on conceptual metaphor has also shown an interdisciplinary, multi-level and refined development trend. Numerous theoretical and applied studies related to conceptual metaphors have emerged in many disciplines, such as history (Sweetser, 1990), literature (Turner, 1996) and cognitive science (Casasanto, 2009). Lakoff has never stopped the pace of metaphor research, and constantly promotes the in-depth development of metaphor. His main theoretical ideas include the initial introduction of CMT in *Metaphors We Live By* (Lakoff, 1980), the pioneering proposal of the idealized cognitive model (ICM) in *Women, Fire and Dangerous Things: What Categories Reveal About the Mind.* (Lakoff, 1987), a comparative study of conceptual metaphor theory with other contemporary metaphor theories (Lakoff, 1993) and the view of the centrality of primary metaphors to conceptual metaphors, metaphors for mental experience and psychological reality in *Philosophy in the Flesh: The Embodied Mind and Its Challenge to Western Thought* (Lakoff, 1999).

With the rapid development of urbanization and industrialization, the political, economic and social exchanges of countries in the world are becoming closer. Scholars have also begun to focus their research on the interdisciplinary role of metaphors in the process of cross-cultural and intracultural communication (Zoltán, 2010). CMT stresses both the embodied nature and cultural embeddedness of metaphor. The latest development of CMT is reflected in the multimodal metaphor theory and ECMT. The former was put forward against the background of the development of multimedia and computer technology, pointing out that CMT is reflected in the study of single-modal language and characters, and it focuses on multi-modal expressions such as gestures, music, pictures and videos. The introduction of ECMT marks the refined development of CMT. Kövecses uses a large English corpus as a research text source, summarizing and solving the current problems of metaphor research, including the interaction of grammar and metaphors in a cognitive language framework, multilevel conceptual structure of metaphor representation and differences in metaphor production and comprehension in multidimensional contexts (Zoltán, 2010).

3. Research significance

There is an old saying in China that food is the most important thing for the people. Franklin once said that eat to live, not live to eat. It can be seen that no matter whether in China or English-speaking countries, people regard food as the top priority in life. The expression and use of metaphors are based on the embodied experience of humans (Zoltán, 2000) and are often used in daily communication (Zoltán, 2015).

There are a lot of linguistic expressions of food metaphors in English and Chinese, and people tend to use the characteristics of food to recognize and represent things around them. Due to the differences in ways of thinking and cultural connotations, people in English countries and China have a certain degree of cognitive convergence when expressing opinions on food, but there are some misunderstandings in different usage situations. Choi compared the similarities and differences of food metaphor expressions in English and Korean. He pointed out that sweet food was referred to as love in most countries, and food could be compared to money, which is unique in Korea (Choi, 2014). Padiernos found that there were similarities in meaning, interpretation, context and usage of food metaphorical expressions in English and Filipino, but at the same time there were certain differences, related to the personalities, psychological states, living conditions, values and ways of thinking of language users (Padiernos, 2018).

For second language learners, it is particularly important to correctly understand and use the metaphorical expressions about food in the two languages in the process of cross-cultural communication. Through the analysis of a large number of examples, the similarities and differences in the expressions of food metaphors in English and Chinese are presented in the paper. In cross-language research, metaphorical expression is an important embodiment of cultural cognition, and the mapping process of metaphorical concepts involves multiple levels of culture, thinking and mind. In the English corpus BOE, there are a large number of metaphorical expressions related to the domain. The use of these food metaphors involves many aspects, such as food, the process of cooking, and methods, which can be broadly grouped into four clusters of metaphorical expression types, namely food preparation, cooker, cooking methods, flavor and taste. The author finds that the classification of the above four types of food metaphors in English has a lot of similarities with the expressions of food metaphors in the Chinese corpus BCC, but there are also certain differences.

4. Similarities and differences of food metaphors in Chinese and English

Cross-lingual studies of metaphorical expressions on different subjects (Yu, 1995; Choi, 2014; Padiernos, 2018; Wang, 2022) mainly conduct a quantitative analysis of the differences in metaphorical expressions between different languages by combining CMT. However, these studies have neglected the deeper exploration of cross-lingual metaphorical expressions to a certain extent.

This paper will analyze and explore the similarities and differences between English and Chinese metaphorical expressions in the source domain Food through the collection of related metaphorical linguistic expressions in the English corpus BOE and the Chinese corpus BCC, combined with the extended CMT (Kövecses, 2020), and then further explore the multiple levels of reasons for their similarities and differences both from conceptual and contextual perspectives. This study is expected to provide some reference for future cross-cultural communication and English-Chinese bilingual teaching.

4.1. THE WEAKENING OF STRENGTH IS THE DILUTION OF FOOD

Before food is cooked, a series of preparatory processes, such as preparing ingredients and cleaning up food, will involve a lot of metaphorical expressions. The similarities between Chinese and English food metaphors in food preparation are mainly reflected in the metaphors about food processing. Taking dilute as an example, the word usually refers to adding water or liquid to food to make it less flavorful (Alice, 1995), which contains many metaphorical expressions. In English, the word dilute can be used metaphorically to express the influence on belief, value, or quality and make them weaker and less effective.

In metaphorical expressions in Chinese, the use of dilute once has a similar effect. The conceptual metaphor THE WEANKENING OF STRENGTH IS THE DILUTION OF FOOD can be seen from the three Chinese-English expressions (1) a, b, c.

The generation of conceptual metaphors is based on people real experience of life. People can perceive the discoloration of the original food after the dilution, so as to map the more specific source domain to the abstract target domain. The process of conceptualizing food dilution is used to refer to the fact that power is weakened. The formation of conceptual metaphors is inseparable from the direct role played by primary metaphors (Grady, 1997), which is based on correlations in experience between an abstract concept and a sensory-motor one (Zoltán, 2021). In the conceptual metaphor, THE WEANKENING OF STRENGTH IS THE DILUTION OF FOOD is made of primary metaphors, THE ABSTRACT FORM IS THE PHYSICAL OBJECT AND THE CONTRACTION IS THE FADING OF NATURE.

(1) a. kai-pi   yixie dijiafang   quyu xishi shichang
    open up some low-price housing   area dilute market
    Open up some low-priced housing areas to dilute the market.

   b. keneng hui xi-shi gudong-de   suoyouquan
    possibe can dilute shareholders ownership
    It is possible to dilute the ownership of shareholders.

   c. jinyibu xishi zhengti fangjia
    further dilute overall house price
    Further dilute the overall house price.

There are also differences in Chinese and English food metaphorical expressions in the process of food preparation. For example, the metaphorical expressions of recipe and ingredient are unique to English. A recipe is a list of ingredients and a set of instructions that tell you how to cook a particular thing (Alice, 1995). In English countries, a recipe can be used metaphorically to refer to the first thing that comes to mind in a given situation, either positive or negative.

The metaphorical expressions about recipe in (2)a, b are unique to English, and there is no similar usage in Chinese. In addition, slice, originally used with food such as bread and sausage, is often used metaphorically in English to modify concrete and abstract things such as money, life, time and luck, which can be seen in (2) c, d, e, f.

(2) a. When asked for his recipe for happiness, he gave very short but sensible answer: work and love.

b. It's a stressful job, and if you don't look after yourself, it's sure a recipe for disaster.

c. Ministers and their departments will have to battle for a slice of funds.

d. Independent travel, when it lives up to its promise, gives you a slice of life as others live it.

e. We each need privacy, a slice of time apart and alone.

f. Even at their best, the team might need a slice of luck.

There are also special metaphorical expressions in the food preparation process in Chinese. Similar to the metaphorical expressions in (1) mentioned above, the special usage of food metaphors in Chinese is also mainly reflected in those related to food cleaning. In Chinese, food cleaning expressions related to the Food domain, such as clean up/shoushi, contain a large number of metaphors unique to Chinese. In (3)a, b, shoushi in Chinese, literally meaning clean up, can be metaphorically expressed as a lesson, but there is no similar use in English.

(3) a. ni   jiushi qian shoushi

you just   owe a lesson

You really should be taught a lesson.

b. wo shou qian   shoushi

my hands owe fight

My hands owe a fight.

4.2. EMOTIONAL STATE IS COOKER

Food-related metaphors naturally involve cookers. In both English and Chinese food metaphors, cookers are used to express concepts, and the most common ones are pressure cooker and kettle. In the metaphorical expressions about the pressure cooker, the usage in Chinese and English is basically the same, both viewing pressure cooker as a state of tension or anxiety, which shows in (4)a and (5)a, b. In (6)a, the metaphorical expressions involving "kettle" in food metaphors is unique to Chinese. When people refer to a person who always lifts the same kettle, it means that this person always likes to discuss the shortcomings of others.

In (6)b, back burner for cooking food is used metaphorically to refer to putting aside the work at hand in order to deal with something, and then do it later when there is time. Such a metaphorical expression is difficult to see in Chinese. Although the metaphorical expressions about the kettle and back burner in (6)a and (6)b are not shared between Chinese and English, they are similar to the metaphorical expressions in (4)a and (5) a, b, which all use cookers to describe the state of people and things.

In the above food metaphorical expressions related to cookers, the conceptual metaphor of THE EMOTIONAL STATE IS A COOKER is revealed. People tend to use the most common cookers in the kitchen to describe the state of things whose primary metaphors can be summarized as THE ABSTRACT STATE IS A PHYSICAL OBJECT.

(4) a. zhengju   shi   kou   gaoyaguo
       politics   is   a   pressure cooker

   Politics is a pressure cooker.

(5) a. He had recently escaped the emotional pressure cooker of the communal flat.

   b. The lid on the pressure cooker of nationalist emotions has now been removed.

(6) a. na   hu   bu-kai   ti   na   hu
       which kettle not boiling lift which kettle

   One speaks only of another's shortcomings.

   b. For ten years she has looked after three children, with her career very much on the back burner.

4.3. LIFE IS METHODS OF COOKING

There are many methods to cook food, including stew, boil, fry, simmer, bake, grill etc. It is a common view to use cooking methods to metaphorically express the development status of things and personal emotional changes. The metaphorical use of cooking up is not uncommon in Chinese and English metaphors. Taking (7) and (8) a, b collected in the corpus as an example, in both English and Chinese, cooking up is often used collocated with other things that has a negative impact, meaning fabrication.

Some more subdivided cooking methods, such as stew, originally refer to cooking slowly by placing food in water for a long time. In the expressions of food metaphors, stew refers to a state suffered by people living in fear or pain for a long time. In both the Chinese metaphorical expression in (9) a and the English metaphorical expressions in (10) a, b, stew maps the state of cooking for a long time to people's experience.

In the expressions of (11) and (12), the concept of boiling point, the peak temperature when food is cooked, is mapped to anger and high emotions. Judging from the above related expressions about food cooking methods, people compare their life experiences with food cooking methods to metaphorically describe life states and emotional attitudes, showing the conceptual metaphor of LIFE IS METHODS OF COOKING whose primary metaphor is THE ABSTRCT PROCESS OF LIFE EXPERIENCE IS THE PHYSICAL METHOD OF COOKING.

(7) a. zhe shi caozuo changxiaoshu-de chaozuo   paozhi
       this is operation bestsellers'   speculation cooking up

   This is the hype of operating bestsellers.

(8) a. He had cooked up some fantastic story.

   b. His lawyer claims that the charges were cooked up.

(9) a. shimian-de   ye   hao-leng   hao-nanao
       Insomnious night chilly   hard to endure

   The night of insomnia is so cold and hard to endure.

(10) a. Should I call him? No. Let him stew.

   b. That was weak of me, for I should have let Marcus stew in his own juice.

(11) a. tade nuqi   dadaole   feidian

   His anger   reached   boiling point

   His anger reached boiling point.

(12) a. His temper was already close to boiling point.

   b. It has brought the present crisis to boiling point.

4.4. A COLORFUL LIFE IS FLAVOR AND THE TASTE OF FOOD

In food metaphors, flavor and the taste of food can best reflect the characteristics of food itself, and these expressions are also the most common expressions in both Chinese and English. *Flavor* usually refers to the distinctive quality of something that is different from other things in English.

In (13)a, flavor metaphorically expresses the characteristics of a metropolis in Shanghai, and (14)a highlights the characteristics of Italy through the metaphorical use of flavor, embodying the conceptual metaphor QUALITY IS THE FLAVOR OF FOOD. Bland is used metaphorically to describe people or things that seem dull or boring and have nothing special or exciting about them, which can be seen both in (15)a and (16)a, b, with the conceptual metaphor A BORING LIFE IS BLAND FOOD.

The above conceptual metaphors can be summarized as CHANGEABLE MOODS ARE THE TASTE OF LIFE with a primary metaphor of A COLORFUL LIFE IS THE FLAVOR AND TASTE OF FOOD.

(13) a. Shanghai you dadushi-de   weida

   Shanghai has a metropolitan flavor.

(14) a. Claude studied and worked in Rome, and his landscapes have a distinctly Italian flavor.

(15) a. xiaorenwu   kanshangqu name putong   pingdan

   little guys   seem   so   ordinary bland

   The little guy looks so ordinary and bland.

(16) a. Are they really that special? Aren't they a little bland?

   b. He was pleasant, bland, and utterly conventional.

(17) a. nianshang-de xiaorong shifen tianmi

   Facial   smile   very   sweet

   Facial smile is very sweet.

(18) a. Her voice was as soft and sweet as a young girl's.

   b. Do tip the barman to keep him sweet.

(19) a. Sam's vocabulary includes some quite salty language.

   b. His work is dense and sharp, with salty dialogue.

5. Multilevel conceptual structure analysis of food metaphors

In CMT, the metaphorical expression is mainly reflected by the choice of domains and the mapping between source domains and target domains.

Taking the conceptual metaphor LOVE IS A JOURNEY as an example, the more specific source domain Journey is selected to represent the more abstract target domain Love based on the perception of people's embodied experience, which derives many related expressions like Our love has reached a dead end and Our relationship is at a crossroads.

The conceptualization process of metaphors is the main link in the development of human cognition. The role of conceptual structure in the formation of metaphors has always been the focus of attention of cognitive linguists, including the introduction of domains (Lakoff, 1980), discussions on mental space in concept blending theory (Fauconnier and Turner, 2002), definition and study of image schema (Talmy, 1988; 2000) and use of frame in cognitive linguistics (Fillmore, 1968; Boas and Dux, 2017). The above-mentioned conceptual structures have further enriched the development of CMT, but they lack certain integration and are loose in actual use. In ECMT, a conceptual metaphor is constituted by a schematical hierarchy composed by an image schema, domain, frame, and mental space level (Zoltán, 2021). The above conceptual structures are incorporated into the analytical framework of conceptual metaphors according to the level of schematic abstraction, which raises the precision of CMT to a new level.

In the above analysis of food metaphors, concepts related to domains, such as food preparation process, cookers, cooking methods and flavor and taste, run through the whole process of metaphorical expressions. The conceptual metaphors, including THE WEAKENING OF STRENGTH IS THE DILUTION OF FOOD, THE EMOTIONAL STATE IS A COOKER, LIFE IS METHODS OF COOKING and A COLORFUL LIFE IS THE FLAVOR AND TASTE OF LIFE, have be summarized in the above analysis as well as the primary metaphors containing AN ABSTRACT FORM IS A PHYSICAL OBJECT, CONTRACTION IS THE FADING OF NATURE, AN ABSTRACT STATE IS THE PHYSICAL OBJECT, THE ABSTRACT PROCESS OF LIFE EXPERIENCE IS THE PHYSICAL METHOD OF COOKING and A COLORFUL LIFE IS FLAVOR AND TASTE OF FOOD.

Food is a domain used in the related food metaphors with the related concept of food preparation, cookers, cooking method, and flavor and taste characterized by image schemas, including OBJECT, CONTAINER and PART-WHOLE, represented in THE WEAKENING OF STRENGTH IS THE DILUTION OF FOOD, THE EMOTIONAL STATE IS A COOKER, LIFE IS METHODS OF COOKING and A COLORFUL LIFE IS THE FLAVOR AND TASTE OF LIFE respectively.

Domains of food metaphors have to be considered in the second hierarchical conceptual structure mentioned in ECMT. When it comes to food domains in food metaphors, some other concepts appear like what we have analyzed above in this paper. Elements in the target so conceptualized may select elements of the source that fit that target element (Zoltán, 2021). For example, food is treated as a recipe ingredient and can be diluted and cleaned up in the preparation of cooking as an object. As a part of a whole, food is bound to be linking to the cooker like pressure cooker, burner and kettle, as well as the cooking methods consisting of cooking up, stewing and boiling. Conceptualized in the container, food is represented in flavor and taste, in the metaphors in the daily communication.

Some frames are involved in Food domain in food metaphors. First of all, food itself has to be viewed as one necessary part of the process of cooking. And then the other frame we should not neglect is the physical participant which can be seen in the whole process of cooking. What's more, the frame parts of cooking play an important role in the cooking, including selection and cleaning of ingredients, mastery of heat and cooking methods. Last but not least, the frame usage of cooking, shows why the food is cooked by people.

As the schematic conceptual structure with the lowest degree of abstraction, different mental spaces are blended in the food metaphors, taking the above frames we have mentioned into consideration. For example, Mother cooked chicken in a pressure cooker can involve the use of the frame parts of cooking, blending the spaces like people who cooked the food and the cooker used in the cooking process. Compared with the three conceptual structures mentioned above, the use of mental spaces does not require much cognitive processing effort and is an important link in the generation and understanding of metaphor.

Conceptual structures, image schema, domains, frames and mental spaces from most schematic to least schematic make up the conceptual metaphors regarding Food, which will be shown next:

Image schema level:
- Abstract emotional forms are objects.
- Abstract emotional forms are containers.
- Abstract emotional forms are whole objects with parts.

Domain level:
- An abstract complex form is a physical object.
- The production of the form is the physical production of food.
- Parts of the form are parts of the physical object.

Frame level:
- One necessary part of cooking is food.
- The abstract participant is the physical participant.
- The usage of cooking is a representation of a physical participant.
- Parts of cooking is the selection of a physical participant.

Mental space level:

(specified examples are provided below)
- Charles life without flavor is Charles food without flavor.
- Mike diluted life is Mike diluted food.

Source Domain: FOOD	Target Domain: ABSTRACT EMOTIONAL FORMS (AEF)
IMAGE SCHEMA: CONTAINER OBJECT WHOLE-PART	AEF
DOMAIN: COOKER FLAVOR INGREDIENT RECIPE COOK USAGE COOKING METHOD HEAT	ABSTRACT PARTS ABSTRACT FORMS ABSTRACT USAGE
FORM: FOOD ingredient, recipe PHYSICAL PARTICIPANT cook, cooker PARTS OF COOKING heat, cooking methods USAGE OF COOKING family, living, strength	LIVING lifestyle mood state attitude relationship value
MENTAL SPACE: CHARLES' LIFE WITHOUT FLAVOR	CHARLES' FOOD WITHOUT FLAVOR

Figure 1. Abstract emotional forms are food

6. Analysis of multidimensional contextual factors on the similarities and differences of Chinese and English food metaphors

The generation of metaphor in CMT depends on the special mapping based on the source and target domains of bodily experience, but this process excludes contextual factors, which makes it difficult to explain the generation and understanding of metaphors, both conceptual and linguistic, in particular situations of discourse (Zoltán, 2015). Metaphor comprehension is highly context sensitive, as experimentally demonstrated by decades of psycholinguistic and psychological research (Zoltán, 2021).

In cross-cultural and cross-language communication, the context is shared by the advocate and the hearer at a given moment, which can be called *current discourse space* (CDS) (Ronald, 2008). Kövecses takes contextual factors and other factors like conceptual structure, cognitive function and embeddedness, embodied character, and neural basis into account in the generation of conceptual metaphors, proposing four types of contexts, including situational context, discourse context, conceptual-cognitive context, and bodily context, which can be seen in Figure 2 (Zoltán, 2020).

The first classification situational context is made up of the physical environment, the social situation, and the cultural situation. The physical environment mainly refers to the living environment in which the metaphor user lives. For example, people in tropical regions tend to use concepts such as coconuts and bananas in metaphorical expressions. The social situation includes all aspects of social life, such as gender, class, education, social organization and social structure which can also play a role in promoting the generation of specific metaphors.

For example, in the United States at the end of the 19th century and the 20th century, a large number of people poured into the western wilderness to pioneer, and there appeared a metaphorical expression describing the western wilderness as a garden to be cultivated (Zoltán, 2020). The cultural situation included the global context (the shared knowledge represented in the conceptual system) and the local context (the specific knowledge in a given communicative situation) (Zoltán, 2021). There are metaphorical expressions of time is money in most countries, but due to the influence of Korean peninsula food culture, the metaphorical expression of food is money is more common in South Korea (Choi, 2014).

There are differences in the expression of food metaphors in Chinese and English. For example, recipe and ingredient mentioned above are concepts often used in English food metaphors, referring to the first things that come to mind in life. It is difficult to see similar usage in Chinese metaphorical expressions, and the reason for this kind of metaphor is related to the social situation in the situational context. Beginning from the 1760s the capitalist countries successively entered into industrialized societies. Their social structure and population distribution continuously optimized with a large number of rural populations flowing into cities. In modern life, people basic necessities of life are affected by the modern way of life. When preparing to cook, people in English-speaking countries mainly went to supermarkets to buy food ingredients and modern packaging products also came with a list of recipes. Food as the top priority for their survival and development was frequently utilized to express metaphors. On the other hand, compared with related concepts in English, the concept of ingredients in Chinese is rarely used as a metaphor, which also reflects the profoundness of Chinese food culture. The cooking methods of the eight major cuisines have their own merits and have been passed down from generation to generation. From mastery of fire to the processing of food, they are extremely complicated. Generally speaking, the first things we do in life tend to be simple, so they will not be used like related metaphorical expressions about ingredients in English.

The differences between Chinese and English food metaphors can also be explained from the perspective of cultural situations, as well as the examples of clean up and kettle mentioned above. Influenced by Chinese food culture, the cleaning of food before cooking is very complicated, including a series of complicated processes such as washing, peeling, shaving, deboning and rolling. Compared with Western catering culture, the cleaning of Chinese food is particularly complicated, and it is even a headache for family members who cook. Therefore, shoushi, literally meaning cleaning up, especially used for food, can be metaphorically expressed in Chinese as punishment for someone or something, which can be seen in (3) a, b.

The example of kettle can be explained from the perspective of physical and cultural situations. It is difficult for English-speaking people to understand why the kettle of water that is not boiling is metaphorically expressed as a shortcoming of people. Due to the relatively slow start of China modernization, related water purification projects like the popularization and use of tap water have only been continuously improved in the past two decades. Before that, people would choose to draw water from wells and rivers. If there are some impurities, people will boil the raw water and drink it. From the perspective of the cultural situation, Chinese people prefer boiled water and believe that boiled water is good for health. Even today, most Chinese people boil pure water before drinking it, which is completely opposite to Americans who generally like to drink cold water. Therefore, water that is not boiled is not healthy enough, and the above reasons explain why a kettle with water not boiled can be metaphorically expressed as shortcomings.

The example of slice mentioned above can be explained from the perspective of conceptual-cognitive context. People are commonly prompted to use particular metaphors relative to their interests and concerns about the world (Zoltán, 2021). In English-speaking countries, people staple food is mostly bread, and when eating bread, they tend to cut it into slices to eat. People in English-speaking countries also mostly choose slices for other foods, such as sausages, barbecues, fruits, etc. So a slice which originally refers to a shape after the food has been divided, has become the most familiar form of things in their lives. When describing abstract or concrete things in life, they prefer to use familiar and interesting slices to express, which is why there is an expression like a slice of time/money.

Different from similar metaphorical expressions in English, the concept of block/kuai is more preferred in Chinese, so metaphorical expressions like wo-men yi-kuai qu meaning, we go together, can be used in Chinese. The related concepts of taste in Chinese and English food metaphors are basically consistent. For example, sweet can be used to metaphorically express happy and joyful things and moments in life, bitter is used to describe difficult and unfortunate encounters, spicy often appears as something dangerous or a slim figure and bland in a food metaphor refers to someone or something boring. Taste is a physical sense that seems to be universally linked to our personal likes and dislikes in the mental world (Sweester, 1990).

Many of the above concepts about taste have basically the same usage in food metaphors, which further demonstrates the point of view that metaphors evolve on the basis of universal properties of the human body in the bodily context (Zoltán, 2021). But the word salty has a special use in English food metaphors. Salty is used metaphorically to describe swearing or offensive language. There is no relevant usage in Chinese, which shows that due to differences in body structure, people perception of the outside world is generally consistent, but at the same time, there are certain differences. This is why lefties prefer to use metaphors like LOVE IS ON THE LEFT SIDE OF THE INTERSECTION.

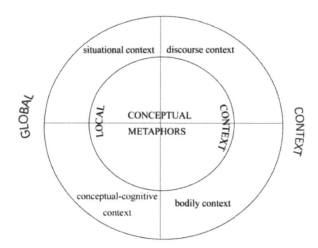

Figure 2. Contextual types in conceptual metaphors (Zoltán, 2021)

7. Conclusion

This paper collects and organizes the related expressions of Chinese and English food metaphors based on the Food domain through BCC and BOE, respectively. The study finds that related concepts of Chinese and

English food metaphors, including the food preparation process with ingredients, recipes, dilution, cleaning and other concepts, cookers like burner and kettle; cooking methods like stew and boil; flavor and taste including sweet, bitter, spicy and salty.

Through qualitative analysis, this study points out that the above-mentioned concepts related to food metaphors have similarities and differences in Chinese-English expressions and summarizes four types of conceptual metaphors: THE WEAKENING OF STRENGTH IS THE DILUTION OF FOOD, THE EMOTIONAL STATE IS A COOKER, LIFE IS METHODS OF COOKING and A COLORFUL LIFE IS THE FLAVOR AND TASTE OF LIFE as well as their primary metaphors including AN ABSTRACT FORM IS A PHYSICAL OBJECT, CONTRACTION IS THE FADING OF NATURE, AN ABSTRACT STATE IS THE PHYSICAL OBJECT, THE ABSTRACT PROCESS OF LIFE EXPERIENCE IS THE PHYSICAL METHOD OF COOKING and A COLORFUL LIFE IS FLAVOR AND TASTE OF FOOD. This paper also summarizes the central conceptual metaphor ABSTRACT EMOTIONAL FORMS ARE FOOD. By combining ECMT, this paper explains the abstract schematic concept system of IM, DM, FR and MS involved in the generation process of the central conceptual metaphor, and its conceptualization operation process is presented through diagrams. Finally, by combining the contextual factors in the process of conceptual metaphors discussed in ECMT, this study analyzes the reasons for the differences in the expression of Chinese and English food metaphors from the perspectives of situational context, conceptual-cognitive context and bodily context. This paper is one exploration of the application of cognitive pragmatics using ECMT, the latest development of CMT, aiming to provide reference for intercultural communication and Chinese-English foreign language teaching.

References

Aristotle. 1954. *Rhetoric and Poetics*. New York: The Modern Library.

Boas Hans C, Ryan Dux. 2017. "From the Past into the Present: From Case Frames to Semantic Frames". *Linguistics Vanguard*, 3(1):1–14.

Casasanto, Daniel. 2009. "Embodiment of Abstract Concepts: Good and Bad in Right and Left Handers". *Journal of Experimental Psychology: General*, 138(3): 351–367.

Choi, Youngju. 2014. "Food as a Source Domain of Metaphor in Korean and English". *The Linguistic Association of Korea Journal*, 22(4): 121-141.

Deignan, Alice. 1995. *Collins Cobuild English Guides 7: Metaphor*. London: HarperCollins.

Fillmore, Charles J. 1968. "The Case for Case". In Bach & R. T. Harm(eds.), *Universals in Linguistic Theory* (pp.1-88). New York: Holt, Rinehart and Winston.

Grady, J. 1997. "Theories Are Buildings Revisited". *Cognitive Linguistics*, 8: 267–290.

Wang, Jianwei. 2022. "A Comparative Study of Animal Metaphors in Chinese and English". *Studies in English Language Teaching*, 10(1): 126-132.

Kövecses, Zoltán. 2000. *Metaphor and Emotion: Language, Culture, and Body in Human Feeling*. Cambridge: Cambridge University Press.

Kövecses, Zoltán. 2010. "A New Look at Metaphorical Creativity in Cognitive Linguistics". *Cognitive Linguistics*, 21(4): 663–697.

Kövecses, Zoltán. 2015. *Where Metaphors Come From. Reconsidering Context in Metaphor*. Oxford and New York: Oxford

University Press.

Kövecses, Zoltán. 2020. *Extended Conceptual Metaphor Theory*. Cambridge: Cambridge University Press.

Kövecses, Zoltán. 2021. "Standard and Extended Conceptual Metaphor Theory". In Wen, Wu., & John R (eds.), *The Routledge Handbook of Cognitive Linguistics* (p.191-203). Routledge. New York.

Lakoff, Gorge. 1987. *Women, Fire, and Dangerous Things. What Categories Reveal about the Mind*. Chicago: University of Chicago Press.

Lakoff, Gorge. 1993. "The Contemporary Theory of Metaphor". In A. Ortony's (eds.), *Metaphor and Thought* (p. 202-251). Cambridge: Cambridge University Press.

Lakoff G, Mark J. 1980. *Metaphors We Live By*. Chicago: University of Chicago Press.

Lakoff G, Mark J. 1999. *Philosophy in the Flesh: The Embodied Mind and Its Challenge to Western Thought*. New York: Basic Books.

Langacker, Ronald. 2008. *Cognitive Grammar: A Basic Introduction*. New York: Oxford University Press.

Padiernos, Maria Olive Gay. "A Comparative Study of Food Metaphors in Filipino and English". *Journal of Linguistic Studies*, 23(3): 141-163.

Reddy, Michael J. 1979. "The Conduit Metaphor—A Case Frame Conflict in Our Language about Language". In A. Ortony (eds.), *Metaphor and Thought* (p. 284–324). Cambridge: Cambridge University Press.

Richards, Ivor Armstrong. 1936. *The Philosophy of Rhetoric*. Oxford: Oxford University Press.

Sweester. 1990. *From Etymology to Pragmatics: Metaphorical and Cultural Aspects of Semantic Structure*. Cambridge: Cambridge University Press.

Turner, Mark. 1996. *The Literary Mind: The Origins of Thought and Language*. New York: Oxford University Press.

Yu, Ning. 1995. "Metaphorical Expressions of Anger and Happiness in English and Chinese". *Metaphor and Symbolic Activity*, 10: 59-92.

A Contrastive Study of Chinese Learners' Implicit Semantic Learning of Shape Classifiers in English and Chinese Contexts

Yaoyu Hu
Sichuan University

Abstract

This empirical study investigates whether native Chinese speakers can implicitly learn the meaning of shape classifiers in different language learning contexts and the factors that affect the implicit learning of the meaning of shape classifiers. This study designs two experiments, and 50 Chinese college students are the subjects of the study. Experiment results show that adult native Chinese speakers fail to learn the meaning of shape classifiers implicitly in both Chinese and English language contexts. The experiment results suggest that the meaning of shape classifiers does not have a processing advantage and is therefore difficult to be learned implicitly. On the other hand, the use of new nouns in the test phase may lead to a transfer decrement effect and attenuate implicit learning. The fact that English does not grammatically encode the meaning of shape classifiers makes it difficult for native Chinese speakers to learn shape classifiers implicitly in English context. Secondly, the amount of learning input also impacts the implicit learning of shape classifiers in English context.

Keywords

English and Chinese contexts, implicit learning, the meaning of shape classifier

1. Introduction

Implicit learning is one of the most fundamental processes in human cognition, and the acquisition of knowledge through implicit learning is a ubiquitous cognitive phenomenon. When people first learn a language, they are largely unconscious. When asked about grammatical phenomena in their native language, they can always communicate with others using the correct grammar. However, they are often unable to summarize the patterns in a very clear and systematic way. Native speakers often attribute this to "language intuition." This is where implicit learning comes into play.

Yaoyu Hu, College of Foreign Languages and Cultures, Sichuan University, Chengdu, Sichuan Province, China. E-mail address: huyaoyuscu@163.com.

Research on implicit learning has mainly been conducted in cognitive psychology and language acquisition, focusing on the characteristics and nature of implicit learning. However, the current understanding of implicit learning is still minimal. First, little implicit learning research involves semantic objects. Second, previous research on implicit learning of language has focused on recognizing the feasibility of learners' implicit learning of language and less on distinguishing between the learning contexts of using a native language and using a foreign language.

This study incorporates the features of the meaning of shape classifiers and focuses on the topic of shape classifiers' semantic learning. The study has two primary purposes: first, to explore the possibility of implicit semantic learning of shape classifiers in adult learners. Second, to distinguish between different language learning contexts and examine the effectiveness of the same learning content in different language contexts.

2. Literature review

The current research on implicit learning in the second language acquisition community can be divided into two main parts: theoretical and empirical studies. The following review is a brief overview of these two areas. At last, a brief overview of the technical tools used in the academic world to measure implicit learning is provided.

2.1. Theoretical research on implicit learning

In terms of theory, research on implicit learning has been conducted for a long time and is rich in research theories, with two significant milestones in its development. The first one is Krashen's (1982) Monitor Theory, which first proposed the role of consciousness on language acquisition and distinguished between the concepts of learning and acquisition. Learning is a conscious process, the outcome of which is conscious knowledge monitored in speech comprehension and output. While acquisition is an unconscious learning process, the outcome of which is unconscious knowledge that is the only knowledge that the learner can apply to the comprehension and output of speech. Krashen's monitor theory has caused widespread controversy in the second language acquisition community but, at the same time, has given rise to a debate about what role implicit and explicit knowledge actually play in second language acquisition.

The second landmark theory is Schmidt's (1990) noticing hypothesis, which proposes that noticing is a minimal combination of attention and lower levels of consciousness, which is necessary and sufficient for transforming input into intake. He argues that language can only be absorbed if it is noticed, and stimuli outside of consciousness may subconsciously activate representations in memory, but subconscious learning is impossible. The noticing hypothesis is also one of the most influential theories in the second language acquisition community. It has been the theoretical basis for many studies, including the interaction hypothesis and the output hypothesis.

Subsequently, usage-based approaches to SLA have been proposed, including connectionist theory, cognitive theory, emergentist theory, etc. This view of acquisition is based on two major assumptions and five core ideas (N. Ellis and Wulff, 2015: 75-76) that language learning and language knowledge are mainly implicit. And most of our cognitive processing is unconscious, and all our language knowledge is constructed based on input (Goldberg, 2009: 93-94). In addition, overseas second language research is increasingly multidisciplinary and multi-perspective. It has proposed skill acquisition theory, information processing theory, sociocultural theory, complexity theory, the declarative/procedural model, and other related theories to affirm the role of implicit learning.

2.2. Empirical research on implicit semantic learning

In terms of empirical research, scholars have conducted prosperous studies. The specific research areas are mainly focused on four primary areas: implicit knowledge representation, grammar, meaning, and phonological implicit learning. This study focuses on the results related to implicit semantic learning.

In the field of implicit semantic learning, there are abundant studies. DeKeyser's (1995) study is one of the first studies in second language acquisition to focus on implicit semantic learning. The study uses Implexan, a 98-word artificial language with nouns with numbers and grammatical variations and verbs with sexual and numerical variations. The researchers train the subjects and subsequently test the representation of pictures in Implexan, and the results show that they do not implicitly learn the meaning of the inflections. William's (2005) study comes to the opposite conclusion, showing that subjects could still learn relevant semantics without awareness of the target semantics. Gong and Guo's (2009) study also shows that learners can unconsciously learn semantic prosody knowledge. Leung and Williams's (2011) Experiment 1 changes how the material is presented and uses a reaction-time method to compare the reaction time of the wrong and right examples to detect whether the subjects have implicit learning and finally prove that the subjects have learned the vitality rule. Chen et al.'s (2011) experiment is built on Williams's (2005) study with Chinese adult learners, and they find that subjects could generalize unconsciously learned vitality meaning to new nouns.

Still, some studies do not support the idea that semantics can be learned unconsciously, arguing that learners must notice form, meaning, and the connections between the two to learn relevant words (Doughty and Williams, 1998). Hama and Leow (2010) replicate Williams's (2005) study but improve it by increasing the subjects' memory load, and the results show that the subjects do not learn the rules. Faretta-Stutenburg and Morgan-Short (2011) replicate Williams's (2005) study exactly, but with contradictory results, where the subjects cannot learn the rules implicitly in the absence of rule awareness. Gai and Wen's (2013) and Lu (2021) and Huang's (2023) research results also indicate that adult learners fail to acquire semantic meaning. Other studies have investigated whether arbitrary semantic features unrelated to language usage can be understood implicitly. Experiment 2 by Leung and Williams (2011) investigates whether learners can implicitly learn the collocation between the size of an object expressed by an article and a noun. Study shows that the feature of the relative size of an object needs to be derived by comparison and is not a property of the object itself and therefore cannot be learned unconsciously. Experiment 3 by Chen et al. (2011) also verifies that the size feature cannot be learned implicitly. Similarly, Leung and Williams (2014) demonstrate that English case and Chinese strokes are not semantic concepts in either language and cannot be acquired implicitly.

2.3. Measurement of implicit knowledge

The measurement methods for implicit knowledge can be divided into three main types: retrospective verbal report, subjective measure, and reaction time test. Each method has its advantages and shortcomings.

A retrospective verbal report asks subjects to state the rules or patterns they may have discovered after completing an experimental task (e.g., Dienes et al.,1991; Ericsson and Simon, 1980). If a subject's performance is above a random level but cannot describe the knowledge that he uses, it is shown that he has learned implicit knowledge (Rebuschat and Williams, 2006, 2009, 2012; Williams, 2005).

The shortcoming of this approach is that there is not necessarily a link between verbal reports and the knowledge used to complete the task, as researchers might imagine. Some scholars have found that subjects do not learn or only partially learn the target implicit knowledge despite completing the task above the random level (Dulany et al., 1984; Perruchet and Pacteau, 1990), in which case it would clearly be inaccurate to take for granted that they have acquired implicit knowledge. Furthermore, the retrospective verbal report requires subjects to recall their thought processes after completing the task, and forgetfulness, interference, and additional processing of describing thought processes may make the reports inaccurate (Ericsson and Simon, 1993).

The subjective measure of implicit knowledge is proposed by Dienes et al. (1995) and is based on the high-order thought theory proposed by Rosenthal (1986). Dienes and Berry (1997) proposed two subjective measures that can be used for implicit learning. The guessing criterion, in which subjects perform above a baseline level but claim that they are merely guessing, indicates that their knowledge is implicit. The zero-correlation criterion, in which the same subjects' confidence and accuracy in making judgments are uncorrelated, suggests that the subject's mental state is implicit.

One problem with the subjective measure is subjective bias. Some subjects may choose to guess because they are not 100% sure of the target item, although they have some awareness of it. On the contrary, some subjects may have a high degree of confidence despite having only a feeling about the target item. Dienes and Scott (2005) argued that the subjects have two types of knowledge when making the subjective measure, structural knowledge and judgment knowledge of the target item. Even if the subjects are unconscious of structural knowledge, their feeling-based judgment knowledge is likely conscious. To solve this problem, confidence evaluation and judgmental basis should perform simultaneously.

Another common way to detect implicit knowledge is the reaction time test, which refers to the time it takes for the body to respond after receiving a stimulus. That is the time distance between stimulus and response, and this method is a widely used research method in psychology and psycholinguistics. Reaction time is also increasingly used in explicit and implicit learning research. This method is more objective and accurate, avoiding the influence of subjective factors, and is therefore also used by many linguists.

The current ways of testing implicit knowledge are imperfect, and almost every method has flaws, so it is best to use multiple methods simultaneously to maximize the validity of the test.

In conclusion, as mentioned earlier, second language acquisition research is increasingly multidisciplinary and multi-perspective, with different theories attempting to explain and predict the phenomena that can be observed in SLA. However, due to the lack of understanding of the process of SLA, SLA and its related theories from multiple perspectives will continue to coexist for some time. The rich empirical studies on implicit learning also keep proving the broad prospect of exploration in implicit second language acquisition. Future generations should continue to innovate and explore based on the previous studies to obtain a breakthrough.

3. Experiment design

This empirical study investigates whether native Chinese speakers can implicitly learn the meaning of shape classifiers in different language learning contexts and the factors that affect the implicit learning of shape classifiers' meanings. From literature review, we can see that there are still some controversies in the academic community about the definition of implicit learning, so we should give a clear definition of implicit learning, the main object explored in this thesis, before the study. According to the theories and studies of scholars in the introduction and literature review, we define *implicit learning* as an "unconscious process of acquiring knowledge in which learners are not conscious of learning knowledge." Still, the knowledge they learn is reflected in their practical use (Chen, 2019: 1). This study is also conducted based on the above definition.

This study focuses on answering the following two research questions:

1) Are native Chinese speakers able to acquire the semantic distinctions of shape classifiers in an implicit way in the context of their native language?

2) Can native Chinese speakers implicitly learn the semantic distinctions of shape classifiers when learning in English?

3.1. Experiment subjects

Considering that the experiments require the subjects to have the ability to use Chinese and English, the subjects of this experiment are 50 students from a university in Sichuan province who are all undergraduates and native Chinese speakers. They are all studying liberal arts, with proficient language application skills. They are divided into two groups. The first group is 25 first-year university students, all native Chinese speakers, who would participate in the Chinese language group of the experiment. The second group is 25 senior students majoring in English, all native speakers of Chinese, who have been studying at the university for four years and have a high level of English proficiency. They will participate in the experiment of the English group. Given the difficulty of implicit learning and the fact that it is not easy to obtain the implicit learning effect when using foreign language learning, the subjects of the English learning environment part of the experiment are senior students majoring in English to obtain an excellent experimental effect.

3.2. Experiment material

The experiment is modeled on Leung and Williams's (2014) experiment, combined with Chen's (2011) study, in which four new words/characters are designed based on alphabetic languages as well as Chinese characters: *gi, ro, ul, ne* and 宁, 夬, 疋, 毛.

Implicit learning is the unconscious learning of new knowledge. To ensure the strangeness of the knowledge, the experiment designer designs four English forms: *gi, ro, ul, ne*, which are not independent words in English and do not have any meaning. Since the combination of English words and Chinese nouns might be slightly unnatural for the subjects, four characters in Chinese, 宁, 夬, 疋, 毛, are selected as qualifiers to make the combination more natural. Since Chinese is not like English, which can randomly combine letters to create unfamiliar words, we could only choose words that are used very infrequently in Chinese to be used as qualifiers. The four unfamiliar words 丁, 夬, 疋, 毛 are from Chen et al.'s (2011) study. These words are selected from the Dictionary Editing Office of the Institute of Language in the Chinese Academy of Social Science, with frequencies lower than 1/1,000,000 (National Language Committee, 1992). So we can say learners have not learned these words before. This can also ensure the strangeness of the experiment material.

These new words appear as qualifiers and are given two meanings, the distance meaning for the explicit learning dimension: "far" or "near," and the shape meaning for the implicit learning dimension: "to describe something is long" (条) or "to describe something is flat" (张). The explicit dimension is the learning dimension that the learner is informed about in advance. The implicit dimension is the dimension that the learner is not informed about in advance.

Table 1. The explicit and implicit dimensions of qualifiers

		Implicit learning dimension	
		to describe something is long (条)	to describe something is flat (张)
Explicit learning dimension	Near	丁/ gi	疋/ ul
	Far	夬/ ro	毛/ ne

The nouns collocated with the qualifiers in this experiment are selected through the Modern Chinese Parallel Corpus of the State Language Commission and finally form 178 items (128 items are in practice phase, and 50 items are in test phase) together with four qualifiers in each group and used as experimental materials. The subjects perform two judgment tasks for each item: "object properties (long/flat)" and "distance (near/far)" judgment tasks. The original designers of the experiment, Leung and William, are consulted about whether the object properties judgments would make implicit learning less rigorous. They conclude that the judgments are merely activation tasks for implicit rule-related information, which do not directly refer to the implicit learning goal of "the meaning of shape classifiers" and do not change the nature of implicit learning.

To avoid the chunk effect of the nouns, none of the nouns of the test items are present in the practice phase. The counter-balanced A/B version of the test is used to compare the reflection time of the same noun's right and wrong items.

3.3. Experiment tools

The experiment is programmed with the psychological experimental software E-Prime 3.0. The reaction time is recorded by the reaction time measurement tool in the software to observe the occurrence of implicit learning by comparing the reaction time change between right and wrong items. For example, "gi stick" in the right item group is changed to "ul stick" in the wrong item group, which also means "a stick in the near." However, since *ul* is usually paired with "something flat," if learners are aware of the word's semantic meaning, they may hesitate when they see *ul* and find that it is different from what they expect. Finally, the reaction time and the error rate will increase.

Leung and Williams (2011) use a questionnaire interview to investigate learners' awareness. Although it is challenging to accurately review awareness during the learning process in offline thinking, the questionnaire method can provide a more intuitive understanding of the subjects' awareness, so this method is also used in this study.

3.4. Experiment steps

This study consists of two experiments. The basic content of Experiment 1 and Experiment 2 are the same; only the language and qualifiers used in each experiment are different. Each experiment takes half an hour and consists of three stages:

1. Explicit rule learning stage: The subjects are expected to get familiar with the explicit rules by reading the experiment instructions. The experiment instructions detail the experiment background, experiment content and experiment operation process as follows:

Experiment Instructions (English Group)
WELCOME TO THIS EXPERIMENT!

Recently, linguists have discovered a new language on a small island. The linguists have translated most of the words in this language. However, there are still a few words that cannot be translated, and the linguists need some knowledgeable people to learn to match these words, and your participation may be helpful to the linguists.

There are four special forms in the language, which are represented by "gi," "ul," "ro," and "ne" for a better understanding of English learners. Linguists know that these words are followed by nouns, with "gi" and "ul" modifying near nouns and "ro" and "ne" modifying far nouns.

This experiment is divided into the learning phase and the testing phase. In the learning phase, the experiment starts with the appearance of a red cross symbol "+" in the center of the computer screen to remind you to start looking at the computer screen, and the stimulus is presented immediately. After the "+" disappears, the center of the screen presents a phrase with qualifiers. You are invited to judge the nature of the object on the test paper and then choose to judge the object near or far in the experimental program. Press the "m" key for near things, and press the "k" key for far things. For example, if the phrase "gi stick" appears, you should check the "long" on the test paper and press "m" for "gi."

Once you understand the above instructions, please notice the position of the "m" and "k" keys.

---

2. Implicit rule learning and testing stage: During the learning phase, a red "+" appears on the computer screen for 500 milliseconds, followed by a phrase consisting of a qualifier and a noun. The subjects then have to make two judgments: first, whether the noun is a "long" or "flat" object, and second, whether the qualifier in the phrase modifies "near" things (key "m") or "far" (key "k"). The learning phase program provides correct/incorrect feedback on the distance judgments. The purpose of providing feedback is to ensure that the subjects understand the nouns correctly and the input is valid. A rest period is set at the end of the learning phase to reduce the fatigue effect that slows down the response during the test phase and affects the response time data.

During the test phase, a red "+" appears on the computer screen for 500 milliseconds, followed by 50 sets of phrases consisting of a qualifier and a noun. The subjects have to determine whether the 50 sets of phrases are correct or not according to what they learned during the study phase. The subjects press "j" for correct and "f" for incorrect. No correct/incorrect feedback is provided for the subjects in this phase.

3. Written questionnaire stage: after the computer task, a written questionnaire test is conducted to investigate the subjects' awareness. The consciousness measurement questionnaire mainly includes the following content:

1) Whether the subjects find the rule (implicit learning dimension) during the experiment. If so, the rule needs to be described in detail, and the specific time period when the pattern is found (instructional phase,

learning phase, testing phase) needs to be reported; if not, the rule needs to be guessed as much as possible.

2) Whether the subjects find any abnormalities in the material during the experiment. If so, a detailed description is required.

3) The subjects need to describe in detail the process of completing the two judgment tasks.

4) Whether the subject had difficulties during the experiment. If so, a detailed description is required.

3.5. Criteria of implicit learning in this study and data processing

Based on the methods commonly used in the academic community to test implicit knowledge summarized in Chapter One, the reaction-time method and the retrospective verbal report method are used in this study.

The first is the reaction time method. The subject's response time in a test will be recorded. The reaction time method is used to compare the reaction time of items that violate the rule ("wrong items") with those that conform with the rule ("right items"), and a significant difference between the two is evidence of implicit learning. The explanation is as follows: During the test phase, if the subjects implicitly learn the rule, when there is a noun pairing that does not match the subject's prediction, this will interfere with the speed of the subject's judgment of the noun, and thus there will be a delay effect, and at the same time, there may be more misjudgments, resulting in less accurate judgment. In contrast, the subjects who do not learn the rule do not experience longer response time or lower accuracy when they encounter nouns that do not conform to the rule. If there is a statistically significant difference between the response time of the judgment in the wrong item and the right item, it can be determined that the subjects have learned the semantic rule. If the difference is not significant, the subjects have not learned the semantic rule. The paired-sample t-test for their right and wrong item response time is counted to see if there is a significant difference between the two.

The following method is the *retrospective verbal report method*. Because verbal reports tend to cause thought interference, a questionnaire is used to investigate subjects' consciousness. Only data from the subjects whose consciousness measurements are unconscious is included in the statistics, meaning that the subjects cannot report or feel any rules in the post-test consciousness measurement session. If the subjects report rules or feel rules, they are considered conscious, and their data are not included in the statistics.

Therefore, implicit learning is considered to happen on the condition that (1) there is a significant difference in the response time between the wrong and right items and (2) the subjects are unconscious of the learning process.

In this study, the psychological reaction time test software counts reaction time, and SPSS is used to analyze the reaction time and learning effect statistically. Because implicit learning is unconscious learning, any data from subjects who report that they find the rule during the experiment will not be included in the statistics.

4. Results

This chapter presents and analyzes the specific data collected from the two experiments introduced in the previous chapter.

4.1. Experiment one: implicit semantic learning of shape classifiers in Chinese context by Chinese learners of English

The basic content of the experiment is described in 2.3. The language of this experiment is Chinese. "丁, 夬, 疋, 毛" are qualifiers, and the qualifiers and the nouns constitute 178 groups of experiment items. The experiment process is the same as the process described in 2.5.

Twenty-five first-year students studying liberal arts participate in this experiment, and all of them successfully finish the experiment. All the reaction time data are recorded, so the valid data of the experiment is 25. The questionnaire reveals that 20 people do not discover the rule, accounting for 80% of the total number, and 5 people think they have found it. Here is the detailed data of Experiment 1:

Table 2 The detailed data of Experiment 1

Number	Wrong items response time	Right items response time	Wrong items error rate	Right items error rate
1	2,099.16	2,077.84	20%	48%
2	2,317	2,766.88	80%	36%
3	1,090.68	918.04	60%	32%
4	705.92	492.2	76%	48%
5	1,544.76	1,792.28	56%	44%
6	3,893.84	4,222.56	76%	40%
7	4,675.4	4,220.48	64%	53%
8	3,881.84	3,854.4	52%	48%
9	4,381.24	4072	52%	64%
10	4,842.24	5,347.72	68%	56%
11	1,528	1,851	64%	44%
12	3,607	1,257	68%	36%
13	2,607.5	2,085.5	60%	24%
14	4,861	1,012.5	60%	36%
15	1,535.5	2,607.5	48%	64%
16	3,230	2,541	80%	20%
17	2,269	1,733.5	80%	44%
18	4,963	5,069.5	44%	60%
19	2,959	4,953.5	40%	40%
20	1,516	1,276	20%	24%
Average	2,448.44	2,475.91	58.4%	43.5%

As we can see from table 2, the subjects showed a large individual difference in the experiment results, such as the maximum value of 4963 in the wrong item response time and the minimum value of 705.92. However, the average data of Experiment One indicate that the difference between the wrong item response time and the right item response time is not large. But there is still a difference between the error rate of wrong items and the error rate of right items, with a difference of 14.9%.

A paired-samples t-test is conducted on the reaction time of right and wrong items of those who do not discover the rule, and the results are as follows:

Table 3. Comparison of right and wrong items response time in Experiment 1 (n=20)

	Wrong items M	Wrong items SD	Right items M	Right items SD	MD	t(499)	Sig. (2-tailed)
Response Time	2448.44	78.65	2475.91	93.37	-27.48	-0.337	0.736*

*$p > 0.05$

Table 4. Comparison of right and wrong items error rate in Experiment 1 (n=20)

Response Time	Wrong items M	Wrong items SD	Right items M	Right items SD	MD	t(19)	Sig. (2-tailed)
	58.40%	3.96%	43.50%	2.84%	15.35%	2.97	0.008*

*p < 0.05

Table 3 shows that the wrong items' response time is *not* significantly different from the right items' response time in Experiment 1 (t(499) = -0.337, p > 0.05). However, table 4 shows that there is a significant difference between the wrong items error rate and the right items error rate of the subjects in Experiment 1 (t(19) = 2.97, p < 0.05).

The results of Experiment 1 are inconsistent with the findings of Leung and Williams, and there is *no* significant difference between learners' right and wrong items response time, indicating that learners failed to experience implicit learning in a native language context.

4.2. Experiment two: implicit semantic learning of shape classifiers in English context by Chinese learners of English

The basic content of the experiment is described in 2.3. The language of this experiment is English. "Gi, ro, ul, ne" are qualifiers, and the qualifiers and the nouns constitute 178 groups of experiment items. The experiment process is the same as the process described in 2.5.

Twenty-five senior students majoring in English participated in this experiment, and all of them successfully finished the experiment. All the reaction time data are recorded, so the valid data of the experiment is 25. The questionnaire reveals that 21 people do not discover the rule, accounting for 80% of the total number, and 4 people think they have found it. Here is the detailed data of Experiment 2:

Table 5. The detailed data of Experiment 2

Number	Wrong items response time	Right items response time	Wrong items error rate	Right items error rate
1	2,315	3,633	72%	28%
2	5,513	4,396	60%	32%
3	12,244	13,076	48%	48%
4	4,714	5,939	72%	32%
5	1,872	4,636.5	60%	52%
6	1,197	16,580.5	52%	48%
7	6,113	2,809	84%	52%
8	2,515	6,494	40%	40%
9	3,545.5	2,497	60%	44%
10	3,268.88	2,677.76	24%	48%
11	2,299.5	3,124	40%	60%
12	1,193	1,288.5	60%	52%
13	5,774.5	5,975.5	40%	52%
14	1,686	9,232	64%	48%
15	3,233	3,583	84%	24%
16	11,532	2,832.5	52%	36%
17	4,469	2,139.5	56%	48%
18	14,785.5	9,145.5	68%	36%
19	5,291	7,181.5	68%	36%
20	3,949.4	2,927	64%	48%
21	2,907.5	3,161.5	72%	28%
Average	3,356.62	2,475.91	59.05%	42.48%

As we can see from table 5, the subjects showed a large individual difference in the experiment results, such as the maximum value of 14,785.5 in the wrong item response time and the minimum value of 1,193. However, the average data of Experiment 2 indicates that the difference between the wrong item response time and the right item response time is not large. But there is still a difference between the error rate of wrong items and the error rate of right items, with a difference of 16.57%.

A paired-samples t-test is conducted on the reaction time of right and wrong items of those who do not find the rule, and the results are as follows:

Table 6. Comparison of right and wrong items response time in Experiment 2 (n=21)

Response Time	Wrong items M	SD	Right items M	SD	MD	t(524)	Sig. (2-tailed)
	3,356.62	160.76	2,475.91	135.86	165.62	1.02	0.307*

*$p > 0.05$

Table 7. Comparison of right and wrong items error rate in Experiment 2 (n=21)

Response Time	Wrong items M	SD	Right items M	SD	MD	t(20)	Sig. (2-tailed)
	59.05%	3.28%	42.48%	2.16%	16.57%	3.48	0.002*

*$p < 0.05$

Table 6 shows that the wrong items' response time is *not* significantly different from the right items' response time in Experiment 2 (t(524) =1.02, p > 0.05). However, table 7 shows that there is a significant difference between the wrong items error rate and the right items error rate of the subjects in Experiment 2 (t(20) = 3.48, p < 0.05).

The present experiment results are inconsistent with the findings of Leung and Williams, where there is *no* significant difference between learners' right and wrong items response time, indicating that learners failed to experience implicit learning in English context.

5. Discussion

The two experiments show that the subjects do not learn the meaning of shape classifiers implicitly in both native language and foreign language learning contexts. Is it true that the meaning of shape classifiers cannot be learned implicitly? Or is it that the meaning of shape classifiers can be learned, but the subjects do not clearly show that they learn it implicitly because of the experimental design and learning effects? Based on these two questions, this part discusses why the subjects in this study cannot implicitly learn the meaning of shape classifiers. Finally, this part examines the differences in the results of the two experiments from the perspective of the learning language environment and explores the possibility of implicit semantic learning of shape classifiers in a foreign language context.

5.1. The possibility of learning shape classifiers implicitly

Here is an interpretation of the experiment results: adult learners have difficulty establishing the connection between form and shape classifiers' meanings through implicit learning.

Other features of the experiment material may also lead to failure in implicit learning of the meaning of shape classifiers. In the experiment, some subjects report that they are disturbed by other features of nouns when judging the shape of nouns, resulting in failure of judgments. In addition to shape, material and size are also common features of nouns, and these features are closely related to human perception. Compared with features such as material and size, the shape features of nouns are less noticeable. They are also particularly susceptible to interference by other features in judging tasks, making it difficult to learn collocation patterns implicitly. Researchers usually strictly control factors outside the implicit learning dimension in previous experiments to prevent other variables from influencing implicit learning (Li et al., 2013; Guo et al., 2013). In this research, no restrictions are made on other variables to make the experiment more closely related to the real learning environment. So other features of the experiment material may affect subjects' judgments of shape and finally lead to difficulties in implicitly learning the meaning of shape classifiers.

Physiologically, the meaning of shape classifiers does not have a processing advantage and is difficult to learn implicitly. The meaning of shape classifiers does not have the same evolutionary significance as other semantic concepts like vitality. Caramazza and Mahon (2003: 360) argued that there is neural specificity in representations of animals, fruit, and vegetables. This differentiation is the result of evolutionary pressure to develop dedicated and highly efficient neural circuits for processing types of stimuli that are of adaptive value. That means evolutionarily meaningful concepts have played an important role in human evolution. Because of this, these concepts occupy an important place in the brain where they can be rapidly activated and processed, facilitating implicit learning. On the other hand, shape classifiers' meaning has little to do with evolution. Many cultures do not distinguish between shape classifiers, and only a very few languages have shape classifiers in their grammatical codes. In most languages, knowledge of the meaning of shape classifiers plays a pragmatic role that expresses the subjective will of the speaker, and it cannot be rapidly activated and processed by the brain to classify the shape features of nouns unconsciously.

5.2. Factors affecting the experimental results during the experiment

Another interpretation of the experimental results: adult learners can differentiate the meaning of shape classifiers implicitly, but they fail to show up clearly in the results.

The author compared the error rates of the subjects in Experiment 1 and Experiment 2 for right and wrong items. It is found that in the two experiments, there is a significant difference between the wrong items error rate and the right items error rate of the subjects (see tables 4 and 7 for details), which can indicate to some extent that the adult learners have learned the meaning of shape classifiers implicitly, but the degree of learning is low, and they cannot be regarded as having completely learned the meaning of shape classifiers. Why does this happen? It may be explained by the following reasons.

First, the difficulty in implicit learning may be caused by new nouns in the testing phase. New nouns make the response time data fluctuate more, which leads to difficulty in implicit learning of shape classifiers. In the previous experiments, Leung and Williams (2014) used nouns that appear in the learning phase during the test phase, which may have caused these nouns to be activated in the brain memory in the learning phase. When the nouns appear for the second time (i.e., in the test phase), the subjects can complete the judgment task more easily. The response time data is less fluctuating and more conducive to implicit learning of the meaning of the shape classifiers.

Second, the *transfer decrement effect* may have occurred. That means, after the use of new test items, the effect of implicit learning decreased. Studies of implicit learning using artificial grammar as learning objects have found that the use of new test items attenuates implicit learning. Knowlton (1996: 169) argued that the reason for the attenuation is that implicit learning is a rule-based and example-based learning that can be transferred to new learning items. When the subjects are tested, they generally make judgments by analogy (i.e., they judge the grammatical correctness of a test item by perceiving the similarity between the learned item and the test item). New test items can lead subjects to believe that the new items are not sufficiently similar to the previously learned items, resulting in less accurate judgments. Implicit learning of the meaning of shape classifiers may also be similar for this reason. If a new test item is used in the test phase, and the new test item is not strongly related to the previously learned item, then the transfer decrement effect may occur. In this experiment, the introduction of new items in the test phase may lead to the transfer decrement effect, affecting the implicit learning of shape classifiers.

Third, the experimental results may be caused by the subjects' failure to complete the experimental tasks in the order of the experimental design. From the questionnaires, we could find that some subjects complete the learning phase task by judging the qualifier first and then the nature of the object. Because the qualifier and the noun appear as a phrase on the computer screen, the qualifier appears on the left side of the computer screen, and the noun appears on the right side of the computer screen. The subjects take a left-to-right approach to do judgment tasks, so they would choose to judge the qualifier first. However, the experiment instructions require the subjects first to judge the noun's shape and then make the qualifier judgment. The subjects may initially follow the experimental instructions. After a period of practice, they may find it more effortless to adopt a left-to-right judgment order, so they judge the qualifier first and then observe the shape of the noun. These explanations are post hoc explanations made in the results of the questionnaires, and future experiments need to explore how the order of judgments specifically affects the experimental results and make more in-depth explanations.

5.3. Influence of English context on the implicit semantic learning of shape classifiers

Implicit learning in the foreign language context is usually more difficult than in the native language context because the learners' limited proficiency leads to different representations in the foreign language and the native language. Foreign language learners tend to make indirect connections through native vocabulary and concepts and thus have less direct and faster access to concepts than native learners. From the perspective of cognition, this is a sign that the degree of the semantic embodied experience of a foreign language is weaker than that of the native language.

From the experiment data, we can see that the subjects in the foreign language learning context have longer reaction times and higher error rates than the native language group in the judgment task, which also explains, to some extent, the difficulty of implicit learning in a foreign language context.

The occurrence of implicit learning is significantly related to whether the learning concept is grammatically encoded in the language of learning. It is found that implicit learning can only occur when the learner's background knowledge is consistent with the target knowledge for implicit learning. It does not occur when the two are not consistent. In the reaction time test, the rapid semantic judgments made by the subjects on phrases are based on the brain's rapid activation of semantics. Grammatically encoded concepts appear to be more active in the brain and are more easily processed and recognized by the brain, facilitating implicit learning. In contrast, the meaning of shape words in English is not grammatically encoded and is difficult for the brain to process and recognize, which may be detrimental to implicit learning.

In addition, the degree of foreign language automation may also be an influential factor. It has been found that the same subjects showed different learning outcomes when completing implicit learning tasks with different levels of automation (Paciorek, 2012), with tasks requiring high levels of automation being more difficult to show implicit learning effects.

Moreover, implicit learning is strongly influenced by the amount of input, and studies have confirmed the important role of input on implicit learning in a foreign language context (Gai and Wen, 2013), as non-native speakers need more input to facilitate implicit learning. Therefore, the limitation of input may also be the reason for the lack of implicit learning effect in the foreign language condition.

6. Conclusion

This study notices that there is no sufficient evidence that native Chinese speakers have learned shape classifiers' semantic distinctions implicitly in L1/L2 learning context. The nature of the meaning of shape classifiers makes it more difficult to form shape semantic generalizations through implicit learning. The task conditions with a high degree of automation make it difficult for learners to break through the decisive role of their own linguistic knowledge (the grammatical encoding state of the target semantics in the learned language) in implicit learning. The above results indicate that subjects fail to learn shape classifiers' meanings through implicit learning in native and foreign language contexts. The findings also suggest that the same learning style has different learning effects. The second language condition is subject to more factors, for example, the lack of input, which often makes it difficult to show the expected results.

Admittedly, there are some shortcomings in this study. The subjects' backgrounds are relatively homogeneous, and more attention should be paid to the individual differences of the subjects. Also, the number of subjects and language proficiency of the subjects should be considered. The input of the experiment is insufficient. On the one hand, future studies should pay more attention to individual factors to explain the different implicit learning results of different subjects under the same learning context. On the other hand, future research should consider improving the design to maximize the amount of learning while maintaining the learners' unconsciousness and obtaining more clear results in the foreign language context.

References

Caramazza A. and Mahon BZ. 2003. "The Organization of Conceptual Knowledge: The Evidence from Category-Specific Semantic Deficits." *Trends in Cognitive Sciences*, 7(8): 354-361.

Chen W, Guo X, Tang J, Zhu L, Yang Z, and Dienes Z. 2011. "Unconscious Structural Knowledge of Form–Meaning Connections." *Consciousness and Cognition*, 20(4): 1751-1760.

Chen Y. 2019. *Explicit and Implicit Second Language Learning*. Beijing: Foreign Language Teaching and Research Press.

DeKeyser RM. 1995. "Learning Second Language Grammar Rules: An Experiment with a Miniature Linguistic System." *Studies in Second Language Acquisition*, 17(3): 379-410.

Dienes Z and Berry D. 1997. "Implicit Learning: Below the Subjective Threshold". *Psychonomic Bulletin and Review*, 4(1): 3-23.

Dienes Z. and Scott R. 2005. "Measuring Unconscious Knowledge: Distinguishing Structural Knowledge and Judgment Knowledge." *Psychological Research*, 69 (5): 338-351.

Dienes Z., Broadbent D, and Berry D. 1991. "Implicit and Explicit Knowledge Bases in Artificial Grammar Learning." *Journal of Experimental Psychology: Learning, Memory, and Cognition*, 17 (5): 875-887.

Dienes Z., Altmann G., Gao S.J. and Goode A. 1995. "The Transfer of Implicit Knowledge Across Domains." *Language and Cognitive Processes*, 10(3-4): 363-367.

Doughty C. and Williams J. 1998. Pedagogical Choices in Focus on Form." In Doughty C and Williams J (eds.). *Focus-on-Form in Classroom Second Language Acquisition*. Cambridge: Cambridge University Press, pp. 114-138.

Dulany D., Carlson R. and Dewey G. 1984. "A Case Of Syntactical Learning and Judgment: How Conscious and How Abstract?" *Journal of Experimental Psychology: General*, 113(4): 541-555.

Ellis N. and Wulff S. 2015. "Usage-Based Approaches to SLA." In VanPatten B and Williams J (eds.). *Theories in Second Language Acquisition: An Introduction* (2nd ed.). New York: Routledge, pp.75-93.

Ericsson K.A. and Simon H.A. 1980. "Verbal Reports as Data." *Psychological Review*, 87(3): 215-251.

---- 1993. *Protocol Analysis: Verbal Reports as Data* (A Bradford Book). London: The MIT Press.

Faretta-Stutenberg M. and Morgan-Short K. 2011. "Learning without Awareness Reconsidered: A Replication of Williams" (2005). In Granena G, Koeth J, Lee-Ellis S, Lukyanchenko A, Botana GP, and Rhoades E (Eds.), *Selected Proceedings of the 2010 Second Language Research Forum: Reconsidering SLA Research, Dimensions, and Directions*. Somerville, MA: Cascadilla Proceedings Project, pp. 18–28.

Gai S. and Wen Q. 2013. "Learning without Awareness by Chinese EFL Learners." *Foreign Language Teaching and Research*, 45(4): 557-567+640-641.

Goldberg A.E. 2009. "The Nature of Generalization in Language." *Cognitive Linguistics*, 20(1): 93-127.

Gong R. and Guo X. 2009. "The Role of Unconsciousness in the Learning of L2 Form-Meaning Connections: An Experimental Study of the Implicit Learning of Semantic Prosody." *Journal of Foreign Languages*, 32(2):68-76.

Guo X., Li F., Yang Z. and Dienes Z. 2013. "Bidirectional Transfer between Metaphorical Related Domains in Implicit Learning of Form-Meaning Connections." *PLoS One*, 8(7): 467-498.

Hama M. and Leow R.P. 2010. "Learning without Awareness Revisited: Extending Williams" (2005). *Studies in Second Language Acquisition*, 32(3): 465-491.

Huang Q. 2023. "Implicit Learning of L2 Semantic Collocation Rules and Influence of Individual Differences." *Foreign Language World*, 215:70-79.

Knowlton B.J. and Squire L.R. 1996. "Artificial Grammar Learning Depends on Implicit Acquisition of Both Abstract and Exemplar-Specific Information." *Journal of Experimental Psychology: Learning, Memory, and Cognition*, 22(1): 169.

Krashen S. 1982. *Principles and Practice in Second Language Acquisition*. Oxford: Pergamon.

Leung J.H. and Williams J.N. 2011. "The Implicit Learning of Mappings Between Forms and Contextually Derived Meanings." *Studies in Second Language Acquisition*, 33(1): 33-55.

---- 2014. "Crosslinguistic Differences in Implicit Language Learning." *Studies in Second Language Acquisition*, 36(4): 733-755.

Li F., Guo X., Zhu L., Yang Z. and Dienes Z. 2013. "Implicit Learning of Mappings between Forms and Metaphorical Meanings." *Consciousness and Cognition*, 22(1): 174-183.

Lu J. 2021. "A Corpus-Driven Experimental Study of Implicit and Explicit L2 Learning of L1-Minus and -Plus Semantic Prosodies." *Foreign Language Teaching and Research*, 53(6):874-886.

National Language Committee. 1992. *Statistics of Word Frequencies in Modern Chinese Language*. Beijing: Language and Literature

Press.

Paciorek A. 2012. *Implicit Learning of Semantic Preferences*. Unpublished Doctoral dissertation. Cambridge: University of Cambridge.

Perruchet P. and Pacteau C. 1990. "Synthetic Grammar Learning: Implicit Rule Abstraction or Explicit Fragmentary Knowledge?" *Journal of Experimental Psychology: General*, 119(3): 264-275.

Rebuschat P. and Williams J. 2006. "Dissociating Implicit And Explicit Learning Of Syntactic Rules." *Proceedings of the Annual Meeting of the Cognitive Science Society*, 28(28): 2594.

Rebuschat P. and Williams J. 2009. "Implicit Learning of Word Order." In Taatgen NA and Rijn H (eds.). *Proceedings of the 31st Annual Conference of the Cognitive Science Society*. Austin, TX: Cognitive Science Society, pp. 425-430.

Rebuschat P. and Williams J. 2012. "Implicit and Explicit Knowledge in Second Language Acquisition." *Applied Psycholinguistics*, 33(4): 829-856.

Rosenthal D.M. 1986. "Two Concepts of Consciousness." *Philosophical Studies*, 49 (3):329-359.

Schmidt R.W. 1990. "The Role of Consciousness in Second Language Learning." *Applied Linguistics*, 11(2): 129-158.

Williams J.N. 2005. "Learning without Awareness." *Studies in Second Language Acquisition*, 27(2): 269-304.

A Study on Vowel Acoustic Phonetics of Elementary English Learners in Chengdu and Chongqing Sub-Cluster in Southwest Mandarin

Mengxing Fu
Sichuan University

Abstract

Taking the perspective of acoustic phonetics, this study is a formant-based investigation of the vowels /ɪ/, /ʊ/, /æ/, and /ɒ/ by examining 30 subjects' pronunciations of Chengdu and Chongqing sub-clusters of Southwest Mandarin. The research adopts a combination of qualitative and quantitative analysis. With the help of the visualization speech software Praat, this research provides F1/F2 graph for acoustic analysis and then conducts retrospective interviews to explore the pronunciation errors of L2 learners in the initial stage of phonology acquisition. The reference of vowels is set by same-aged Cambridge native speakers' pronunciations from the IViE corpus, and the Native Language Magnet Model and Perceptual Assimilation Model were employed to explain the specific change in tongue position caused by Southwest Mandarin. These findings contribute to providing more empirical support for the dialectal negative transfer of Southwest Mandarin at the syllabic level in the future and also shed light on the localization of English teaching in various dialect areas.

Keywords

Southwest Mandarin; formant; Perceptual Assimilation Model; Language Magnet Effect; acoustic phonetics

1. Introduction

The 1950s witnessed the development of the concept of "mother tongue influence" in the field of second language acquisition (SLA), and Lado, who proposed the Comparative Analysis Hypothesis in 1957, promoted the theory of language transfer to the spotlight of SLA. Lado pointed out that the similarities with the mother tongue in second language acquisition are easy to learn, while the differences are difficult to learn (Wang, 1999). And it is axiomatic that sound is the foundation of any language, phonetic transfer is one of the common phenomena of language transfer, and phonological interlanguage has always been the focus of SLA. At the end of the 20th

---

Mengxing Fu, College of Foreign Languages and Cultures, Sichuan University, Chengdu, Sichuan, China. E-mail address: 1282163067@qq.com.

century, the theory of L2 phonetic acquisition developed rapidly and formed two categories: (1) the output category, which is based on typological markedness features and (2) the perception category, which is based on the similarity of different phonemes. And tremendous effort has been put into exploring the relationship between the perception and production of phonemes. And respectively, the output category is represented by the markedness differential hypothesis proposed by Eckman (1977) and the optimality theory proposed by Prince and Smolensky (2004), and the perception category is developed around four mainstream perceptual models, namely the native language magnet model proposed by Kuhl (1993), the perceptual assimilation model proposed by Best (1993), the speech learning model proposed by Flege (1995), and the automatic selective perception model proposed by Strange (1995) (Wang, 2008). Previously, many studies have been based on the speech learning model to explain the final results of L2 learners' phonetic acquisition, but the experimental subjects in this study are in their initial stage of learning English, so the native language magnet model and the perceptual assimilation model are used to explain how the differences of the acquisition of English target vowels emerge.

The native language magnet model believes that the phonetic prototype in the native language has a magnetic effect, and in the process of acquiring a second language, perceptual processing "attracts" non-native phonemes with similar acoustic distance to the vicinity of the prototype in the native language. And the higher the similarity of the two phonemes, the shorter the perceived distance, and the more difficult it is to distinguish the two phonemes. Moreover, the linguistic experience of the mother tongue changes the acoustic perception space of the second language, and this distortion of hearing discrimination ultimately leads to erroneous output. The perceptual assimilation model explores the influence of articulatory gestures in native language experience on second language acquisition. It is acknowledged that Chinese and English have different phonetic patterns, especially vowels. Chinese and its various dialects have a wider division of vowels and fewer phonemes than English, and each vowel assumes more functions and a wider distribution in the vowel space, so the area it represents is larger. Therefore, native Chinese and dialect speakers are not sensitive to the perception of tongue position, because their tongue cannot perceive many slight articulatory gestures in nature, which eventually leads to deviations in English vowel production. And L2 learners rely on the phonetic category built in the native phonetic system to perceive L2 phonetics, and when learning the second language, the non-native phonemes with large similarity in the perception space will be assimilated to the nearest native vowel representation.

According to the authoritative explanation of the "Overview of Chinese Dialects (2021 Edition)," about 80% of the pronunciation of various dialects in China is different. Different dialect backgrounds exert different effects on the learner's target language phonetic acquisition (Marinescu, 2012). The interference of the native dialect on the English phonology is enormous because the "vernacular sound" inevitably has an impact on the accuracy of the pronunciation of the new phonetics. However, previous studies mostly relied on the Official Mandarin vowel pattern as a comparative basis and did not summarize the general formant graph of the average vowel pronunciation in dialect areas. Only a few studies pointed out the difference between dialects and the Official Mandarin pronunciation. Besides that, the current research on phonetic transfer in dialects in SLA is relatively weak. Zhai and Zhao (2015) sorted out 260 papers between 1957 and 2013 that studied the influence of Chinese dialects on English phonetic acquisition. They found that, in terms of paper sources, there are few high-end research results, and core journal papers account for only 7.7%; in terms of research methods, most papers in this field are mainly descriptive, and there are only 12 acoustic experimental studies. I continued to search for related research and found that among 443 articles between 1983 and 2022, the proportion of focus on the Official Mandarin was as high as 46%, nearly half. Among the other dialect regions, except for Cantonese, which accounts for 12%, the rest are between 3% and 8%, and there is no significant difference in the number of paper publications. In the intragroup distribution of Mandarin Chinese, Southwest Mandarin enjoys the largest number of speakers (up to 270 million) and has the widest geographic distribution, but there are only 44 studies on the influence on English phonetic acquisition. Among these, most of them are based on classroom teaching and application. There is almost no research from the perspective of acoustic output. Overall, the research on the influence of Southwest Mandarin on English phonology acquisition is not comprehensive and systematic.

2. Experimental design

2.1. Research questions

The influence of native dialects on second-language phonetic acquisition has always been the focus and difficulty of learning English, and the influence of vowels is more complicated than that of consonants. This study uses a combination of qualitative analysis and quantitative analysis and uses the speech visualization software Praat to explore the problems of vowel pronunciation in the initial stage of English learners of the Southwest Mandarin mother tongue from the perspective of experimental phonetics. The pronunciation of vowels mainly emphasizes the change in the position of the tongue and the degree of roundness of the lips. The subtle adjustment of the tongue position causes a change in vowel quality, and each vowel has a corresponding set of formants. Among them, the most influential are the first two formants (F): F1, which is inversely proportional to the height of tongue raising (high, mid, low), and F2, which is proportional to the fronting of the tongue (front, central, back). The formant can be used as an acoustic parameter to visually compare the differences in phonological output between L2 learners and native speakers. The research questions are as follows:

i. What are the pronunciation problems of L2 learners in dialect area when pronouncing /ɪ/, /ʊ/, /æ/, and /ɒ/? How difficult is it to pronounce the four target vowels?

ii. How do gender and region affect the acoustic parameters of the target vowels? How does the tongue position change in specific?

iii. How do certain dialect phonemes affect target vowels' pronunciation?

2.2. Research methods

a) Experimental Subjects

The subjects in this study are first-year students from Dafo Middle School in Lezhi County, Sichuan Province. Fifteen males and fifteen females were selected based on their similar scores on two midterm and one final English test. The subjects were all between 13 and 15 years old, their English pronunciation was in the initial formation and development stage, Southwest Mandarin was the most commonly used language for students in the region, and the Official Mandarin was rarely used. Therefore, Southwest Mandarin can be considered as their mother tongue, and the influence of Official Mandarin on English vowel acquisition can be largely ignored.

    b)   Defining the Chengdu-Chongqing sub-cluster vowel of the Southwest Mandarin

Based on the division of Chinese entering tone, Southwest Mandarin is divided into 6 clusters and 22 sub-clusters. In this experiment, the Chengdu-Chongqing sub-cluster in the Chuan-Qian cluster was selected as the research object. The reason for choosing it is because the phonological characteristics of this sub-cluster are concise, the internal consistency is higher than that of other areas, and it is the most typical Southwest Mandarin (Li, 2009). Unlike in English, there is no fixed division to induce Chinese phonological structures, and controversy over vowel categories has a long history because the phonemic divisions range from 2 to 8 in terms of different research purposes, theoretical models, or teaching purposes. In this study, based on the "Sichuan Dialect Phonology," the vowels of the Chengdu-Chongqing sub-cluster of Southwest Mandarin were summarized into 8 phonemes, expressed as [ɿ] 日, [ɚ] 二, [a] 大, [o] 我, [ɛ] 黑, [i] 一, [u] 五, and [y] 鱼 respectively, and the Chinese characters that followed can help pinpoint their pronunciations. When collecting the formant data of 30 subjects, F1 and F2 in the single words of the above 8 Chinese characters were first extracted twice, and then the words were put into the declarative sentences of daily life language, and F1 and F2 were extracted from these sentences twice again, and finally, the average value of the two formants was taken (Jiang, 2010).

    c)   Defining the vowel corpus

In order to objectively reflect the general picture of the sensitivity of the tongue position in the whole vowel space, /ɪ/, /ʊ/, /æ/, and /ɒ/, which were distributed in the four corners of the vowel pattern, were selected as experimental materials. Since the formant will vary greatly in different contexts, speech rates, and intonation, in order to obtain relatively stable F1 and F2 values, the vowel-bearing carrier words formulated by phonetics scholars were selected as the test corpus (Zhou, Shao and Chen, 2010). Vowels can usually appear at the beginning, at the middle, and at the end of syllables, but in the context of the beginning and the end, the vowel in the RP inventory sometimes does not hold. And only in the CVC structure can any vowel form a meaningful phrase. Therefore, in the experiment, /ɪ/, /ʊ/, /æ/, and /ɒ/ were placed in the structure of CVC: /h_d/ and the corresponding stimulus were selected as hid, hood, had, hod. When arranging the tone in which the vowel is located, the descending tone at the end of a sentence is preferred, because this is where the vowel pronunciation is most prominent and stable. During the experimental period, each participant reads the carrier sentence "I say ____ now," which provides the same speech environment for vowel pronunciation. English words are replaced by hid, hood, had, hod in sequence, and the sentence materials are "I say hid now," "I say hood now," "I say had now," "I say hod now."

    d)   Defining the formant standard

Since the school's junior high English textbook is the PEP edition, in which the vowels of RP are used as the phonetic standard, the experiment uses the RP vowel inventory as a reference. This study extracted phonetic data from the IViE corpus. Established by the Oxford University Phonetics Laboratory, the IViE corpus recorded nine major British dialects, and the native speakers within were about 15 years old, which was the same age as the subjects in this experiment, so the frequency of the formant itself was not much different. Words containing /ɪ/, /ʊ/, /æ/, and /ɒ/ in the Cambridge corpus that was closest to the RP pronunciation were selected, and the influence of co-articulation of adjacent phonemes was minimized (Jiang, 2010). F1 and F2 values were extracted five times both in male and female voices, and then the average value was taken.

e) Experimental Procedures and Research Tools

The experimental equipment used is the HUAWEI MateBook D14 with a built-in microphone and a matching FreeBuds Bluetooth headset. In Praat software, the sampling rate is set to 44100 Hz, and the recording of sounds is performed in a quiet classroom so as to reduce ambient sound. The ten most stable waves in the wideband spectrogram of the recorded WAV file were selected, from which we took the average F1 and F2 values. After the recording, five male and five female subjects were randomly selected to conduct a retrospective interview in order to get information on their phonetic learning habits and acquisition environment, so as to explore how errors emerge in vowel production, and the content of the questionnaire is detailed in Annex I. Finally, SPSS and EXCEL software are employed for data statistics and analysis.

3. Data analysis

3.1. Quantitative comparative analysis of male subjects in dialect area and IViE male corpus

As can be seen from figure 1, there is no difference in the pronunciation characteristics of vowel /ɪ/ in the F1 frequency, but there is a significant difference in the F2 frequency, with a standard deviation of 310.599, indicating that when male subjects pronounce the vowel /ɪ/, they are not sensitive to the difference between the front and back positions of the tongue, and their tongue position is generally more forward. The formant values of the vowel /æ/ were the most discrete, and the participants had huge differences in F1 and F2 frequencies, with a standard deviation of 98.006 for F1 and 124.530 for F2. The vowel /æ/ was clearly problematic and has the lowest precision. The formant values for the vowels /ʊ/ and /ɒ/ are more concentrated, the two groups have a large overlap, and /ɒ/ is all near RP /ɒ/ except for a singular pronunciation. All male subjects deviated from the pronunciation of RP /ʊ/, and the F1 frequency was comparable to RP, but the F2 frequency was much lower than that of RP. This indicates that the tongue is further backward than the standard pronunciation when producing the /ʊ/ sound.

Figure 1. Formant comparison between subjects and IViE corpus (male, n=15)

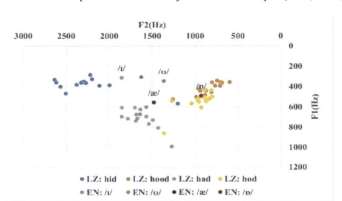

3.2. Quantitative comparative analysis of female subjects in dialect area and IViE female corpus

It can be seen from figure 2 that similar to the male subjects' pronunciation characteristics, the vowel /ɪ/ of females have little difference in F1 frequency, with a standard deviation of only 49.513, but a significant difference in F2 frequency, with a standard deviation of 333.362. It shows that female subjects are not sensitive to the difference in tongue fronting when pronouncing the vowel /ɪ/. With lower pronunciation accuracy and precision, the female vowel /æ/ pronunciation was even more discrete than the male subjects', which has a standard deviation of 164.687 on F1 and 408.835 on F2. And vowel /æ/ also has the lowest acquisition rate among the four target vowels. The formant values for the vowels /ʊ/ and /ɒ/ are more concentrated, partially overlapping, and also near RP /ɒ/. The pronunciation of /ʊ/ deviated from the pronunciation of RP /ʊ/ in all female subjects just as in males, and the F1 frequency was higher than that of RP and lower in F2 frequency than RP. This indicates that the tongue is lower and further back than the standard pronunciation when producing the /ʊ/ sound.

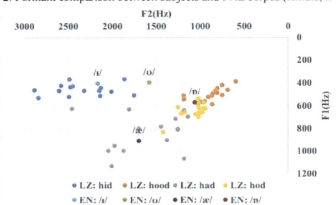

Figure 2. Formant comparison between subjects and IViE corpus (female, n=15)

3.2. Comparison of the mean value of the formant of native speakers in the dialect area and the IViE corpus

Table 1. Mean Formant Value of Dialect Area Subjects and IViE corpus (female, n=15)

vowels	LZ F1(Hz)	LZ F2(Hz)	IViE F1(Hz)	IViE F2(Hz)
ɪ	457	2346	424	2192
ʊ	497	870	357	1576
æ	835	1600	899	1686
ɒ	636	1074	519	1107

Table 2. Mean Formant Value of Dialect Area Subjects and IViE corpus (male, n=15)

vowels	LZ F1(Hz)	LZ F2(Hz)	IViE F1(Hz)	IViE F2(Hz)
ɪ	375	2217	314	1914
ʊ	412	826	335	1512
æ	708	1625	583	1520
ɒ	543	951	492	911

The difference in formant between the pronunciation of experimental subjects and the IViE corpus was first tested by an independent sample t-test, the F1 and F2 values of the target vowel were used as the test variables, and the region (whether the sound came from the dialect area or the corpus) was used as the grouping variable. The results showed that the frequency of regional differences in F1 was higher than that of F2; that is, for participants from the dialect area, the mastery of the height of the tongue was less sensitive than that of the fronting of the tongue. The specific data are as follows: for vowel /ɪ/, pF1=0.09, pF2=0.04; for vowel /ʊ/, pF1=0.01, pF2=0.01; for vowel /æ/, pF1=0.477, pF2=0.882; for vowel /ɒ/, pF1=0.001, pF2=0.917. Gender was then used as the grouping variable to test the difference in formants between male and female subjects. The results show that for vowel /ɪ/, pF1=0.001, pF2=0.011; for vowel /ʊ/, pF1=0.01, pF2=0.579; for vowel /æ/, pF1=0.01, pF2=0.236; for vowel /ɒ/, pF1=0.004, pF2=0.001. In general, F1 had sex differences more frequently than F2, which means female subjects were less sensitive to the high and low positions of the tongue than the fronting of the tongue.

The difference in formant between the pronunciation of experimental subjects and the corpus was then analyzed by univariate multivariate ANOVA, and F1 or F2 of the four target vowels were set as the dependent variables and gender and region were set as fixed factors (Chen, 2021). The results showed that the main effects of sex and region were mixed, and the frequency of sex differences in F1 was higher than that of F2, which confirmed the results of the independent sample t-test. The specific data are as follows:

With regard to /ɪ/, F1 values differ as a function of gender and region, which both yields a $p < 0.05$, indicating that F1 will have significant changes with these two factors, but the interaction effect of the two is not significant ($p = 0.265$). F2 values did not differ concerning gender ($p > 0.05$), but they differ as a function of the region ($p < 0.05$), indicating that there was no significant difference in sex in F2 values, and the interaction effect between the two fixed factors was not significant ($p=0.308$). For the vowel /ʊ/, F1 values differ as a function of gender and region ($p < 0.05$), showing that F1 will change significantly with these two factors, and there is a group interaction ($p=0.058$). F2 values did not differ with regard to gender ($p > 0.05$) but differed as a function of the region ($p < 0.05$), and there is no interaction effect between the two factors ($p= 0.757$), illustrating that there was no significant difference in F2 in gender. With regard to /æ/, F1 values differ as a function of gender ($p < 0.01$), but did not differ concerning region ($p= 0.294$), and the interaction effect between the two was significant ($p < 0.01$). F2 values did not differ both as a function of gender and region ($p > 0.05$ respectively), and the interaction effect of the two was not significant either ($p=0.113$). And this result is consistent with the results of the previous independent sample t-test. And for the vowel /ɒ/, F1 values differ significantly as a function of gender and region, which both yields a $p < 0.01$, and the interaction effect of the two was significant also, with a $p < 0.05$. F2 values differ with regard to gender ($p < 0.05$) but did not differ as a function of the region ($p > 0.05$), demonstrating that there was no significant difference in F2 between the dialect area subjects and corpus speakers, and the interaction effect of the two was not significant, with a $p > 0.05$.

4. Conclusion

The influence of gender and region on acoustic parameters is very complex and sometimes interacts. However, in general, the frequency of significance on both regional and gender differences in F1 was higher than that of F2, indicating that female subjects in dialect areas were generally more sensitive to the height of tongue position than to the fronting of tongue position. However, there was a great similarity between males and females in the pronunciation of target vowels. In terms of pre-vowel pronunciation, when pronouncing the vowel /ɪ/, the difference in F1 frequency is smaller than the difference in F2 frequency, and the sensitivity to the height of tongue position than to the fronting of tongue position. The acquisition rate of /æ/ was the lowest in both male and female subjects, but when pronouncing vowel /æ/, there were huge individual differences in F1 and F2 frequencies between different gender subjects, and female subjects had more discrete acoustic data and lower speech precision. In terms of the back vowel, when pronouncing the vowel /ʊ/, all participants deviated from the RP /ʊ/ pronunciation and were closer to the pronunciation of RP /ɒ/, and neither male nor female subjects could distinguish between the pair of lax and tense vowels of /ʊ/ and /ɒ/. However, as can be seen from the concentration of formant parameters, the vowel /ɒ/ has the highest acquisition rate.

On a formant graph, a vowel space does not represent a point but rather represents a range of points that contain specific phonemes and phonemic variants of that vowel (Zhang, 2002). And after excluding gender differences, 3 kinds of acoustic data were condensed in figure 3, and the formant parameter of subjects' English and Chinese vowel sounds and IViE corpus were illustrated in different colors, respectively. This three-way comparison chart will help explain how certain dialect phonemes affect target vowels' pronunciation (Ma and Tan, 1998).

From the perspective of the native language magnet effect, figure 3 explicitly revealed that the pronunciation of vowel /ɪ/ was "attracted" by the phoneme [ɛ] of the Southwest Mandarin and thus deviated from the corpus RP /ɪ/ pronunciation, and the tongue position was further back, but the dialectal phoneme [ɛ] had no effect on the sensitivity of tongue fronting. The articulatory gesture of the vowel /ɒ/ was affected by the magnetic effect of the phoneme [o] of Southwest Mandarin, and the tongue position became slightly lower, but the vowel /ɒ/ had the highest acquisition rate overall. The pronunciation of the vowel /ʊ/ was "attracted" by the phoneme [u] of Southwest Mandarin, which caused the F2 frequency to be greatly lowered, and the tongue position was significantly more forward. In general, the smaller the perceived distance and the greater the magnetic effect, the more difficult it is to acquire those phonemes.

From the perspective of perceptual assimilation, figure 3 showed that the pronunciation of /ʊ/ seriously deviated from corpus RP /ʊ/ and closer to the category of Southwest Mandarin [u] in vowel space, indicating that when the subjects pronounced the /ʊ/ sound, the perceptual result of this vowel was assimilated into the articulatory gesture of the Southwest Mandarin phoneme [u], resulting in the tongue position of /ʊ/ being significantly more backward. The formant dispersion of the vowel /æ/ was the largest, the negative transfer at the F1 and F2 frequencies was complicated, and the degree of influence was different for each individual. Due to vowel /æ/'s unique degree of mouth opening, it is colloquially known as the "plum blossom sound." However, in the Chengdu-Chongqing subcluster of Southwest Mandarin, there is no such sound. And the acoustic distance between dialectal phonemes [ɚ] and [a] and RP vowel /æ/ is relatively large; that is, the articulatory gesture near vowel /æ/ is missing, and the original phonological materials for establishing the second language phonological category are insufficient, so it is difficult for the subjects to master the standard opening gesture, resulting in the lowest acquisition rate of vowel /æ/. So it is impossible to determine which dialectal phoneme exerts an influence on vowel /æ/. Meanwhile, because the overall mean of dialectal phoneme [æ] is exactly around the RP /æ/ mean value, it explains why the p-value of the vowel /æ/ is greater than 0.05 in the independent sample t-test.

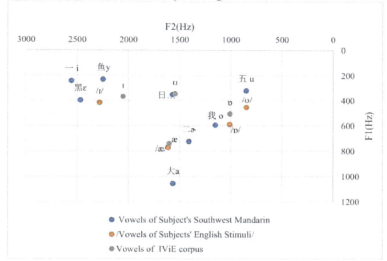

Figure 3. Formant comparison between subjects' English and Chinese vowel sounds and IViE corpus

5. Discussion

From the perspective of acoustic linguistics, this study takes the comparison between the same-age pronunciation of subjects from the Chengdu-Chongqing sub-cluster of the Southwest Mandarin and IViE corpus and compares the first and second formants of /ɪ/, /ʊ/, /æ/, and /ɒ/. The research aims to analyze the acoustic differences of (a) the dialectal intra-group as a function of gender and (b) the pronunciations of dialectal subjects and IViE corpus as a function of gender and region and (c) explores the negative transfer of specific dialectal phonemes on the target vowel formants and then determines the source and degree of production errors.

The study found that the situation of vowel acquisition in the Chengdu-Chongqing sub-cluster is not optimistic, and the questionnaire survey after the testing revealed the reasons that restrict the second language phonology acquisition of local students. On the one hand, in terms of subjective factors, (1) only 30% of interviewees noticed the difference between the correct and incorrect vowel pronunciation, and almost all of the interviewees thought language experience of dialect only affects speaking and were not aware of the negative transfer on English spelling and listening, and this can be explained by the native language magnet model. It is because they cannot perceive the difference that they cannot pronounce it correctly. Native language experience will distort the perceived difference of the second language, and L2 learners can only establish new phonetic categories if they perceive the difference between the native and target language. The accuracy of perception greatly restricts the accuracy of second-language acquisition, which is, accurate perception is the prerequisite for standard output. (2) After being demonstrated the negative transfer of dialects on the target vowel, the interviewees said that this negative effect was difficult to eliminate and they lack confidence in their phonetic level. Moreover, they lack motivation to receive systematic phonetic training, thinking it is of little use to their final scores. (3) Most of the interviewees showed the habit of directly labeling English words with Chinese characters or Chinese Pinyin. This bad learning strategy overemphasizes the role of the mother tongue, and the excessive reliance on the experience of the mother tongue leads to a fossilized pronunciation, which further rigidizes their sensitivity to the tongue and decreases the accuracy of L2 perception. Moreover, the overreliance on Pinyin can also be explained by the perceptual magnet effect. Because after hearing the pronunciation of a foreign language, the brain will first find a similar sound from its familiar native language to replace it. And each time the incorrect pronunciation is reinforced, the only remaining ability to distinguish pronunciation will continue to weaken until it disappears completely.

On the other hand, in terms of objective reality, (1) the English textbooks employed locally are mixed with American and British accents, and the textbooks spell words according to British English standards, but the accompanying audio tapes are American English, and the inconsistency of British and American accents will cause great obstacles to the perception of tongue position of beginners. (2) English learning in Chinese secondary schools is test oriented, and teachers spend most of the time on vocabulary and grammar learning, neglecting systematic phonetic training. (3) The lacking teaching conditions and the poor accent of local English teachers themselves leads to little phonetic training, and the situation is even worse in undeveloped areas. (4) In the classroom, participation in oral activities is low, and students are reluctant to interact.

Each dialect has a different impact on English phonological acquisition, different native language experiences will form different phonological articulatory gestures, and the phonological category of interlanguage learners established will limit the accuracy of L2 phonetic output. Therefore, when fossilized perception already rigidized pronunciation, only listening to standard English is of little use. So in practical teaching applications, teachers can use the formant shown on Praat to establish a reference system between Southwest Mandarin and English by using the standard parameters as coordinates to pinpoint the correct pronunciation pattern of English vowels and to specify the movement of the tongue. Moreover, at a macro level, the mainstream English textbooks that middle and high schools use nationwide are only applicable to Official Mandarin speakers. However, a large number of empirical studies have confirmed that dialects have different effects on English pronunciation in different parts of China. Therefore, in order to localize pronunciation teaching, it is necessary to find teaching methods based on different mother tongue experiences that are suitable for learners in different dialect areas (Fa, 2011). This study provides a reference for improving the English teaching application in dialect areas and provides more empirical support for research on the negative transfer of Southwest Mandarin at the syllabic level in the future.

Annex I: Questionnaire

1. Do you think your dialect is negatively affecting your English pronunciation?
   (A: clearly aware of   B: slightly aware of   C: have no idea)
2. Do you think that the negative transfer of dialects on English pronunciation is difficult to eliminate?
3. Are you confident in your English pronunciation?
4. Have you ever marked English words directly with Chinese characters or Pinyin?
5. Do you think that dialect affects your English listening, speaking and spelling ability?
6. Do you think your hometown English teacher has a vernacular accent?
7. Have you received systematic phonetic training/are you willing to accept it?

References

Chen M. 2021. "The Influence of Official Mandarin on Learners' English Vowel Pronunciation." *Modern Communication*, 21(02): 14-17.

Fa X.Y. 2011. "A Study on the Negative Transfer of Chinese Dialects to Phonetic Acquisition in English Phonetic Segments." *Journal of Hunan Finance and Economics University*, 27(04).

Jiang Y.Y. 2010. "Corpus-Based Research on Vowel Acoustic Characteristics of English Learners." *Journal of Beijing International Studies University*, 32(04): 23-27+22.

Jiang Y.Y. 2010. "Experimental Study on Vowel Acoustics of English Learners in Min and Wu Dialect Areas." *Foreign Languages Research*, 122(04): 36-40.

Li L. 2009. "Classification/Distribution of Southwest Mandarin." *FangYan*, 31(01): 72-87.

Ma C.D. and Tan L.H. 1998. "A Preliminary Comparative Study of Sichuan Dialect Phonology and English Phonology." *Journal of Sichuan Normal University Social Sciences Edition*, (03):13-18.

Marinescu I. 2012. "Native Dialect Effects in Non-Native Production and Perception of Vowels." University of Toronto.

Wang W.Y. 1999. "Review and Reflection on the Phenomenon of Language Transfer." *Foreign Language Education*, 99(01): 7-13.

Wang Y.J. 2008. "Cross-Language Comparison and L2 Speech Acquisition: Theories and Issues." *Proceedings of the 8th Chinese Phonics Conference and International Symposium on Frontier Issues in Speech Science*, 898-903.

Zhai H.H. and Zhao J.L. 2015. "Review of the Influence of Chinese Dialects on English Phonetic Acquisition." *Foreign Language World*, 15(01): 88-95.

Zhang J.S. 2002. "English-Chinese Vowel Contrast and English Phonetic Teaching." *Journal of PLA University of Foreign Languages*, 02(01): 56-59.

Zhou W.J., Shao PF and Chen Hong. 2010. "An Empirical Study on RP Vowel Perception of English-Majored College Students." *Journal of PLA University of Foreign Languages*, 33(06): 45-49+128.

Foreign Language Learners' Emotions in China (2012-2022): A Review and the Prospect

Xilin Xu

Sichuan University

Abstract

Emotions can be an influential factor in foreign language learning (FLL), and the past decade has seen an "affective turn" in second language acquisition (SLA). The scoping review method and the visualization tool CiteSpace are used in this paper to sort out studies on foreign language learners' emotions (FLLE) from 2012 to 2022 in China. The selected 114 articles from 19 journals are analyzed from the perspective of the general trend, keywords changes, research types, and research methods. Based on findings, four characteristics of recent FLLE research are summarized: (1) "positive turn" of research variables; (2) "holistic approach" to the studies of emotions; (3) interdisciplinary application of "broaden-and-build theory" and "control-value theory"; (4) rise of research on foreign language learning (FLL) boredom. In addition, the paper puts forward some suggestions to optimize future research: (1) to pay more attention to the dynamicity of FLLE; (2) to increase research on the effects of psychological interventions in regulating FLLE; (3) to enrich research methods by using dynamic and ecological tools, autonomic measurements, and emotion-stimulating methods.

Keywords

foreign language learners' emotions; positive emotions; negative emotions; positive psychology

1. Introduction

Emotions are "involuntary excitations and sensations that arose from various personal biological and social experiences" (Prior, 2019). Language learning, which requires both individual comprehension and social interactions, can be greatly influenced by emotions. Therefore, emotions play a fundamental role in language learning (Dewaele and Li, 2020). The student-centered orientation emphasizes the center status of the process of learning. Knowing what emotions learners may experience and how emotions change along with different variables can give much inspiration to foreign language (FL) teaching. The understanding of emotions' effects on FLL progress can partially reflect the development of SLA. For instance, at the initial stage of studying FLLE,

---

Xilin Xu, College of Foreign Languages & Cultures, Sichuan University, Chengdu, Sichuan Province, China. E-mail address: xxchoumin@163.com.

FLL anxiety attracted the most attention (Brown, 1973) because researchers believed emotions could mostly be a hindering factor for FLL. With more researchers devoting themselves to revealing the complicated relationship between emotions and FLL, SLA has witnessed an increase in research on various emotions in FLL from different aspects in the past decade. This is because a new perspective, positive psychology, was introduced in SLA (MacIntyre and Gregersen, 2012). Since then, an "affective turn" has gradually emerged in SLA research. Emotions other than anxiety have been paid more attention to, such as pleasure, shame, guilt, boredom, pride, interest, anger, love, hope, etc. (MacIntyre and Vincze, 2017; Teimouri, 2018; Li et al., 2020). The more emotions have been explored, the more detailed and thorough knowledge researchers have obtained to better understand the process of FLL.

This paper will attempt to give future researchers an overview of China's latest developments in FLLE research and offer preliminary guidance on methodology. To meet this end, the first part will give a review to demonstrate the recent trends, topics, and commonly used methods in FLLE research. Based on these, the second and third parts will sort out the main characteristics of the developing direction in FLLE research in China and propose related suggestions, hoping to benefit the further exploration of this research in China.

2. Review of research on FLLE in China

This review is organized by adopting the *scoping review method*, which is an ideal tool to give an overview of a body of literature on a given topic (Munn, 2018). In total, 114 papers from 19 journals published between 2012-2022 have been selected as samples. Of all these 19 journals, 13 are indexed in the CSSCI[①]. The other 6 are also representative journals of foreign languages[②] from the database of CNKI. All the papers are encoded and classified based on the publishing information of the paper (title, author, published periodical, publication year), theoretical basis, keywords, subjects' information (grade, number), and research methods (research type, period, research tools, data analysis methods). Based on the coding data, the following analysis was launched.

2.1. Overall developing trend

The change in the number of FLLE research studies in China from 2012 to 2022 is shown in figure 1. The line graph shows the year-to-year change, and the histogram stands for the number of studies involving positive and negative emotions each year.

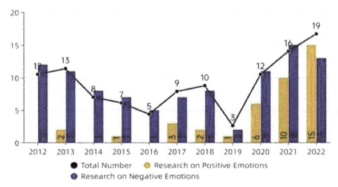

Figure 1. Distribution of papers related to FLLE in China from 2012 to 2022[③]

Here, *positive emotions* refers to "pleasant or desirable situational responses" (Cohn MA and Fredrickson BL, 2009), while *negative emotions* are the opposite. Overall, the research on FLLE from 2012 to 2019 declines with fluctuation, which suggests that it is necessary to seek new growth points after many years of development. From 2019 to 2022, the downward line begins to rebound. A more prominent feature is that the number of positive emotions-related studies increases significantly after 2019. In 2022, that number is larger than that of negative emotions for the first time. All the trends indicate that the study of FLLE will still be one of the hotspots in the field of SLA in the future, and the research on positive emotion will continue to be paid much attention to by researchers.

2.2. Change in keywords

In order to show the change of themes of FLLE research directly in recent years, CiteSpace, a visualization tool, is used to analyze the keywords of sample literature. Using CNKI as the database, besides the 114 sample papers, 104 related papers in other journals are added as supplements to enlarge the sample size to get more accurate results. In total, 218 articles are selected as sample data. The keyword distribution graph is automatically drawn using the "Timeline View" function of CiteSpace (Chen C, Song M, 2019). The result is shown in figure 2. Words in this figure are edited by the author because the original version is in Chinese.

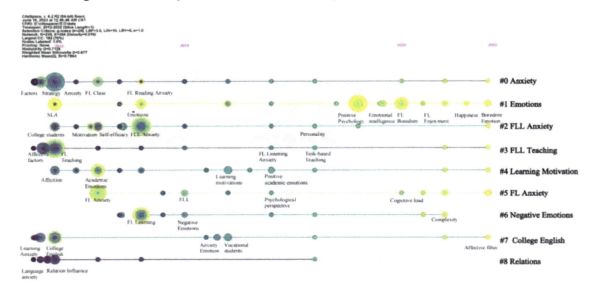

Figure 2. TimeLine view of keywords in FLLE research from 2012 to 2022

In figure 2, nine clusters of keywords are listed on the right side with an icon "#," and the band on the top is the timeline. The axes can show the beginning and end time of each keyword cluster. The nodes on each axis are the main keywords whose frequency is greater than or equal to 13 times, and the larger the nodes are, the more times they appear. To have a closer look at this figure, the node density is relatively high from 2012 to 2018, and the main keywords before 2017 are "anxiety," "learning anxiety," "language anxiety," "FL learning anxiety," "FL reading anxiety," "negative emotions," and "academic emotions." In 2017, "positive academic emotions" and "psychological perspective" emerged. From 2019 to 2022, the nodes are sparse, among which the main nodes are "positive psychology," "FL boredom," "emotional intelligence," "happiness," and "FL enjoyment." From the distribution of keyword nodes, it can be seen that the research on the number of FLLE decreases in a wave-like pattern and then rises, and the turning point of the rise lies at the emergence of "positive psychology" in 2019, which indicates that the introduction of positive psychology has imported growth points for the study of FLLE.

2.3. Types of research

Types of research refers to from what perspective the research is conducted. Based on the coding results of 114 papers, it is found that scholars mainly carry out FLLE research around the following nine aspects. The detailed categories and the number of articles are shown in table 1[④].

Table 1. Types of FLLE research from 2012 to 2022[④]

Category	Number	Main content
1. The relationship between emotions and other variables	40	To explore the relationship between emotions and learners' traits, and between emotions and environmental variables. (such as FL capability, gender, motivation, self-efficacy, second language communication intention, teaching methods, interaction ways, etc.).
2. Description of learner's emotional experience	35	To explore the type, degree, or change of emotions of a particular group of second language learners in a specific learning environment or language skill-using situation.
2. The effect of training and intervention	19	To explore the effect of specific training or intervention on emotion regulation and other variables.
3. Emotion regulation ability and strategy	14	To explore a specific group's emotion regulation strategies and abilities.
4. Reviews	12	To summarize the development of research on FLLE, reflect on the deficiencies of the relevant research, and discuss the future development prospects.
5. The correlation between emotions and academic achievement	11	To explore the predicting effect or influence of emotions on FL performance.
6. The analysis of the factors that trigger emotions	10	To explore the contributing factors and psychological mechanisms of how FLLE is triggered.
7. Theoretical discussion and comments	10	To publish new theories and suggestions based on the existing theories and research results, and try to put forward some guidance for the future research direction.
8. Development and verification of emotion measurement scales	5	To develop emotion-related measurement tools suitable for specific purposes with good reliability and validity. Or through factor analysis, spherical tests, and other ways to test the validity of the existing scale.

Overall, the sample studies can be divided into three tiers based on the number of studies. In the first tier (with over 30 articles), category 1 "The Relationship between Emotions and Other Variables" and category 2 "Description of Learner's Emotional Experience" are included. The second tier (10 to 30 articles) consists of category 3–8. The last tier (less than 10) is category 9, "Development and Verification of Emotion Measurement Scales." These indicate that researchers are most concerned about the relationship between emotions and various factors that affect the effectiveness of FLL, such as the research on the relations among achievement goal orientation, English learning anxiety, and self-access learning behavior (Wei, 2014). Many researchers have also explored the types and degrees of emotions a certain group experiences when they are in specific learning environments or language-skill-using situations. A small number of scholars have devoted themselves to the development and validation of emotion measurement scales, indicating that the tools developed by previous researchers have been widely recognized and applied. On the other hand, it also indicates that with the development of practice, there is still a need to develop scales that meet specific purposes.

2.4. Research methods

The sample papers on FLLE can be divided into empirical and non-empirical research. Among the 114 papers selected in this article, the majority use empirical research methods, accounting for 76.3% (87) of the total, while papers using non-material research methods accounted for 23.7% (27). This indicates that practical material collection, data collection, and statistical analysis are the first choices for scholars in this field. Among the 86 empirical studies, 56 were quantitative studies, 7 were qualitative studies, and the remaining 23 were mixed studies.

Secondly, the proportions of each range of sample size used in empirical research are shown in table 2. This indicates that a sample size ranging from 100 to 500 is the most commonly used one and a sample size within this range can be most efficient for conducting an experiment. Studies with sample sizes of less than 30 are qualitative or mixed studies, which are now a supplement for large sample studies.

Table 2. Sample size range in empirical research

Sample size	Over 2000	1000-2000	500-1000	100-500	30-100	1-30
Proportion	1.1%	3.5%	18.6%	46.5%	22.1%	8.1%

In terms of research tools, apart from regular tools like SPSS, AMOS, ANOVA, NVivo, and Mplus, questionnaires and scales are the most frequently used ones. To offer a reference for future researchers about what scales they can apply to their experiment design, some frequently used scales in sample research are summarized in table 3. There are reliable scales to measure emotional intelligence, academic emotions, anxiety, enjoyment, and burnout. Among all the scales, only anxiety scales are further subdivided into the anxiety measurement in the FL classroom, writing, listening, speaking, and reading, which could reflect the richness of studies on anxiety.

Table 3. List of frequently used questionnaires

Measurement factors	Frequently used questionnaires
Emotional Intelligence	Trait Emotional Intelligence Questionnaire, TEIQue (Petrides and Furnham, 2010) Trait Emotional Intelligence Questionnaire—Short Form, TEIQue—SF (Petrides, 2009)
Academic Emotion	Academic Emotion Questionnaire, AEQ (Pekrun et al., 2011) Academic Emotion Regulation Questionnaire, AERQ (Burić et al., 2016) Positive and Negative Affect Scale, PANAS (Watson et al., 1988) General Academic Emotion Questionnaire for College Students (Ma, 2008)
Anxiety	The Foreign Language Classroom Anxiety Scale, FLCAS (Horwitz, 1986) Foreign Language Listening Anxiety Scale, FLLAS (Elkhafaifi, 2005) Second Language Writing Anxiety Inventory, SLWAI (Cheng, 2004) Foreign Language Reading Anxiety Scale, FLRAS (Saito et al., 1999) Spoken Foreign Language Anxiety for Undergraduate Students Scale (Wu et al., 2009)
Enjoyment	Foreign Language Enjoyment Scale (Dewaele and Macintyre, 2014)

	The Chinese version of Foreign Language Enjoyment Scale, CFLES (Li, et al, 2018)
	Foreign Language Enjoyment Scale (Jiang and Dewaele, 2019)
Burnout	Maslach Burnout Inventory Student Survey, MBI-SS (Maslach and Jackson, 1981)
	Foreign Language Learning Burnout Scale, FLLBI (Yang, 2015)
Boredom	Foreign Language Learning Boredom Scale, FLLBS (Li et al., 2023)

In terms of research time frame, there are 65 cross-sectional studies (75.6%) and 21 longitudinal studies (24.4%) among 86 empirical studies. However, emotions are of great complexity and dynamicity. To better reveal these features of FLLE, more longitudinal studies need to be conducted.

This section briefly reviews domestic research from four aspects, trying to give a clear and understandable overview of current trends, hotspots, types, and methods of FLLE research. Having summarized what Chinese researchers have done based on the superficial research content, the next section discusses more overall research tendencies in the field of FLLE.

3. Future orientations and suggestions

Based on the review above, this section includes four developing directions of FLLE research in China, namely: (1) the "positive turn" of research variables; (2) the holistic approach to FLLE research; (3) the interdisciplinary application of "broaden-and-build theory" and "control-value theory"; (4) the rise of research on FL boredom. Then, suggestions for future research would be proposed from the perspective of research themes and methods.

3.1. Developing orientations

By analyzing current research developing trends, those showing an upward tendency can give guidance for future research. From the sample papers, the following four trends have been distilled in research on FLLE in China since 2012.

3.1.1. "Positive turn" of research variables

According to 2.1, it can be seen that before 2017, most Chinese scholars were mainly concerned with the factors that hinder FLL under the influence of a "problem-oriented" thinking mode. In recent years, with the development of positive psychology (PP), research on FLLE has gradually broken the old limitation that focuses on negative emotions, especially FLL anxiety. Combining the changes in the number of studies on positive emotions in figure 1 and the changes in research keywords in figure 2, it concludes that positive emotions and PP have received much attention in FLLE research in recent years. PP was first put forward by the humanistic psychologist Abraham Maslow (1954), and its focus is on the positive qualities that enable human beings to succeed, satisfy and realize their ambitions. MacIntyre and Gregersen (2012) first introduced PP into the SLA field. To help scholars have a more comprehensive understanding of PP, MacIntyre and Mercer (2014) systematically explained PP's concept, research scope, and research methods in the context of SLA. In terms of empirical research in 2013, Lake (2013) took the lead in conducting empirical research to explore the FL positive L2 self, positive global self, and second language motivation of Japanese FL learners from a PP perspective.

Gradually, researchers have realized how rich learners' emotional experiences could be during the process of learning; thus positive emotions such as FL pleasure, hope, interest, and satisfaction have received more attention (Dewaele, et al. 2019).

Compared to the international prevalence of PP in SLA research, China's PP research started relatively late but has shown strong growth momentum in recent years. In the sample literature, Jiang and Li's (2017) article "SLA Research in the Perspective of Positive Psychology: Review and Prospects" first sorted out the history of the convergence of SLA and PP and summarized the main contributions of PP to SLA research. In the same year, Xiong (2017) conducted empirical research from the perspective of PP to explore the complex relationship between emotions and motivation based on the control-value theory. More relative reviews and studies have been raised in recent years. Except for some theoretical reviews (Li, 2021; Qin, et al., 2022), empirical studies have been conducted to figure out learners' emotional experiences and emotional regulation strategies while writing (Han & Xu, 2020), to explore how teachers affect students' FL pleasure (Jiang, 2020), to trace the positive L2 self-development (Jiang & Zhan, 2021), and to figure out the predictive effect of FL pleasure emotions on learning outcomes (Li & Han, 2022). Now, more and more scholars have shifted their thinking from focusing on defective qualities to positive ones, and this trend will continue.

3.1.2. "Holistic approach" to the studies of emotions

The "holistic approach" refers to not discussing a particular emotion at one time, but considering emotions as a whole and accessing the coexistence and transformation of multiple emotions. After analyzing the keywords in figure 2, it was found that in recent years, keywords that do not distinguish the types of emotions, such as "academic emotions," "emotional intelligence," "FL emotions," "negative emotions," and "positive emotions" start to emerge. Secondly, when working on specific emotions, scholars recognize the coexistence of multiple emotions in the FLL process; thus, they combine more emotions and analyze them together in one study. This trend correlates to the increasing application of PP in SLA. PP emphasizes the dynamicity and correlation of emotions, which means that positive and negative emotions can coexist, interact, and even transform (Oxford, 2016). Dewaele and MacIntyre (2014) found that a moderate negative correlation exists between FL enjoyment and FL anxiety. Li (2020) also verified this conclusion.

In addition to studying positive and negative emotions at one time, Pekrun et al. (2007) proposed a conceptual framework of academic emotions that evaluates emotions with a dimensional method. Academic emotions are classified into three dimensions: valence (positive vs. negative; or pleasant vs. unpleasant), activation (physical or/and cognitive activation/deactivation), and objective focus (activity-related or outcome-related). Based on this classification, Xia and Xu (2018) explored the impact of eight types of classroom environmental factors on negative high-arousal and low-arousal emotions. Han and Xu (2020) found that written corrective feedback awakens different levels of academic emotions across positive, neutral, and negative valence. The research above does not take a specific emotion as the object. Instead, it treats emotions as a whole and distinguishes them by different dimensions.

Thirdly, the "holistic approach" in FLLE also emphasizes the individual's ability to regulate emotions, that is, how learners reduce the adverse effects of negative emotions and elevate positive emotions to promote language learning. Therefore, emotional intelligence (EI) has received increasing attention. EI refers to an individual's ability to recognize, perceive, access, understand, and regulate their own and others' emotions (Mayer and Salovey, 1997). Both Shao et al. (2013) and Yu et al. (2015) found that EI can affect academic achievement by influencing learners' emotions. In addition, Li and Dewale (2020) explored the predictive role of EI on FL classroom boredom, while Wei et al. (2021) studied the impact of EI on second language communication intention. Generally, learners with high EI are more likely to regulate and control their emotions.

In sum, the holistic perspective enables scholars to view emotions as a dynamic and transformable whole. It requires a more sophisticated experiment design and data collection method. There is still a lot of room remaining for exploration in future research.

3.1.3. Interdisciplinary application of "broaden-and-build theory" and "control-value theory"

Both the "positive turn" and "holistic approach" are to some extent based on the "broaden-and-build theory" (Fredrickson, 2001) and the "control-value theory" (Pekrun, 2006) originally from educational psychology. In the sample literature, there is little theoretical principle in FLLE research before these two theories are introduced into SLA. In recent years, there has been a significant increase in research using these two theories as theoretical guidance. Here is a brief introduction and actual application of these two theories.

Firstly, the broaden-and-build theory differentiates the effects of positive emotions and negative emotions. Positive emotions can broaden one's perspective, help individuals absorb new information, and facilitate the building of resources. On the contrary, negative emotions narrow learners' focus and restrict the range of potential language input (Fredrickson and Branigan 2015). Besides, the "undoing hypothesis" (Fredrickson, 2003) from this theory points out that positive emotions can undo the lingering effects of negative emotions. Under the guidance of the broaden-and-build theory, Wei et al. (2022) distinguished the effects of FL enjoyment and FL anxiety on second language communication intention; Dewaele and Li (2022) discussed how FL enjoyment and FL anxiety are linked to overall FL achievement and self-perceived achievement in six different domains. This theory emphasizes the promoting effects of positive emotions and the importance of good utilization of them.

The control-value theory stresses that academic emotions are awakened in the learning process by learners' sense of control over academic activities and their learning outcomes (Pekrun, 2006). With its emphasis on the origin and influencing factors of emotions, this theory plays a vital role in understanding the causes and impact of emotions. Guided by these two theories, Liu and Guo (2021) worked on the relationship among teachers' support, student engagement, and FL enjoyment; Dong and Liu (2022) focused on the causes of emotions and explored the predictive role of control appraisal and value appraisal on anxiety and pleasure in FL classrooms.

The research above can prove the increasing importance and feasibility of the interdisciplinary theoretical application. Appropriate theories can make the research more logical and systematic. Aside from psychology, other disciplines, such as pedagogy and sociology, can also provide new approaches to FLLE research.

3.1.4. Rise of research on FL boredom

Boredom is an emotional state comprised of unpleasant sensations, lack of stimulation, and low physiological arousal (Preckel et al., 2010). As early as 1992, scholars have pointed out that boredom, as a negative inhibitory emotion, can hinder the stimulation and maintenance of students' learning motivation. However, as boredom is a kind of "silent emotion" (Goetz et al., 2007), students only feel faintly unpleasant, so it has not received much attention. In recent years, scholars have brought forward that FL boredom widely exists in the learning process, which has a negative impact on learners' engagement, self-efficacy, and academic achievement (Pekrun, 2010). Pawlak et al. (2020) and Li et al. (2020) constructed the conceptual structure and developed a measurement scale of FL boredom, providing theoretical and instrumental support for research in China. Some scholars have conducted a detailed review of FL boredom (Li and Lu, 2022; Liu and Li, 2021). Existing empirical research primarily focuses on the relationship between FL boredom and other variables, as well as its predictive effect on academic achievement. For example, Li et al. (2020) discussed the predictive effect of trait EI and online learning achievement perception on FL boredom. Xia and Chen (2022) examined perceived classroom affordance, control-value appraisals, and emotional experiences of boredom. Compared with the research on FL anxiety and enjoyment, the study of FL boredom is still in its infancy, and there is still much to explore.

Under the trend of a positive turn in FLLE research, boredom can still become a new research focus, and the reasons behind it are worth considering. Based on Pekrun's (2007) categorization of academic emotions, boredom is a negative emotion with an extremely low degree of activation/arousal that arises from ongoing activities that are typically over-challenging or under-challenging (Li et al., 2020). Unlike anxiety, a high-arousal negative emotion, FL boredom arises during the learning process, and it could prevent rather than activate students' responses. Therefore, it is easier to intervene. Future research can focus on how to convert other procedural and low-arousal negative emotions into positive emotions and how to reduce students' boredom during the teaching process to improve the effectiveness of teaching practice.

3.2. Suggestions for future research

Research on FLLE has shifted to a more holistic and comprehensive study in the past decade. This section will provide suggestions for the future breakthrough of FLLE research in China from three aspects.

3.2.1. Adopting dynamic approaches

Language learning is an emotionally and psychologically dynamic process influenced by many changing variables producing moment-by-moment fluctuations in learners (Gregersen et al., 2014). It is necessary to adopt dynamic research approaches to reveal the changing nature of the emotions of FLL during the acquisition process. In the sample literature, only 24.4% are longitudinal studies. A few Chinese researchers, such as Dong and Liu (2022), have investigated the developmental trajectories of FLLE. Internationally, more studies are now conducted with some newly developed research methods from the ecological perspective of complex system theory. For example, within the framework of the nested ecosystem model, Saghafi et al. (2017) found that EFL learners' writing anxiety fluctuates within the interactive relation of the individual and environmental variables. Further, Elahi Shirvan et al. (2020) employed a time-based sampling scheme of ecological momentary assessment to explore the dynamism of FLE among EFL learners across different time scales. Both studies expose the dynamicity of FLLE.

Longitudinal research is necessary to track the changes and fluctuations of emotions. However, it requires a huge time commitment and is relatively difficult to carry out. In practice, the time frame could be expanded in research designs to reach a balance between efficiency and reliable outcomes. For instance, the microgenetic method can be adopted in the FLLE studies. This method features a sufficiently long observation span, a high density of observations, and an intensive analysis of the observation data (Wen, 2003). Here the observation span can be time for one class or task as long as enough data is collected. For instance, Shirvan and Talebzadeh (2020) used the technique of retrospective qualitative modeling and moment-to-moment ratings to analyze the signature dynamics of FLE and FLA. In addition, the pseudo-longitudinal method can be an option. This method is viewed as an advanced form of cross-sectional study where the change in "time" is measured by proxy, using a characteristic such as proficiency level or age, and thus can increase efficiency by obtaining data of similar quality using fewer resources (Bandyopadhyay and Mukherjee, 2021). Based on this method, Dewaele and Dewaele (2017) carried out a pseudo-longitudinal investment to explore the dynamic interactions in FL classroom anxiety and FFL enjoyment and how these two emotions evolve over time. Both methods can reflect the dynamic characteristics of emotional changes in a relatively short period of time.

3.2.2. Increasing psychological interventions in FL

In China, the current research on intervention in FLLE mainly focuses on variables in the classroom, such as task modes (Rui and Ji, 2017), teaching methods (Guo, 2016), ways of interaction (Zhang and Zhao, 2021), etc. Emotions are more thoroughly studied in psychology. Theories and methods from this discipline can, to some extent, be applied to the research on FLLE, just like the application of the "broaden-and-build theory" and the "control-value theory." At present, only a few scholars in China have applied psychological intervention methods in FLLE research. For example, Meng and Chen (2014) adopted cognitive-behavioral therapy in their intervention case study. Results show that the student's anxiety in English learning and test preparation has reduced considerably. Besides, inspired by the psychological outpatient technology for the treatment of general social anxiety, Jin et al. (2021) took a positive psychology approach and found that reminiscing about language achievements could decrease the learners' FL classroom anxiety. The above research has transcended the limitation of SLA and utilized more effective ways of intervention from the perspective of psychology and cognitive science, and it proves the feasibility of the interdisciplinary application of methods and theories. There is more waiting to be explored in the future study.

3.2.3. Enriching and innovating research methods

Given a large proportion of research is empirical research, appropriate methods and efficient tools are of crucial importance. Based on the review above, there are three main problems in the existing empirical research: (1) longitudinal study is insufficient, and it is difficult to reflect the dynamic characteristics of emotional changes; 2) the measurements of emotions mostly use retrospective research tools, which can lead to retrospective bias; (3) the measurement mostly focuses on triggered emotions. In response to these issues, suggestions will be made below.

The first issue has been mentioned in 3.2.1, and the solution is to "adopt dynamic approaches to FLLE research." To restate this from a perspective of research method, more dynamic and ecological tools need to be applied to future research, such as self-organizing maps (De Ruiter et al., 2019), which capture how intra-individual dynamics are situated in a changing context; ecological momentary assessment (Elahi Shirvan et al., 2022), in which a classroom is examined as an interdependent whole to fully understand the forces surrounding a developing individual; and latent growth curve modeling, which focuses on mean trends as the nomothetic aspects of change over time and individual variability as idiographic aspects of change (Elahi Shirvan and Taherian, 2021). These techniques are proven to be appropriate ways to reveal the complexity and dynamicity of learning emotions.

Secondly, existing measurement tools used in China are mainly verbal or textual self-reports such as questionnaires, interviews, and reflective diaries. These tools can collect data in a simple way and conduct quantitative or qualitative analysis on a large scale. But these tools rely on the retrospection of subjects and are prone to cognitive bias. In contrast, autonomous measurement can compensate for these shortcomings. It adopts physiological and behavioral indicators to objectively analyze real-time emotional experiences. For example, Shirvan and Talezadeh (2018) and MacIntyre and Gregersen (2022) adopted the idiodynamic method to explore subjects' anxiety. It requires video recording a research participant and then using specialized software to play the video back while collecting contemporaneous self-reported ratings. In addition, the experience sampling methodology (ESM) used in psychological research can also be applied to FLLE research. EMS is a method of collecting instantaneous assessments of events experienced by people in a relatively short period of time and recording them in the real context of events (Bolger and Laurenceau, 2013). Participants need to answer measurement questions as soon as they receive the signal. These methods can also be used in qualitative research to avoid the drawbacks of quantitative research, which may lead to preconceived assumptions about the existence of certain emotions due to specific research questions and assumptions. With continuous observation during the learning process and the help of these methods, researchers can draw a more objective and accurate conclusion in FLL.

Lastly, to respond to the third issue mentioned above, stimulating learners' certain types of emotions is feasible. If emotion can be stimulated in the participants before the experiment, it can not only make the experimental results more prominent, but it can also help to explore how teachers can interact with students properly to activate their positive emotions. So far, there is not much related research, but researchers have developed a series of experimental methods (such as film, music, the Velten method, autobiographical recall, etc.) to stimulate transient emotional states (Banos et al., 2006). Theoretically, these emotional states can simulate certain emotions in real scenes.

4. Conclusion

In this paper, the current developing trends and features of FLLE research in China from 2012 to 2022 are demonstrated by using the scoping review method and a visualization tool. A review of future research orientations and some further suggestions are proposed. Overall, PP has a significant influence on the research of FLLE, making scholars in the SLA shift their focus from exploring how emotions hinder FLL to how to use positive emotions to promote FLL. At present, there are still limitations in research methods. As an intersection of psychology and SLA, FLLE can be studied from an interdisciplinary perspective in terms of theory and methods. The aim of this review is to provide inspiration for future research on FLLE.

Notes

① 13 journals indexed in the CSSCI: *Foreign Language Teaching and Research, Modern Foreign Languages, Foreign Language World, Foreign Language Education, Foreign Language Research, Foreign Languages and Their Teaching, Foreign Languages in China, Foreign Language Learning Theory and Practice, Technology Enhanced Foreign Language Education, Journal of PLA University of Foreign Languages, Foreign Languages Research, Foreign Languages and Literature,* and *Foreign Language Education in China*

② 6 other representative journals of foreign languages: *Chinese Journal of Applied Linguistics, Foreign Languages Research, Contemporary Foreign Language Studies, Research in Teaching, Journal of Xi'an International Studies University,* and *Journal of Beijing International Studies University*

③ The studies on EI, academic emotions, and positive psychology all discuss both positive and negative emotions, so they can be counted twice in this graph.

④ As the content of one study can involve multiple research aspects, the total number of articles in the table will be greater than the sample size of the literature.

References

Abraham M. 1954. *Motivation and Personality.* Nueva York: Harper & Row, Publishers.

Bandyopadhyay A. and Mukherjee A. (2021. "Pseudo-Longitudinal Research Design: A Valuable Epidemiological Tool in Resource-Poor Settings." *Rural and Remote Health,* 21: 6977.

Baños R.M., Liaño V., Botella C., Alcañiz M., Guerrero B. and Rey B. 2006 May 18–19. "Changing Induced Moods Via Virtual Reality." In *Persuasive Technology: First International Conference on Persuasive Technology for Human Well-Being, PERSUASIVE 2006,* Eindhoven, The Netherlands.

Bolger N. and Laurenceau J.P. 2013. *Intensive longitudinal methods: An introduction to diary and experience sampling research.* Guilford Press.

Brown H.D. 1973. "Affective Variables in Second Language Acquisition." *Language Learning,* 23 (2): 231-244.

Burić I., Sorić I. and Penezić Z. .2016. "Emotion Regulation in Academic Domain: Development and Validation of the Academic Emotion Regulation Questionnaire (AERQ)." *Personality and Individual Differences,* 96: 138-147.

Chen C. and Song M. 2019. "Visualizing a Field of Research: A Methodology of Systematic Scientometric Reviews." *PLOS One,* 14(10): e223994.

Cheng Y. 2004. "A Measure of Second Language Writing Anxiety: Scale Development and Preliminary Validation." *Journal of Second Language Writing,* (4):313-335.

Cohn M.A. and Fredrickson B.L. 2009. "Positive Emotions." In Lopez SJ and Snyder CR (Eds.), *The Oxford Handbook of Positive Psychology* (2nd ed.), Oxford University Press. pp. 13-24.

De Ruiter N.M.P., Elahi Shirvan M. and Talebzadeh N. 2019. "Emotional Processes of Foreign-Language Learning Situated in Real-Time Teacher Support." *Ecological Psychology,* 31(2): 127-145.

Dewaele J.M. and Dewaele L. 2017. "The Dynamic Interactions in Foreign Language Classroom Anxiety and Foreign Language Enjoyment of Pupils Aged 12 to 18." A pseudo-longitudinal investigation. *Journal of the European Second Language Association,* 1(1): 11-22.

Dewaele J.M. and Li C. 2022. "Foreign Language Enjoyment and Anxiety: Associations with General and Domain-Specific English Achievement." *Chinese Journal of Applied Linguistics,* 45(01): 32-48, 150.

Dewaele J.M. and Macintyre P. 2014. "The Two Faces of Janus? Anxiety and Enjoyment in the Foreign Language Classroom." *Studies in Second Language Learning and Teaching,* 4(2): 237-274.

Dewaele J.M., Chen X., Padilla A.M. and Lake J. 2019. "The Flowering of Positive Psychology in Foreign Language Teaching and Acquisition Research." *Frontiers in Psychology,* 10(1): 1-13.

Dong L. and Liu M. 2022. "Developmental Trajectories of Foreign Language Reading Anxiety and Reading Strategy Use: Latent Growth Modeling." *Foreign Languages and Their Teaching,* (04): 134-144, 150.

Dong L. and Liu M. 2022. "Effects of Foreign Language Enjoyment on Foreign Language Test Performance: A Moderated Mediation Model." *Modern Foreign Languages,* 45(02): 195-206.

Elkhafaifi H. 2005. "Listening Comprehension and Anxiety in the Arabic Language Classroom." *The Modern Language Journal,* 89(2):206-222.

Elahi Shirvan M. and Taherian T. 2021. "Longitudinal Examination of University Students' Foreign Language Enjoyment and Foreign Language Classroom Anxiety in the Course of General English: Latent Growth Curve Modeling." *International Journal of Bilingual Education and Bilingualism,* 24(1): 31-49.

Elahi Shirvan M. and Taherian T. 2022. Affordances of the Microsystem of the Classroom for Foreign Language Enjoyment." *Human Arenas,* 5(2): 222-244.

Elahi Shirvan M. and Talezadeh N. 2018. Is Transparency an Illusion? An Idiodynamic Assessment of Teacher and Peers' Reading of Nonverbal Communication Cues of Foreign Language Enjoyment." *Journal of Intercultural Communication Research,* 1-19.

Elahi Shirvan M., Taherian T. and Yazdanmehr E. 2020. The Dynamics of Foreign Language Enjoyment: An Ecological Momentary Assessment." *Frontiers in Psychology,* 11: 1391.

Fredrickson B.L. 2001. "The Role of Positive Emotions in Positive Psychology. The Broaden-and-Build Theory of Positive Emotions." *The American Psychologist,* 56(3): 218-226.

Fredrickson B.L. 2003. "The Value of Positive Emotions—The Emerging Science of Positive Psychology in Coming to Understand Why It's Good to Feel Good." *American Scientist,* 91(4): 330-335.

Goetz T., Frenzel A.C., Pekrun R., Hall N.C. and Lüdtke O. 2007. "Between-and Within-Domain Relations of Students' Academic Emotions." *Journal of Educational Psychology,* 99(4): 715-733

Gregersen T., Macintyre P.D. and Meza M.D. 2014. "The Motion of Emotion: Idiodynamic Case Studies of Learners' Foreign Language Anxiety." *Modern Language Journal,* 98(2): 574-588.

Guo S. 2016. "An Empirical Study on the Influence of AAWP Teaching Model on English Majors' Writing Anxiety." *Journal of PLA University of Foreign Languages,* 39(04): 111-118, 160.

Han Y. and Xu Y. 2020. "Emotional Experiences and Emotion Regulation Strategies in Second Language Writing Classrooms from the Perspective of Positive Psychology: What Can We Learn from Written Corrective Feedback Situations?" *Foreign Language World,* (01): 50-59.

Horwitz, E.K., Horwitz M.B.H. and Cope J. 1986. "Foreign Language Classroom Anxiety." *Modern Language Journal,* 70(2): 125-132.

Jiang G. and Li C. 2017. "SLA Research in the Positive Psychology Perspective: Review and Prospects." *Foreign Language World,* (05), 32-39.

Jiang L. and Zhan J. 2021. A Case Study of Positive L2 Self in the Iterative Continuation Task." *Foreign Language World,* (06): 23-30.

Jiang Y. 2020. "An Investigation of the Effect of Teacher on Chinese University Students' Foreign Language Enjoyment." *Foreign Language World,* (01): 60-68.

Jiang Y. and Dewaele J.M. 2019. "How Unique Is the Foreign Language Classroom Enjoyment and Anxiety of Chinese EFL Learners?" *System*, 82(1):13-25.

Jin Y., Dewaele J.M. and MacIntyre P.D. 2021. "Reducing Anxiety in the Foreign Language Classroom: A Positive Psychology Approach." *System*, 101: 102604.

Kruk M. 2016. Variations in Motivation, Anxiety and Boredom in Learning English in Second Life." *The EuroCALL Review*, 24(1): 25-39.

Li C. 2020. "Emotional Intelligence and English Achievement: The Mediating Effects of Enjoyment, Anxiety and Burnout." *Foreign Language World*, (01): 69-78.

---- 2021. "Looking Back and Looking Forward: SLA Research from a Positive Psychology Perspective Over the Past Decade (2012–2021)." *Foreign Language Education*, 42(04): 57-63.

Li C. and Dewaele J.M. 2020. "The Predictive Effects of Trait Emotional Intelligence and Online Learning Achievement Perceptions on Foreign Language Class Boredom Among Chinese University Students." *Foreign Languages and Their Teaching*, (05): 33-44, 148-149.

Li C. and Han Y. 2022. "The Predictive Effects of Foreign Language Enjoyment, Anxiety, and Boredom on Learning Outcomes in Online English Classrooms." *Modern Foreign Languages*, 45(02): 207-219.

Li C. and Lu X. 2022. "Foreign Language Learning Boredom: A Scoping Review." *Foreign Language Education*, 43(06): 70-76.

Li C., Dewaele J.M. and Hu Y. 2023. "Foreign Language Learning Boredom: Conceptualization and Measurement." *Applied Linguistics Review*, 14(2): 223-249.

Li C., Jiang G. and Dewaele J.M. 2018. "Understanding Chinese High School Students' Foreign Language Enjoyment: Validation of the Chinese Version of the Foreign Language Enjoyment Scale." *System*, 76: 183-196.

Liu H. and Li J. 2021. "Foreign Language Learning Boredom: Review and Prospects." *Journal of PLA University of Foreign Languages*, 44(05): 10-17, 160.

Liu X. and Guo J. 2021. "Teacher Support, Interaction Engagement and Learning Enjoyment in Online EFL Teaching. "*Journal of PLA University of Foreign Languages*, 44(05): 34-42, 160.

Ma H. 2008. "Development of the General Academic Emotion Questionnaire for College Students." *Chinese Journal of Clinical Psychology*, 16(06):594-596, 593.

Macintyre P. and Gregersen T. 2012. "Emotions That Facilitate Language Learning: The Positive-Broadening Power of the Imagination." *Studies in Second Language Learning & Teaching*, 2(2): 193-213.

MacIntyre P. and Gregersen T. 2022. "The Idiodynamic Method: Willingness to Communicate and Anxiety Processes Interacting in Real Time." *International Review of Applied Linguistics in Language Teaching*, 60(1): 67-84.

Macintyre P. and Mercer S. 2014. "Introducing Positive Psychology to SLA." *Studies in Second Language Learning and Teaching*, (2): 153-172.

Macintyre P.D. and Vincze L. 2017. "Positive and Negative Emotions Underlie Motivation for L2 Learning." *Studies in Second Language Learning & Teaching*, 7(1): 61-88.

Maslach C. and Jackson S.E. 1981. "The Measurement of Experienced Burnout." *Journal of Organizational Behavior*, 2(2): 99-113.

Mayer J.D. and Salovey P. 1997. *Emotional Development and Emotional Intelligence*. Nova Iorque: Basics Books.

Meng C. and Chen L. 2014. An Intervention Case Study of a College Student's Anxiety in EFL Learning." *Foreign Language World*, (04): 21-29.

Munn Z., Peters M.D., Stern C., Tufanaru C., McArthur A. and Aromataris E. 2018. "Systematic Review or Scoping Review? Guidance for Authors When Choosing Between a Systematic or Scoping Review Approach." *BMC Medical Research Methodology*, 18: 1-7.

Oxford R.L. 2016. "Powerfully Positive: Searching for a Model of Language Learner Well-Being." *Positive Psychology Perspectives on Foreign Language Learning and Teaching*, Springer, Cham. pp. 21-37.

Pawlak M., Kruk M., Zawodniak J. and Pasikowski S. 2020. "Investigating Factors Responsible for Boredom in English Classes: The Case of Advanced Learners." *System*, (91): 1-10.

Pekrun R., Frenzel A.C., Thomas G. and Perry R.P. 2007. "The Control-Value Theory of Achievement Emotions: An Integrative Approach to Emotions in Education." *Emotion in Education*, Academic Press. pp. 13-36.

Pekrun R., Goetz T., Daniel L.M., Stupnisky R.H. and Perry R.P. 2010. "Boredom in Achievement Settings: Exploring Control-Value Antecedents and Performance Outcomes of Neglected Emotions." *Journal of Educational Psychology*, 102(3): 531-549.

Pekrun R., Goetz T., Frenzel A.C., Barchfeld P. and Perry R.P. 2011. "Measuring Emotions in Students' Learning and Performance: The Achievement Emotions Questionnaire (AEQ)." *Contemporary Educational Psychology*, 36(1): 36-48.

Pekrun R. 2006. The Control-Value Theory of Achievement Emotions: Assumptions, Corollaries, and Implications for Educational Research and Practice." *Educational Psychology Review*, 18(4): 315-341.

Petrides K.V. 2009. "Psychometric Properties of the Trait Emotional Intelligence Questionnaire" (TEIQue). *Springer US*: 85-101.

Petrides K.V. and Furnham A. 2010. "Trait Emotional Intelligence: Psychometric Investigation with Reference to Established Trait Taxonomies." *European Journal of Personality*, 15(6): 425-448.

Preckel F., Thomas G. and Frenzel A.C. 2010. "Ability Grouping of Gifted Students: Effects on Academic Self-Concept and Boredom." *British Journal of Educational Psychology*, 80 (3): 451-472.

Prior M.T. 2019. "Elephants in the Room: an "Affective Turn," or Just Feeling Our Way?" *The Modern Language Journal*, 103(2): 516-527.

Qin L., Yao L. and Niu B. 2022. "A Critical Review of L2 Learners' Emotion." *Foreign Language Education in China*, 5(02): 51-58, 92-93.

Rui Y. and Ji H. 2017. "The Impact of Multimodal Listening & Speaking Teaching on English Speaking Anxiety and Classroom Reticence." *Technology Enhanced Foreign Language Education*, (06): 50-55.

Saghafi K., Adel S.M.R. and Zareian G. 2017. "An Ecological Study of Foreign Language Writing Anxiety in English as a Foreign Language Classroom." *Journal of Intercultural Communication Research*, 46(5): 424-440.

Saito Y., Thomas J. and Horwitz E. 1999. "Foreign Language Reading Anxiety." *The Modern Language Journal*, (2): 202-218.

Shao Y. and Ji Z. 2013. "An Exploration of Chinese EFL Students' Emotional Intelligence and Foreign Language Anxiety." *Modern Language Journal*, 97(4).

Shirvan M.E. and Talebzadeh N. 2020. "Tracing the Signature Dynamics of Foreign Language Classroom Anxiety and Foreign Language Enjoyment: A Retrodictive Qualitative Modeling." *Eurasian Journal of Applied Linguistics*, (1): 23-44.

Teimouri Y. 2018. "Differential Roles of Shame and Guilt in L2 Learning: How Bad Is Bad?" *Modern Language Journal(S1)*, (4): 632-652.

Watson D., Clark L.A. and Tellegen A. 1988. "Development and Validation of Brief Measures of Positive and Negative Affect: The PANAS Scales." *Journal of Personality and Social Psychology*, 54: 1063-1070.

Wei X. 2014. A Structural Analysis of College Students' Achievement Goal Orientation, Learning Anxiety and Self-Access Learning Behavior in Foreign Language Learning." *Foreign Language World*, (04): 12-20, 38.

Wei X., Chen X. and Yang Y. 2022 "The Roles of Emotional Intelligence and Class Social Climate in L2 Willingness to Communicate: Evidence From the Moderating Model." *Foreign Languages and Their Teaching*, (06): 88-99, 147-148.

Wei X., Wu L. and Chen X. 2021. "A Structural Analysis of Emotional Intelligence, Language Mindsets and L2 Willingness to Communicate" (L2 WTC). *Foreign Language World*, (06): 80-89.

Wen Q. 2003. "The Microgenetic Method and Second Language Acquisition Research." *Modern Foreign Languages*, (03): 312-317, 311.

Wu W., Lu J. and Guo W. 2009. "A Cluster Analysis of Various State of Spoken Foreign Language Anxiety for Undergraduate Students." *Psychological Science*, 32(05):1091-1094.

Xia Y. and Chen X. 2022. "The Relationship between Perceived Classroom Affordance and Boredom in CLI Classrooms: The Mediating Role of Control-Value Appraisals." *Foreign Language Education*, 43(03): 44-49.

Xia Y. and Xu Y. 2018. "On the Influence of Classroom Environment on Negative Academic Emotions of English Majors." *Foreign Languages and Their Teaching*, (03): 65-76, 144-145.

Xiong W. 2017. "From 'Motivation Exhaustion' to 'Motivation Reconstruction' in Foreign Languages: A Perspective of Positive Academic Emotions: Based on the Control-Value Theory." *Contemporary Foreign Language Studies*, (04): 61-65.

Yang T. 2010. *The Relationship Between Foreign Language Learning Burnout and Motivation*. Ph.D Thesis, Southwest University, China.

Yu W., Shao K. and Xiang Y. 2015. The Relationships Among Chinese EFL Learners' Emotional Intelligence, Foreign Language Anxiety and English Proficiency." *Modern Foreign Languages*, 38(05): 656-666, 730.

Zhang J. and Zhao K. 2021. "Exploring Learners' Experience in an Online Oral English Task." *Foreign Languages and Their Teaching*, (05): 68-77, 149.

On the English Existential and Presentational Constructions: An Interactive Construction Grammar Perspective

Ziyan Li, Xia Guo
Sichuan University

Abstract

The English existential and presentational construction (abbreviated as EEPC) is a classical issue in linguistic research and one of the key problems in syntactic research. The EEPC is a construction indicating existence and presence guided by *there*, and can be written as *There + BE/V +NP (+ PP)*. The research on EEPC in the past decades has mainly been conducted from the perspectives of formal linguistics and functional linguistics, exploring a series of issues such as the syntactic generation process of the constructions, the grammatical status of *there* at the beginning of the sentence, the restriction of the noun after the existential verb, the discourse function of the constructions, and the information transfer, which have advanced the development of some syntactic theories and hypotheses. However, only a small number of scholars have attempted to examine the relationship between the construction and its constituents and explore the interaction between EEPC and its mental representation. Over the course of the last ten years, cognitive linguistic researchers have undertaken a number of studies, based on the corpus and using new research methods such as construction collocation analysis to cognitively study the EEPC, and these studies have laid a solid foundation for the development of the thesis. Collectively, the paper integrates construction grammar theory, interactive construction grammar theory, and figure-ground theory, and uses holistic and reductive analysis methods, with the aim of systematically explaining how the EEPC interacts with its mental representations. Two main conclusions are drawn from this study. The interaction between EEPC and mental representations based on figure-ground theory is mainly reflected in the following. On the one hand, EEPC coerces the mental representation, forcing its temporal configuration to change in order to conform to the characteristics of EEPC. On the other hand, the reversed allotment of the existential subject and the existential place in this mental representation also provide a meaning for this construction that indicates "prominence." The meaning is not derived from the constituents of the construction and reflects that "the whole is greater than the sum of its parts."

Corresponding author: Xia Guo, the College of Foreign Languages and Cultures, Sichuan University, Chengdu, Sichuan, China.

E-mail address: 542316748@qq.com.

Keywords

interactive construction grammar; English existential and presentational construction; mental representation; cognitive model.

1. Introduction

A construction is a conventional form-meaning pair. Any linguistic pattern should be considered a construction as long as some aspect of its form or function cannot be fully predicted from its constituents or from other constructions already established (Shi, 2021:6). Moreover, even if some linguistic patterns are sufficiently predictable, they are still stored as constructions as long as they occur frequently enough.

Everything exists in time and space, which can be expressed by existential and presentational constructions (abbreviated as EPC as follows) in language. As the name implies, an existential and presentational construction is a construction that denotes "existence" and "presence" (Zhang, 2006:60). It is a traditional topic in linguistic research that, due to its intricacy and distinctiveness, has garnered a lot of interest and debate. The English existential and presentational construction (abbreviated as EEPC as follows) is a particular type of sentence led by *there*. It is classified as a semi-open construction, which refers to "a form in which part of the components of the construction have been largely fixed" (Hou, 2021: 92). Scholars generally refer to the EEPC as the existential sentence or *there* construction (Quirl et al., 1985; Hannay, 1985; Lumsden, 1988; McNally, 1997), while Bimer & Ward (1998), Huddleston and Pullum (2002) and Zhang (2006) distinguish *there*-guided sentence structures into existential *there* constructions and presentational *there* constructions. The existential *there* construction states that "something/someone exists somewhere"; the presentational *there* construction states that "something/someone appears somewhere," which are collectively called existential constructions.

As theoretical linguistics has advanced, researchers' studies of existential constructions have revealed a trend toward multi-perspective, multi-dimensionality, and diversity. Scholars have conducted a series of research on EEPC from the perspectives of formal linguistics, functional linguistics and cognitive linguistics, and these studies have been successful in examining the grammatical and semantic properties of existential sentences as well as the semantic types of verbs. Through sorting out the previous literature, it can be found that there are still many problems in EEPC that deserve further exploration. English existential constructions are the basic structures in language, and verbs expressing the meaning of presence are also one of the basic verb types. Linguists have mostly studied the grammatical functions and varieties of collocational verbs in EEPC (Yang and Xu, 2020: 11). The paper discovers that so far, little research has taken the mental representation of EEPC as a dimension and aims at exploring its interaction mechanism with schematic EEPC. Therefore, this study will attempt to provide a relatively unifying analytical framework under the perspective of interactive construction grammar and incorporate mental representation as one of the dimensions in order to acquire a deeper insight into the cognitive rationale of EEPC.

2. Literature review

The research on EEPC is generally on the rise. In the early studies, scholars focused more on "existential sentences," usually from the syntactic role of "there," noun phrases, whether existential sentences are subject-predicate sentences and so on. Since then, the functional linguistic school has started to study EEPC, extending from syntactic to semantic and functional levels. In recent years, there has been an increasing number of studies comparing EEPC among multiple languages, and the trend of exploring the issue in the framework of construction grammar is more obvious. The study on EEPC has gradually shifted from the initial focus on the insertion of dummy subjects at the beginning of sentences and the derivation on the generation of such constructions to functional discourse and discourse analysis from the perspectives of cognitive linguistics in recent years.

Looking at the previous studies, it is not difficult to find that the research on EEPC has developed from the initial superficial understanding to the current more mature argumentation. It is clear that a variety of ideas, theoretical models, methodologies, and approaches have been used to investigate EEPC. The categorization, syntactic, semantic, and discourse roles of them have all been discussed extensively up to this point. The research methods and approaches have also kept pace with the development of the research techniques, and some studies have started to adopt a corpus-based approach for quantitative research. The trend in the last decade has been to study the EEPC from a cognitive linguistic perspective. However, a whole new analytical framework is undoubtedly required to understand the issues with EEPC since only a small number of scholars have attempted to examine the relationship between the construction and its constituents from the standpoint of interaction. The study will also employ a cognitive strategy to address the research issues, drawing on the interactive construction grammar theory in an effort to offer a reasonable explanation for the interaction of the EEPC with its mental representations.

Many results have been achieved in the theoretical community regarding the study of constructions, but the research perspective can continue to be innovative. The thesis summarizes some of the remaining problems that have not been explored in depth as the following two points:

Firstly, the definition of the *there be/v* structure is still controversial, and previous studies usually regard the structure as an existential clause, while fewer studies explore the structure from the perspective of construction grammar. In the study, it is agreed that *There + BE/V +NP (+ PP)* is a complete construction.

Secondly, regarding the interaction analysis of EEPC, it has not yet seen any research on the interaction between EEPC and its mental representations from the vertical dimension which means to investigate the interaction between linguistic dimension and mental dimension.

Based on the emerging theory of interactive construction grammar, the paper comprehensively analyzes EEPC, expecting to describe the interdependent interactions among the elements of the constructions.

3. Research target

English existential and presentational constructions have been set as the target of the current research. An EEPC is a construction that indicates the existence, appearance, and disappearance of a thing or event in a certain time and space, and the basic form of this construction is *There + BE/V +NP (+ PP)*. The EEPC consists of two different subconstructions: the existential construction, which indicates the existence of a thing, and the presentational construction, which indicates the appearance or disappearance of a thing or event. For example:

*(1) I believe **there is** a link between stereotypes and violence against whatever group is being stereotyped.*

*(2) I certainly think **there are** some similarities with his ability to make difficult shots.*

*(3) **There comes** a moment, early in his career at the River Company of the Caribbean when . . .*

*(4) In any case, with a communist organization of society, **there disappears** the subordination of the artist to local and national narrowness, which arises entirely from . . .*

The above sentences (1)(2) are existential constructions, where the predicate verb expresses a static "existential sense"; (3)(4) are presentational constructions, where the predicate verb is mainly a verb of appearance and disappearance, and the key to decide whether they are existential or presentational constructions lies in the semantic characteristics of the predicate verb itself in the construction.

In order to demonstrate that *there* constructions are not just variations of simple phrases employed in various situations, Lakoff (1987) sorts out *there* constructions into two categories: indicative *there* and existential *there*, and compares them with simple sentences. The indicative *there* can indicate direction, i.e., *I went **there***. All English sentences that comprise non-repeated, non-indicative words are referred to as *existential sentences* by Milsark (1977).

Despite the fact that "existence" and "presence" were highlighted in earlier studies, the term "existential and presentational construction" is still not commonly utilized in English. The study agrees that *There + BE/V +NP (+ PP)* is a complete construction and utilizes the term "English existential and presentational construction" and depicts it as follows: *There + BE/V +NP (+ PP)* is a construction guided by *there* and expresses the meaning of "existence" or "presence."

4. The interaction between EEPC and mental presentation

Based on the literature review of existential and presentational constructions, following the realization of mental representations based on figure-ground theory, in the implementation of ontological interaction analysis, the paper focuses on how the long-used and solidified linguistic representation of English existential and presentational constructions constrains its mental representation, and how the mental representation contributes to the linguistic representation of EEPC. By combining conceptual and methodological interactions with ontological interactions, a unified analytical framework can be developed for the EEPC. Integrating construction grammar with figure-ground theory and concerned with the realization and expression of the figure-and-ground mental representation in EEPC, the paper analyzes the interaction between the components of the figure-ground mental representations in the EEPC in the horizontal dimension and explains how the linguistic EEPC interacts with the specific mental representations in the vertical dimension. Under this analytical framework, the analysis of the form and meaning of EEPC is unified and reduced to horizontal and vertical interactions (Liu, Luo and Wu, 2021:61), in order to make the research object more systematic, the research content more adequate, the research perspective more comprehensive, and the research concept and method more convincing.

In the following, a cognitive model of the EEPC will be constructed based on the analytical framework mentioned above, and the different interactions and effects in the operation of the model will be analyzed.

Through explaining the realization path of the figure-ground mental representations in the EEPC, the rationale for constructing a cognitive model of EEPC has been clarified.

4.1. Mental representation

Reality representation, mental representation and linguistic representation are three closely related concepts. *Mental representation* is a subjective reflection of the objective world and a conceptualization of existence; *linguistic representation* is the linguistic realization of mental representation, which refers to words, phrases and sentences. Thus, the three concepts, in turn, have logical dependence; that is, mental representation is based on real representation, and linguistic representation is predicated on mental representation (Liu and Wang, 2005:14).

Mental representations are based on real representations, which are internalized in the human brain. Mental representations are more abstract than real representations. For example, when describing a dog, its mental image includes four legs and a tail, while many specific features are actually missing, such as its coat color and gender. In the study, the mental representation will be hypothesized based on figure-ground theory.

Humans always assign some basic properties and characteristics to the objective world with themselves as the reference point. In terms of spatial relations, man takes the orientation of himself and establishes a three-dimensional spatial relationship, i.e., front-back, left-right, and up-down. Sometimes, the reference frame of reality representation shifts from speaker-centered to object-centered. For example, in EEPC, in the sentence, "There is a market just across the road to the restaurant," "the road to the restaurant," is the reference frame that indicates the location of the market.

Figure-ground relations have been regarded as a basic cognitive principle for organizing spatial relations (Zhang, 2009: 8), and the cognitive basis of EEPC, regardless of the language, is always to express the existential relation of things. A pair of existential relations can be regarded as an existential event, which consists of the event role of the existential event and the relationship between the roles. An "existential event" refers to the phenomenon that something in the real world continues to occupy a certain spatial position during the period from its appearance to its disappearance. In an existential event, the existential subject and the existential place are two elements that necessarily appear. Among them, the existential subject is the focus of the description of the existential event and is part of cognitive prominence, and the existential place reveals the background element in the existential event, which provides a spatial reference point for the existential subject. Without the existential place, no existential subject exists, and without the existential subject, the existential place becomes meaningless, and there is a dependency relationship between the two, expressing the concept of space (Cao and Wen, 2022:32). Therefore, it is justified to analyze the EEPC by the figure-ground theory. Combining the previous definitions of existential subject and existential place, the paper sets the former as the figure and the latter as the ground in the figure-ground relation. In addition to the existential subject and the existential place, the existential mode is also an element in the existential event. The existential event implies the existence of a certain thing, and it must exist in a certain way or state in a spatial location. In the EEPC, the existential mode is expressed by an existential verb.

According to the figure-ground theory of cognitive linguistics, Zhang(2006) summarizes the English existential constructions as TtFG constructions, and distinguishes two categories of existential TtFG constructions and presentational TtFG constructions. Both types of TtFG constructions embody a cognitive spatio-temporal framework. However, existential TtFG constructions embody a static spatio-temporal framework, expressing locative relations, indicating that an entity (figure) exists statically in a certain spatio-temporal range (ground). The presentational TtFG construction is a dynamic spatio-temporal frame that shows that a certain entity (figure) dynamically moves from one (implied) spatio-temporal range (ground 1) into another (ground 2), either in a certain pose or in a certain spatio-temporal range (ground), or moves out of a spatio-temporal range (ground 1) and fades into a (implied) spatio-temporal range (ground 2). According to Zhang Keding's classification, TtFG constructions contain four components within them, and the interaction between the components affects the formation of the spatio-temporal frame. Among them, the existential verb (t) acts most on the formation of the spatio-temporal frame.

The paper hypothesizes three mental representations and the map of movement relations in more detail with reference to Zhang's classification of spatio-temporal frames:

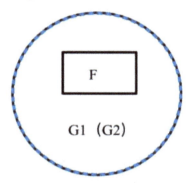

Figure 4.1 Schematic diagram of the static existence of EEPC

Figure 4.1 represents a static cognitive mental representation in which the rectangle represents the figure (F), the black circle represents the actual ground formed by *there* (G1), and the blue dashed circle represents the implicit ground formed by the prepositional phrase (G2). G1 and G2 are in a co-reference relationship, and the figure (F) exists statically in the ground. In the sentence "There are three white hairs on my head," *there*, as the existential place (G1), provides a reference ground for the existent subject "three white hairs" (F), while the prepositional phrase "on my head" (G2) at the end of the sentence forms a co-reference, together with *there*, serving as the ground of the existential subject.

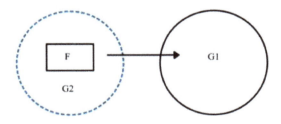

Figure 4.2 Schematic diagram of the dynamic presence of EEPC

Figure 4.2 represents a dynamic cognitive mental representation, where the blue dashed circle containing the figure (F) represented by the rectangle is the implied ground and the black circle is the actual ground. The frame illustrates that the figure (F) dynamically moves from the implied ground into the actual ground represented by the black circle (G1). For example, in the sentence, "There came a voice from heaven," "There" is the actual ground (G1), which is the destination of the voice; the prepositional phrase "from heaven" is the implied ground (G2), which represents the place from which the subject comes; and the existential verb "came" reflects a movement relationship.

If an EEPC in which the verb depicts an entity existing in a certain ground fades from it, then such a, EEPC is called a *fading EEPC*.

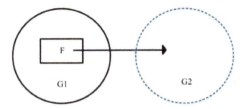

Figure 4.3: Schematic diagram of the dynamic fading of EEPC

Figure 4.3 illustrates a cognitive process in which an entity (F) exists in a ground (G1) then moves out of it and fades into an implied ground (G2). For example: "There disappears the subordination of the artist to local and national narrowness."

4.2. The cognitive model of the interaction between the EEPC and the mental representation

In the thesis, the EEPC is a construction indicating existence and presence guided by *there*, that is, *There + BE/V +NP (+ PP)*. The semantics of existential verbs opens one or more grounds, namely, the actual ground and the implicit ground. In the thesis, it is argued that both *There* and *PP* denote the existential place, and their semantics enrich the content of grounds, which sometimes overlap. In the mental representation of EEPC, the interaction between the components is mainly reflected as follows: On the one hand, the interaction between existential place and existential verbs forms the grounds of EEPC; on the other hand, the formed grounds reflect how the existential subject exists and completes the relationship between existential subjects and existential place. For example: "There exists a freedom of religion clause in the constituent."

According to the item "exist," it is not difficult to understand that the whole EEPC sentence represents a statistic cognitive mental representation. "There" and the phrase "in the constituent" are in a co-reference relationship and together form the ground of the whole sentence. As to the relationship with the existential subject, it can be analyzed that the existential subject "a freedom of religion" exists statically in the ground.

In the process of forming an EEPC, the interaction between the linguistic EEPC and the mental representation formed on the basis of the figure-ground theory is mainly reflected in the fact that, on the one hand, the linguistic EEPC coerces the mental representation and makes it conditional for access, and on the other hand, the allotment relationship between the existential subject and existential place in the mental representation provides the constructional meaning. The main motivation for the linguistic constructional coercion of mental representations is that when linguistic communication is generated, linguistic constructions can assimilate components that are essentially compatible but differ in some aspects, so that they conform to the semantic needs of the construction by means of apposition and variation, which results in constructional coercion (Shi 2015).

Linguistic EEPC must activate and invoke specific mental representations and make them conform to the requirements of constructions as components for forming EEPC.

In linguistic descriptions, the figure-ground is a cognitive structure or cognitive model in which the figure is the object to be described, which is more cognitively salient, and the ground is its environment, which is less cognitively salient. Sentences in human language are usually arranged in a certain order, and the linear feature makes the symbolic arrangement appear in chronological order. In terms of syntax, the subject is the realization of the figure in the language; the object or complement is the realization of the ground in the language, and the predicate is the intermediate link used to represent the relationship between the two. Therefore, "Figure–Intermediate link–Ground" is the cognitive schema of natural order sentences. However, in the EEPC, the natural order is changed and the ground is placed at the beginning of the sentence, forming the order of "Ground—Intermediate link—Figure." Moreover, in the dynamic temporal frame, it is the ground in which the figure is supposed to act (i.e., the FVG structure, e.g., "A teacher comes there."), but its syntactic structure is reversed (i.e., the GVF structure, "There comes a teacher"), which also seems to violate the temporal configuration. It means that the EEPC coerces its temporal frame, forcing its temporal configuration and degree of prominence to change in order to conform to the constructional features as in the following sentence: (5) "Look! There comes a bus!"

"A bus" seems to be the existential subject of the whole sentence and surely the focus of EEPC. Human beings tend to pay attention to the focus, which means that "a bus" should be noticed at the first time and placed at the beginning of the sentence as a subject, which makes "A bus comes there" in the order that should have been. However, the EEPC coerces its temporal frame, forcing it to adapt to the constructional features.

Not only does the EEPC coerce its mental representation, but the relationship between the components of that mental representation also provides a constructional meaning for the EEPC, thus creating an interaction between the construction and the mental representation. The constructional meaning of the EEPC reflects a meaning of "prominence" that does not come from the constituents of the construction. The thesis argues that the constructional meaning is formed by the inverted collocation relationship between the existential place *there* and the existential subject. That is to say, the existential place is in the subject position of the basic sentence pattern, while the existential subject is in the object position. In the conventional case, the existential subject is placed at the beginning of the sentence as a figure with prominence. However, in the EEPC, the existential place appears first in the sentence as the known information, and then the unknown information (the existential subject) is introduced. As in the above example, because of the reversed allotment, the existential subject "A bus" becomes more prominent for people to notice.

In summary, the study has constructed a cognitive model of the EEPC as follows:

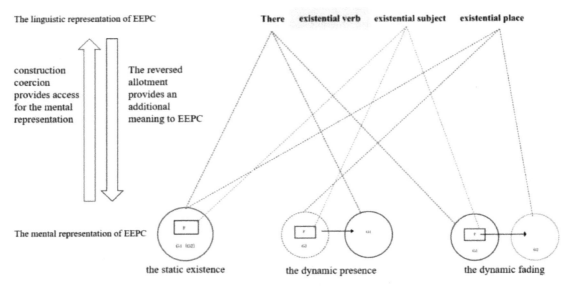

Figure 4.4 A cognitive model of the interaction between the EEPC and the mental representation

In figure 4.4, the existential verb triggers three kinds of mental representations. When the existential verb expresses the meaning of static existence, "There" (connected with G1 by the red line) and existential place (connected with G2 by the blue line) coincide and cooperate to form the ground. And the existential subject becomes the figure (connected by the green line). When the existential verb expresses the meaning of dynamic presence, "There" forms G1; the existential place forms G2; and the existential subject forms the figure. They jointly show a process of occurrence. When the existential verbs mean "something disappears from somewhere," "There," the existential place and the existential subject represent G1, G2 and figure, respectively.

5. Major findings

The basic concepts, forms, semantics and functions of EEPC have been explored and discussed from different theoretical perspectives, which have enriched the observation of EEPC to some extent and provided worthwhile research ideas.

The present study takes a small step forward from the previous studies by examining EEPC and drawing two main conclusions.

The interaction between EEPC and mental representations in the process of forming EEPC is mainly manifested in the following ways. On the one hand, the linguistic EEPC coerces mental representations and makes them gain access. The EEPC produces constructional coercion and changes the cognitive schema of the natural sequence of "Figure—Intermediate—Ground" by placing the ground at the beginning of the sentence and forming the sequence of "Ground—Intermediate— Figure." This means that the EEPC coerces the sentence's mental representations, forcing its temporal configuration and degree of prominence to change in order to conform to the constructional features. On the other hand, the inverted allotment of the existential subject and the existential place in this mental representation also provides a constructional meaning for this construction that indicates "prominence on the subject." This constructional meaning is not derived from the constituents of the construction and reflects that "the semantics of the whole is greater than the sum of its parts." According to Shi (2016), it is important to further explore the reasons for the "greater than" in construction grammar. The present study argues that the constructional meaning is formed by the inverted collocation relationship between the existential place *there* and the existential subject; i.e., the existential place is in the subject position of the basic sentence type, while the existential subject is in the object position. In the conventional case, the existential subject is placed at the beginning of the sentence as a figure with prominence. However, in the EEPC, the existential place appears first in the sentence as the known information, and then the unknown information (the existential subject) is introduced.

6. Conclusion

The study of constructions is a top-down approach, along which we can unify the holistic and extended features of constructions under the concept of constructions. At the same time, examining the form and semantics of its components from the constructions can provide a more detailed examination of the prototypical and extended meanings of the constructions. The research findings may offer new perspectives on the syntactic, semantic, and pragmatic functions of the EEPC and can possibly obtain some future research attempts based on linguistic facts that have not been the focus of previous studies. These findings have some implications for further research and teaching of English syntax.

Nevertheless, the study still has some research limitations which need to be improved in further study. For example, the mental representation of EEPC in the study is still in hypothesis, and the interrelationship between language and mind still needs to be further explored through empirical studies, laying a solid foundation for future interdisciplinary and multidisciplinary research.

Funding

*The research has been funded by the teaching reform and research project "Exploring Curriculum Design of Advanced Academic English Writing Based on the Theory of the Content and Language Integrated Learning."

References

Birner, Betty J. and Gregory W. 1998. *Information Status and Noncanonical Word Order in English*. Amsterdam: John Benjamins Publishing Company.

Cao, Y. and Wen, X. 2022. "Representations and Cognitive Features of Existential Sentence in Chinese Sign Language". *Foreign Languages and Literature*, 38 (02):31-41.

Hannay, M. 1985. *English Existentials in Functional Grammar*. Dordrecht: Foris Publications Holland.

Huddleston, R. and Geoffrey P. 2002. *The Cambridge Grammar of the English Language*. Cambridge: Cambridge University Press.

Lakoff, G. 1987. *Women, Fire and Dangerous Things: What Categories Reveal about the Mind*. Chicago: The University of Chicago Press.

Liu, Y., Luo, J. and Wu, F. 2021. "The Construction of the Cognitive Model of the Syntactic-semantic Mismatched Resultative Constructions: From the perspective of the interaction Construction Grammar". *Foreign Language Education* 42 (06):60-66.

Liu, Y, and Wang, Z. 2005."Factual Representation, Psychological Representation and Linguistic Representation". *Journal of Xiangtan University (Philosophy and Social Sciences)*, 29 (01): 147-150.

Lumsden, M. 1988. *Existential Sentences: Their Structure and Meaning*. London: Croom Helm.

McNally, L. 1997. *A Semantics for the English Existential Construction*. New York: Garland Press.

Milsark, G. 1977. "Toward an Explanation of Certain Peculiarities of the Existential Construction in English." *Linguistic Analysis*, 3: 1-29.

Quirk, R., et al. 1985. *A Comprehensive Grammar of the English Language*. London: Longman.

Hou, W. 2021. "A Study on Chinese Wh-Conditional Construction and Its Constructionalization." *Journal of Tongji University (Social Science Edition)*, 32.04 (2021): 90-99.

Shi, C. 2015. "Linguistic Value on the Analysis of Construction Coercion." *Contemporary Rhetoric*, 02 (2015): 12-28.

Shi, C. 2016. "Rationales and Research Path of Interactive Construction Grammar." *Contemporary Rhetoric*, 02 (2016): 12-29.

---- 2021. "The Basic Ideas of Construction Grammar." *Journal of Northeast Normal. University (Philosophy and Social Sciences)*, 04 (2021): 1-15.

Yang, L. and Xu, H. 2020. A Cross-Linguistic Comparison between Chinese and English Existential Verbs on the Interaction Between Event Types, Grammatical Aspect and Existential Construction." *Foreign Language and Their Teaching*, 01 (2020): 11-19+146.

Zhang, K. 2006. "English existential/Presentational Constructions Revisited: A Cognitive Approach." *Foreign Language and Literature*, 06 (2006): 60-64.

Zhang, K. 2009. "Chinese Existential Constructions from the Perspective of Figure-Ground Relations. *Foreign Language and Literature*, 05 (2009): 8-12.

A Cognitive Approach to the Syntactic Features and Semantic Functions of Chinese Noun Classifier *Tiao*

Qiuyi Huang
Sichuan University

Abstract

As one of the distinctive features that sets Chinese apart from other non-Sino-Tibetan languages, the system of the Chinese classifier represents the abundant Chinese culture and reflects the unique thinking patterns and cognitive processes of Chinese speakers. Based on the data collected from Beijing Language and Culture University Corpus Center (BCC Corpus), this paper, under the guidance of prototype theory, analyzes one of the most commonly used noun classifiers, *tiao* (条), in modern Chinese in terms of its syntactic features and semantic functions. This paper first provides an overview of previous studies on Chinese classifiers and *tiao*, the feasibility of prototype theory to reveal the underlying cognitive rationale behind *tiao*, and the source of data and statistical results. Then, by examining the distributional patterns of numerals and nouns in the "numeral-*tiao*-noun" structure, this paper discovers that among numerals, the frequency of specific numbers is much greater than that of approximate numbers. In general, the bigger the number is, the lower its frequency of occurrence; among nouns, concrete nouns are more frequent than abstract nouns. The most frequently used words are "lines and routes," which are the prototypical members of the *tiao* category. Then, this paper emphasizes and explains the categorizing function and quantifying function of *tiao* and further explains the cognitive basis for the above-mentioned syntactic features and semantic functions in light of prototype theory.

Keywords

prototype theory; Chinese classifier; *tiao*; syntactic features; semantic functions

1. Introduction

1.1. Research background

Through millennia of development, the system of Chinese classifiers is extensive and sophisticated, which distinguishes Chinese from other non-Sino-Tibetan languages. It is not only a gem of Chinese culture, but also an

---

Qiuyi Huang, College of Languages and Cultures Sichuan University, Chengdu, Sichuan Province, China. E-mail address: huangqiuyi4@gmail.com.

epitome of the cognitive method that Chinese speakers exert in perceiving the world. Classifiers originated in the Pre-Qin and Han dynasties, matured during the Northern and Southern dynasties, and were further promoted and developed during the New Culture Movement in the early 20th century (Dong, 2015: 134; Gao, 2020: 136). Though classifiers have enjoyed a long history as a part of the Chinese language, they were not considered as an independent category but as a subclass of nouns for a long time (Zhou, 2006: 49). It was not until the publication of Zhang Zhigong's *A Preliminary Outline of the Chinese Grammar System for Teaching* (《暂拟汉语教学语法系统简述》) in 1956 that they were finally established as a separate category (Gao, 2020: 137). Scholars then became aware of the special significance of classifiers and conducted extensive and in-depth research on them. To this day, classifiers remain the hotspot in Chinese linguistics.

1.2. Research significance

Theoretically, this study incorporates prototype theory into the research of Chinese classifiers, broadening its application scope and providing new research ideas for the study of Chinese classifiers. Practically, by conducting a cognitive analysis of the classifier *tiao*, this study can offer new teaching approaches for the instruction of Chinese classifiers.

1.2.1. Theoretical significance

Most studies on Chinese classifiers, both at home and abroad, have adopted a macroscopic approach to research the entire classifier system, or at least one type of classifier, to clarify the general development trend of classifiers. Research at the individual level on specific classifiers is exceptionally rare and thereby needs to be enriched urgently. Based on prototype theory, this study investigates the syntactic features and the semantic functions of the Chinese classifier *tiao* (条), which can further expand the scope of application of prototype theory on one hand and provide new ideas for the research of Chinese classifiers on the other.

1.2.2. Practical significance

The teaching of classifiers has always been one of the cruxes in Chinese language teaching for primary and secondary schools as well as for teaching Chinese as a foreign language. The collocations of classifiers and nouns seem to have no regularity and can only be explained as conventional. The root of this is the lack of clarification of the cognitive basis behind the use of classifiers as well as the neglect of cognitive differences in the grammaticalization of different classifiers. Although this study only involves one single classifier, the reproducibility of its research method allows other researchers to carry out research on other classifiers as well. Thus, cognitive reasons for the differences in the collocations can be found and new approaches for classifier teaching can be proposed.

1.3. Research object

Before being used as a classifier, *tiao* referred to the slender branch of a tree as a noun. It was discovered to be first used as a non-noun in the Eastern Han Dynasty and eventually developed into a classifier with fixed syntax and scope of usage in the Tang Dynasty. As a member of strip-based classifiers, *tiao*, compared with other analogous classifiers (*zhi* (枝), *gen* (根), and *lü* (缕)), enjoys a higher degree of usage in modern Chinese, hence possessing greater representativeness and research value.

The emergence of classifiers during the Pre-Qin and Han periods triggered the "noun-numeral-classifier" structure, which became the mainstream structure during the Wei-Jin, Northern, and Southern dynasties. During the Tang dynasty, influenced by the rule that modifiers in Chinese always precede the modified elements, numerals, together with classifiers, were placed before nouns, forming the "numeral-classifier-noun" structure, which gradually replaced the "noun-numeral-classifier" structure as the mainstream quantifying structure and has retained its popularity to this day. This study focuses on the "numeral-classifier-noun" structure of *tiao*, with no other structures involved.

1.4. Organization

The body of this research consists of four parts. Part one is a literature review, which summarizes the previous studies on the system of Chinese classifiers at large and the research on *tiao* in particular. Part two, the theoretical basis, briefly introduces the significance of category and prototype theory in cognitive linguistics and emphasizes the explanatory power of prototype theory and its feasibility in conjunction with the study of Chinese classifiers. Part three introduces the source of the research data, the collection and selection process, and the final data results. Followed by conclusions, Part four is a data-based discussion, which, based on prototype theory, expounds upon the distribution features of numerals and nouns in the "numeral-*tiao*-noun" structure and the categorizing function and quantifying function of *tiao*.

2. Literature review

Due to the lack of research on Chinese classifiers by foreign scholars, in lieu of categorizing previous studies according to their origins, this literature review categorizes them by research objects and divides them into two kinds: studies on Chinese classifiers and studies on *tiao*.

2.1. Studies on Chinese classifiers

2.1.1. Enumeration perspective

The first group of people to conduct research on Chinese classifiers were missionaries who came from Europe to China. To learn Chinese, they compiled manuals comprised of lists of commonly used classifiers and their respective usage. The earliest known study on classifiers was conducted by an Italian missionary named Martion Martini in 1653 (Gao, 2020: 136). Domestically, the enumeration stage began with *Ma's Grammar* (《马氏文通》) by Ma Jianzhong (1898), where he listed classifiers and their respective grammar, collocations, and scope of usage. Meanwhile, some scholars noted the close relationship between classifiers and nouns and have discussed the relationship between the two. Although scholars then only focused on enumerating classifiers, they pioneered the study of classifiers and laid a solid foundation for subsequent research.

2.1.2. Description perspective

The second stage, the description stage, started in 1956 with the establishment of classifiers as a separate category. Treatises on classifiers were written and published, Liu Shiru's *A Study on Chinese Classifiers in the Wei,*

Jin, Northern, and Southern Dynasties (《魏晋南北朝量词研究》) and He Jie's *A Study of Chinese Classifiers in Modern Chinese* (《现代汉语量词研究》) for example. At the same time, the rhetorical functions of classifiers were extensively discussed. For instance, in *Exploration of Chinese Grammar Rhetoric* (《汉语语法修辞新探》), Guo Shaoyu (1979) discussed in detail the rhetorical features of classifiers and pointed out their special role in counter-restricting nouns. Li Huixin (1994) discussed the unconventional use of classifiers by writers to achieve unique modifying effects. Researchers then did not confine themselves to enumerating classifiers but spotlighted the rhetorical function of classifiers, providing rich materials for subsequent research. Regretfully, their studies were nothing but linguistic facts, with no explanations being provided.

2.1.3. Explanation perspective

Stepping into the 21st century, the explanation stage began. Scholar James H.Y. Tai (1990, 1994), inspired by Allan (1977) as well as Adams and Conklin (1973), who attempted to incorporate cognitive and semantic theories into the study of classifiers, analyzed *tiao* (条) and *zhang* (张) from a semantic perspective and demonstrated that the classification and collocations of classifiers are not conventions but reflections of the cognitive categorization of Chinese speakers. Shao Jingmin (1993) proposed a semantic bidirectional selection principle to explain the selective-restrictive relationship between classifiers and nouns. This research was groundbreaking in that instead of depicting classifiers statically, it explored them within the dynamic relationship of classifiers and nouns. Then, with the rise of cognitive linguistics, grammaticalization theory, linguistic typology, and generative grammar, more and more scholars began to apply these theories to the study of classifiers, discussing different facets of classifiers from various perspectives. Shi Yuzhi (2001) conducted the earliest cognitive research on Chinese classifiers. By analyzing two-dimensional shape-based classifiers *tiao* and *zhang* (张) as well as three-dimensional shape-based classifiers *kuai* (块) and *pian* (片), she proposed that the primary cognitive foundation of shape-based classifiers is the proportion between dimensions, and materiality is the secondary. Zong Shouyun (2008, 2011, 2014) systematically analyzed Chinese classifiers from the perspective of prototype theory, regarding metaphors, metonymies, schema transformations, and fixed images as motivations for the categorization of Chinese classifiers.

For the grammaticalization of Chinese classifiers, there are generally two study approaches. The first one takes a macroscopic perspective to deduce the historical development pattern of the classifier system and explore the underlying reasons for grammaticalization. Key viewpoints include the quantifying function theory (Huang, 1964), which emphasizes that the quantifying function is the fundamental reason for the origin of classifiers; the individual marker theory (Jin and Chen, 2002; Zhang, 2012), which posits that the individual marker is the fundamental reason for the existence of classifiers in Chinese; and the categorization theory (Erbaugh, 1986), which contends that classifiers add quantitative information by categorizing the central nouns. The second approach focuses on the diachronic evolution of specific classifiers. For example, Li Xiaojun (2016) discussed the semantic evolution of the classifier *ge* (个) based on historical materials and dialect evidence. Chen Xianglan and Yu Hang (2018) used a diachronic corpus to explore the production and development process of the classifier *tao* (套). Currently, research on the generative grammar and construction of classifiers is burgeoning, such as the comparative study of "X *shuang/dui/fu* N" classifier constructions (Wang et al., 2022).

2.2. Studies on *tiao*

2.2.1. Studies using "tiao" as an example

As *tiao* is a commonly used classifier, it has been used as an example by many scholars. Shi Yuzhi (2001) introduced function Y/X (X is the longer side) to quantify the dimensional proportion of objects when analyzing the cognitive foundation of shape-based classifiers and argued that *tiao* is used to measure the object when its dimensional proportion approaches zero. Jin Fufen and Chen Guohua (2002) used *tiao* as an example when analyzing the grammaticalization of classifiers from the perspective of structural code adjustment and semantic evolution. Also, Luo Lin (2007) used *tiao* as an instance to explore the construction of metaphors in the collocations of noun classifiers and nouns.

2.2.2. Comparative studies of strip-shaped classifiers

This type of research focuses on the differences among strip-based classifiers. Zhou Shao and Shao Jingmin (2014) explored the effects of cognitive selection on the semantic divisions of *tiao*, *gen* (根), and *dao* (道). In order to find the cognitive foundation of the syntactic divisions of strip-shaped classifiers *tiao* (条), *zhi* (枝), *zhi* (支), *si* (丝), and *hao* (毫), Hou Ruilong (2010) interpreted the cognitive prototypes of them on the basis of imagery theory.

2.2.3. Studies on "tiao" in particular

The earliest research on *tiao* can be traced back to James H.Y. Tai and Wang Lianqing's semantic examination of the classifier (1990). They argued that the combination of individual classifiers and nouns is closely related to the dimensionality of objects, and the extension of objects in one, two, and three dimensions is the cognitive foundation of individual classifiers. And *tiao*, according to them, refers to strip-based objects that extend in one dimension. Meng Fansen (2009) analyzed the process of the emergence and historical evolution of *tiao* based on extensive linguistic data from a diachronic perspective, clarifying the path of *tiao* from a noun to a classifier.

Overall, after the stages of enumeration and description, with support from various linguistic theories, research on Chinese classifiers has become increasingly rich over the last twenty years. However, scholars have mostly taken a macroscopic perspective, attempting to fathom the rules behind the entire system of Chinese classifiers while neglecting the uniqueness of individual classifiers. Even when some scholars have approached the study of individual classifiers from a microscopic perspective, they have mostly focused on the historical evolution of them, with few exploring their usage in modern Chinese from a synchronic perspective. Based on this, using corpus as a foundation, this research studies the syntactic features and semantic functions of the classifier tiao in modern Chinese, so as to provide new insights for the study of Chinese classifiers.

3. Theoretical basis

The formation of human language can be roughly summarized as "reality – interactions – image schema – category – concept – meaning – language" (Wang, 2007: 171). From the selection of a single word in a practical communication scenario to the cognitive rules behind language formation, category, as a major component in language formation, has great explanatory power in all sorts of linguistic phenomena. The study of categories has thus become one of the main contents of cognitive linguistics.

The understanding of category and categorization can generally be divided into two major systems: the classical theory of categories and the prototype theory.

The classical theory holds that categories are constructed from a set of common features. Specifically, a category is a set with clear-cut boundaries, of which each member shares a certain feature and an equal status. But as scholars found that it fails to explain many phenomena in natural categories, such as language, prototype theory emerged.

Based on the family resemblance of Wittgenstein and the research on color words by Berlin and Kay, cognitive psychologist Eleanor Rosch (1973, 1975, 1978), through a series of experimental studies, proposed prototype theory, which later became a significant facet of cognitive psychology. The basic content of prototype theory is diametrically opposed to that of the classical view. Prototype theory holds that categories are not established through common features but through similar attributes. No clear-cut distinctions could be drawn among different categories, for they are developed upon a "cross-cutting network of similarities" (Wang, 2007: 119). As one of the founders of cognitive linguistics, Lakoff (1987), in his work *Women, Fire, and Dangerous Things*, extensively affirms the importance of categorization and prototype theory, thereby incorporating prototype theory as a fundamental part of cognitive linguistics.

Prototype theory has great explanatory power in explaining many language phenomena that classical category theory cannot, playing a pivotal role in both uncovering the cognitive processing in language use and exploring the basic cognitive rules behind language development. It can not only explain how humans establish categories based on interactions with the external world, but also, combined with cognitive theories such as metaphor, illuminates how human beings complicate concrete categories, form abstract categories, and ultimately form languages. Thus, by incorporating prototype theory into the analysis of the classifier *tiao*, new insights into the cognitive processes of *tiao* and the system of the Chinese classifier at large can be provided.

4. Data description

4.1. Source

The corpus used in this study is sourced from the Beijing Language and Culture University Corpus Center (BCC Corpus), which contains approximately 9.5 billion characters from various fields. It is a large-scale corpus that can comprehensively reflect the language used in modern Chinese.

4.2. Collection

To comprehensively analyze the usage of *tiao* in modern Chinese, this paper utilizes the multi-domain search function of the BCC corpus and searches for instances of "m 条 n" (where m represents a numeral and n represents a noun), resulting in 24,468 entries. With a threshold of 100, 167 entries are sifted. It is discovered that in some entries, *tiao* is not followed by a noun but by modifying elements inserted between it and the noun it modifies, such as "一条经济" (an economic) and "一条红色" (a red). After manually filtering out 14 invalid entries, 153 entries are finally selected (see appendix for details).

4.3. Results

After classification, a total of 12 numerals are found, including 9 specific numerals and 3 approximate numerals. Specific statistical results are shown in table 1.

Table 1. The distribution of numerals

Category	Numeral	Frequency	Total
Specific Numerals	一 (one)	44,693	
	两 (two)	16,178	
	三 (three)	1,465	
	四 (four)	734	
	五 (five)	576	
	九 (nine)	154	
	八 (eight)	135	64,042
	千 (thousand)	107	
Approximate Numerals	半 (half)	905	
	几 (several)	709	2,139
	整 (whole)	525	
Total			66,181

Regarding nouns, after collating the corpus, a total of 110 nouns are found (see appendix). They are then divided into two main categories: concrete nouns and abstract nouns. The former includes lines and routes, body parts, objects, animals, natural things, and humans, while the latter comprises abstract lines, messages, and lives. The specific results are presented in table 2.

Table 2. The distribution of nouns

Category	Word Class	Frequency	Total
Concrete Nouns	Lines and Routes	25,199	
	Body Parts	7,447	
	Objects	5,676	49,054
	Animals	4,635	
	Natural Things	3,393	
	Humans	2,704	
Abstract Nouns	Abstract Lines	7,467	
	Messages	5,600	17,127
	Lives	4,060	
Total			66,181

5. Discussion

5.1. The syntactic features of "tiao"

It is generally believed that there have been five changes in the quantifying structure of Chinese, which are referred to as the "numeral-noun" structure, the "noun-numeral" structure, the "noun-numeral-noun" structure, the "noun-numeral-classifier" structure, and the "numeral-classifier-noun" structure. In modern Chinese, classifiers are always used in conjunction with numerals and nouns, forming the "numeral-classifier-noun" structure. Analyzing the distributions of numerals and nouns when they collocate with *tiao* in the structure "numeral-classifier-noun" can clarify the development of *tiao* and the underlying cognitive basis.

5.1.1. The distribution of numerals

The statistical results in ***table 1*** show that: (1) among the numerals collocated with *tiao*, specific numbers (64042/66181=96.77%) far outweigh approximate numbers (2139/66181=3.23%). (2) The numeral "一" (one) has the highest frequency, accounting for 69.79% (44693/64042) of the specific numbers and 67.53% (44693/66182) of all numerals. (3) In general, for specific numbers, the larger the number, the lower its frequency.

Based on spatial understanding, the cognitive ability of human beings develops along a path from concrete to abstract. Humans in their infancy first encounter things that are discrete, tangible, and concrete, to which words are learned to refer. As their life experience expands, abstract concepts come into being, and as such, the vocabulary they have learned to refer to concrete objects progressively falls short of expressing themselves. In dealing with the scant vocabulary, more words are mastered in referring to both concrete and abstract concepts as more complex concrete categories and abstract categories gradually form synchronically.

The construction of the quantity category undoubtedly follows this pattern. When interacting with the external world, discrete and complete entities present human beings with exact numbers. Based on this, human beings first establish the natural number category and then use mathematical operation rules upon the center members (0 to 9), who are with generativity, to generate other members (Lakoff, 1987), eventually obtaining the entire number category, forming the concept of number and acquiring explicit numerical meanings. Within the center members, except for the negating zero, the smaller the number, the lower its information density, the shorter the cognition processing, and the higher its usage frequency among people. However, anomalies in the data can be observed that seem to contradict the aforementioned path of cognitive development. Data shows that the numeral "五" (five) is not followed by "六" (six) but by "九" (nine), which is then followed by "八" (eight) and "千" (thousand). Through the corpus (see appendix), it can be found that "九" (nine) only appears in the phrase "九条命" (nine lives), "八" (eight) in "八条规定" (eight regulations), and "千" (thousand) in "千条线" (a thousand of lines), all of which are fossilized linguistic units with fixed meanings due to frequent use.

Acquiring the natural number category is not the end of understanding the concept of quantity. As the cognitive level deepens and mindsets become more complex, human beings gradually realize that though specific numbers are very precise in expressing quantity, when a number gets too large, the information it contains undermines the effectiveness of cognitive processing. Therefore, driven by the cognitive economy, they expand the number category from the natural number category to the approximate number category, creating characters such as "几" (several) and "一些" (some) to represent approximate quantities.

To sum up, the quantity category is established on the basis of the natural number category and gradually expands to the approximate number category. The natural number category is at the center, while the approximate number category is at the periphery, explaining why the frequency of specific numbers is much higher than that of approximate numbers. Within the natural number category, the status is also unequal. By and large, the smaller the number, the closer it is to the center and the higher its frequency in usage.

5.1.2. The distribution of nouns

It can be seen from the statistics in ***table 2*** that: (1) *Tiao* has an extensive scope of modification; both concrete nouns and abstract nouns are within its stretch. (2) The frequency of concrete nouns (49054/66181=74.12%) is higher than that of abstract nouns (17127/66181=25.88%). (3) The most frequently used words among both concrete and abstract nouns are "lines and routes." (4) There are no plant nouns that appear.

Categorization is based on prototypes and built up through family resemblance, so there must be some similarities among the members of the *tiao* category even though they seem to be diverse and have nothing in common. Some scholars have already explained this issue. Based on a large amount of literature, Meng Fansen (2009) argued that *tiao* was grammaticalized on two bases, one on its original meaning as "thin branches," and another on its derivative meaning of "regulations." Following the first path, *tiao* was grammaticalized as a classifier that can be used to modify entities with the attribute of "strip," spanning through different categories like fabrics, animals, and people. In the second path, *tiao* was endowed with the ability to modify legal terms, informational events, and texts. Jin Fufen and Chen Guohua (2002), however, held different opinions. They argued that the function of *tiao* modifying abstract nouns such as laws and texts came not from its derivative meaning as "regulations" but from its metaphorical sense of "writing." On top of these, Zhou Shao and Shao Jingmin (2014) believed that regardless of whether they are abstract or concrete, the nouns modified by *tiao* all possess the attribute of "one-dimensional extension" in space or time, which is the result of spatial-temporal metaphor.

Albeit there are differences in the specifics, these views unanimously follow the absolute paths and relative paths for classifiers' categorization proposed by Zong Shouyun (2011). Motivated by metaphors, metonymies, and fixed images, the categorization of most noun classifiers follows the path that it proceeds from central members, most of which are concrete nouns, and extends gradually to abstract nouns in the margin (Zong). This tendency explains why the frequencies of concrete nouns are higher than that of abstract nouns in the nouns that collocate with *tiao* and provides hints in finding similarities between seemingly unrelated word classes. Concrete nouns such as "街道" (street), "河流" (river), "胳膊" (arm), "围巾" (scarf), and "鱼" (fish), all evoke a linear, elongated image. Among abstract nouns, "信息" (message) and "法律" (law) can be regarded as chains of text, "经验" (experience) as streams of words (Ma), and "人命" (human life) as a long linear object along the time axis. They all possess the attribute of "strip," either in a concrete or abstract sense, which is the very reason why they are categorized into the *tiao* category.

This regularity, however, cannot explain the results reflected in 3 and 4. The original meaning of *tiao* is "slender branch," thus its earliest use as a classifier should be to modify nouns about plants. Therefore, plant nouns should have been at the center of the *tiao* category and should have had the highest usage frequency. But the data shows that the most frequently modified nouns by *tiao* are nouns about "lines and routes," in both concrete and abstract noun categories, while plant nouns are absent from the collected corpus. To explain this phenomenon, it is necessary to not only focus on the *tiao* category itself but also analyze it within the entire system of noun classifiers.

Prototype theory posits that, based on the interaction between human beings and the objective world, categories are subjective abstractions made by cognitive subjects regarding the attributes of external objects (Wang, 2007: 91). Categories are not immutable and will change as the subject's cognition deepens or as the objective world changes. New members may join a category as old members leave, and prototypical members who were once at the center of a category may become marginalized while marginal members may gradually become central. When viewed in conjunction with 3 and 4, it can be seen that plant nouns were originally at the center of the *tiao* category, but "lines and routes" later overtook them, replacing them as the central members of the *tiao* category.

Internally, at the outset of *tiao* as a classifier, plant nouns were the closest to *tiao* semantically and were at the center of the *tiao* category. It was, however, not the cognitive model (CM) "part of a tree" but the CM "strip" was emphasized as *tiao* was grammaticalized, the latter of which was thence retained as the basic semantic meaning of *tiao*. After *tiao* became a classifier, "lines and routes" got the upper hand over plant nouns, best fitting the prototype of the *tiao* category. Externally, due to the higher degree of abstraction and greater extension capability of *tiao*, its semantic differentiation is not clear. As a result, though having a wider range of applications in a macro sense, *tiao* lost its competitiveness in certain specific noun categories. When modifying plant nouns, instead of choosing *tiao*, people prefer to choose more precise and directional classifiers such as "*ke*" (棵) and "*zhu*" (株). Under the joint influence of internal and external factors, nouns of "lines and routes" gradually replaced plant nouns as the central members of the *tiao* category, while plant nouns were marginalized to the point of exiting the category.

5.2. The semantic functions of "tiao"

As a type of functional word, a classifier undoubtedly has its semantic functions. It is generally agreed that classifiers have more than one semantic function, yet scholars hold different views on which function is the primary one. Erbaugh (1986) believed that classifiers serve the function of adding information to central nouns to classify and categorize them. Li Ruohui (2000) regarded classifiers as the combined result of modification and semantic representation. Meanwhile, some scholars hold the opinion that the function of classifiers is similar to that of measurements: to quantify the nouns. Based on corpus data, this study believes that *tiao* has two functions: the categorizing function and the quantifying function.

5.2.1. The categorizing function of "tiao"

Regardless of concrete or abstract nouns, the nouns modified by *tiao* all possess the attribute of "strip." Therefore, the basic function of *tiao* is to utilize the CM of "strip" to categorize nouns with this attribute into the *tiao* category.

The ability of categorization is not fixed but fluctuates in the presence of different nouns. First, not all nouns with the same attribute will be included in the same category, for that a noun (a concept) corresponds to not a single attribute but many. A concept is essentially an idealized cognitive model (ICM) that is constructed through multiple cognitive models, each of which correlates with one attribute. So a concept can be seen as an aggregation of multiple attributes. The multiplicity of attributes leads to a bi-selectional relationship between nouns and noun classifiers and a competitive relationship among classifiers. In the complex dynamic selection network, noun classifiers attract nouns that possess their basic semantics while nouns are doing the same. Not until they find the best match will the course of selecting terminate. For instance, "笔" (pen) is eligible to be categorized into the *tiao* category, but "一枝/支笔" (a pen) is the preferred expression. It is because that, though *tiao*, to some extent, can manifest the attribute "strip" of "pen," it is overshadowed in the presence of *zhi* (枝/支) that has both the attribute of "strip" and "made of wood" that a pen possesses.

From the perspective of *tiao*, the closer the nouns are to the prototype of it, the less likely they are to be attracted by other classifiers, making them more easily to be categorized into the *tiao* category. As shown in **table 2**, among concrete nouns, *tiao* has the strongest categorizing ability over lines and routes, followed by body parts, items, animals, and finally, natural things and humans. The more complex the modified noun is, the more attributes it possesses and the higher the possibility of itsbeing included in other classifier categories, resulting in a weaker categorizing ability for *tiao* and a lower frequency of occurrence within the category.

If delving deeper, it will be found that the degree of *tiao*'s categorizing ability is also manifested in its ability to modify nouns at different levels of a specific noun category. Rosch and Mervis (1975) proposed that humans form categories at three levels: basic level, superordinate level, and subordinate level, among which the basic level, with the highest informativeness and practicality, relies on humans' fundamental perceptual abilities, thereby serving as the cornerstone for human understanding of the world and forming prototypes. Since *tiao* has the strongest categorizing ability over "lines and routes," it can not only quantify various types of "lines and routes" at the basic level ("一条红线" [a red line], "一条丝线" [a thread] etc.) but can also quantify the concept of "line" itself ("一条线" [a line]), which is at the superordinate level. In the meantime, for nouns with relatively weak categorizing ability, *tiao* can only modify concepts at the basic level of the category. For example, for the "animal" category, *tiao* not only cannot modify the superordinate concept "animal" (when we say "一条动物" [an animal], we are not using *tiao* to modify the noun "animal" per se, but have limited "animal" to certain species), but also has limited ability in categorizing the concepts at the basic level, where only a few concepts, such as "狗" (dog), "鱼" (fish), "虫" (worm or insect), and "蛇" (snake), can be modified.

5.2.2. The quantifying function of "tiao"

According to Yasuhiro Okochi (1993), the semantic meaning of nouns in Chinese is non-countable. In order to achieve counting, it is necessary to first quantify the substance into discrete individuals, and this is where the noun classifier plays the role of quantifying the central nouns. It should be noted that the quantifying function here does not mean to express a specific amount but rather refers to the way the quantity category is acquired. Shao Jingmin (1993) believed that a classifier, in its essence, is the result of people observing things from different perspectives. For example, both "一条虫" (a worm) and "一只虫" (an insect) are correct expressions, but they exhibit different psychological impressions. "一条虫" focuses on the exterior shape of a "虫," so when hearing this expression, the image that comes to mind tends to be a centipede or a worm. On the other hand, "一只虫" compared with *tiao zhi* (只) takes a more comprehensive perspective in observing "虫" and emphasizes the "虫"

itself, giving hearers a psychological impression that would lean toward beetles or other analogous insects. Hence, when *tiao* is used to quantify a noun, it indicates that the noun is quantified from the perspective of highlighting its attribute of "strip."

Some may use classifiers like *shuang* (双) or *qun* (群) to rebut the above-mentioned view, claiming that classifiers themselves have the function of quantifying the nouns. It is true that shuang or qun, to a certain extent, include quantitative information, either specific or approximate, at their basic semantic meaning. Nevertheless, this information still only indicates how human beings obtain the quantity category and cannot take over the quantifying function of numerals. Shuang, though it includes the quantity information of "two," only implies that the noun being modified by it has to have the attribute of "paired." When expressing a specific quantity, numerals are still in need. ("两双手套" [two pairs of gloves] is the correct expression when there are two pairs of gloves.) The same is true for *qun*.

Another ostensibly convincing objection is the sentence "这有条蛇." (There is a snake.) No numeral appears in this sentence, but the quantitative information "一" (one) can still be comprehended. Does this not show that *tiao* itself has its quantifying function and can independently endow the nouns with a specific number? To disprove this argument, the following three sets of examples are presented.

(1) a. 这里有蛇
    zhe li you she
    "There are snakes."

    b. 这里有一条蛇
    zhe li you yi *tiao* she
    there is a-classifier snake
    "There is a snake."

    c. 这里有一蛇*
    zhe li you yi she*
    "There is a snake."

    d. 这里有条蛇
    zhe li you *tiao* she
    there is-classifier snake
    "There is a snake."

(2) a. 这里有蛇
    zhe li you she
    "There are snakes."

    b. 这里有两条蛇
    zhe li you liang *tiao* she
    there are two-classifier snake
    "There are two snakes."

    c. 这里有两蛇*
    zhe li you liang she*
    "There are two snakes."

    d. ?

(3) a. 这里有蛇
    zhe li you she
    "There are snakes."

    b. 这里有 m 条蛇 (m stands for numerals)
    zhe li you m *tiao* she
    there are m-classifier snake
    "There are m snakes."

    c. 这里有 m 蛇*
    zhe li you m she*
    "There are m snakes."

    d. ?

In the first set of examples, neither numeral nor classifier appeared in a, and no quantitative information can be obtained from it. Examples b, c, and d in the first set all convey the quantity "one," but through different means: b includes both a numeral and a classifier, c only has a numeral, and d only has a classifier. Compared with c, d is more consistent with the syntactic rules. In light of the analysis above, it seems that *tiao* itself carries the quantitative information of "one," while the numeral "一" (one) is a reiteration of this information. However, when switching the number from "一" (one) to "两" (two) (as a–d in the second set), it can be seen that even though c does not strictly fit the syntactic rules, it still conveys the information of "两" (two). Yet with solely the classifier *tiao*, such a sentence cannot even be constructed (as in d), not to mention conveying the concept of "两" (two). The same is true for other numerals (as a–d in the third set). The sentence "这里有条蛇" is essentially an abbreviated form of "这里有（一）条蛇." The quantitative information "一" (one) is automatically added, as it is located at the very center of the numerical category and has been internalized as a latent component in cognitive processing.

In summary, *tiao* itself does not carry any quantitative information. Its quantifying function is not to designate a specific quantity to the noun, which is the function of numerals, but to indicate how the quantity category is acquired.

6. Conclusion

Based on the previous discussion, it can be inferred that with respect to syntactic features, with regard to numerals, the vast majority of numerals that collocate with tiao are specific numbers, with their frequency of occurrence roughly inversely proportional to their value. However, some numerals have relatively higher frequencies of occurrences due to being used in fixed collocations. With respect to the nouns modified by tiao, they cover a wide range, with concrete nouns more common than abstract nouns, and "line and routes" having the highest frequency of occurrence. In terms of semantic function, tiao has functions to categorize and quantify the nouns it modifies. Its categorizing function fluctuates with changes in the type of noun, with its ability to categorize nouns closest to the prototype being the strongest. Its quantifying function does not assign a specific quantity to the central noun, but rather implies the cognitive pathway for the modified noun to acquire a quantity category. Amenable to prototype theory, above-mentioned linguistic phenomena are then dissected cognitively, with the unique cognitive strategies of Chinese speakers in perceiving the world being revealed and insights into a corner of the seemingly disorganized yet essentially coordinated system of Chinese classifier provided. Limitations and inadequacies of this paper are supposed to be pointed out. Firstly, the corpus used in this study may not be comprehensive enough, thus lacking representativeness. Secondly, the limited academic proficiency of the author leads to a less-than-optimal fit between the theory employed and the research subject, resulting in some linguistic phenomena observed in the corpus being unexplained. In addition, tiao is just one type of classifier within the vast system, and extending the cognitive basis behind it to the entire classifier system may result in biases.

More synchronic research is needed to enrich the study of the cognitive foundation of classifiers. It is hoped that future scholars, in conducting research on Chinese classifiers, can expand their corpus to increase its representativeness and integrate theory with research objects more closely, thereby providing new research perspectives for the study of Chinese classifiers.

References

Adams K.L. and Conklin N.F. 1977. "Towards a Theory of Natural Classification." *Proceedings from the Annual Meeting of the Chicago Linguistic Society*, 1: 1-10.

Allan K, 1977. "Classifiers." *Language*, 2: 285-311.

Chen X. and Yu H. 2018. "A Diachronic-Corpus-Based Study of the Evolution and Underlying Metonymic Mechanism of the Chinese Classifier Tao." *Technology Enhanced Foreign Language Education*, 3: 26-32.

Dong Z. and Li Y. 2015. "On the Chinese Quantifiers." *Academic Exploration*, 9: 134-137.

Erbaugh M. 1986. *Talking Stock: The Development of Chinese Noun Classifier Historically and in Young Children*. Amsterdam: John Benjamins Publishing Company.

Gao Y. and Liu H. 2020. "The Research Trend and Exploration Space of Chinese Classifiers." *Journal of Liaoning University (Philosophy and Social Sciences)*, 2: 136-142.

Guo S. 1979. *Exploration of Chinese Grammar Rhetoric*. Beijing: The Commercial Press.

Huang Z. 1964. "Examination of the Origin and Development of Chinese Classifiers from the Application of Classifiers in Oracle Bone Scripts and Chinese Bronze Inscriptions." *Studies of the Chinese Language*, 6: 432-441.

Hou R. 2010. "On the Syntactic Cognitive Basis of 'Strip-Based' Classifiers—A Case Study Series on Teaching Chinese Classifiers to Foreigners V. "*Journal of Zhenzhou University (Philosophy and Social Sciences)*, 6: 126-128.

Jin F. and Chen G. 2002. "On Grammaticalization of Chinese Classifiers." *Journal of Tsinghua University (Philosophy and Social Sciences)*, S1: 8-14.

Lakoff G. 1987. *Women, Fire, and Dangerous Things: What Categories Reveal about the Mind*. Chicago: The University of Chicago Press.

Li H. 1994. "On the Superlative Collocation of Classifiers." *Language Teaching in Middle School*, 3: 40-41.

Li R. 2000. "A Probe into Classifiers in the Yin Dynasty" (殷). *Research in Ancient Chinese Language*, 2: 79-84.

Li X. 2016. "The Semantic Evolution Model of Quantifier 'Ge' in Chinese." *Linguistic Sciences*, 2: 150-164.

Luo L. 2007. Construction of Metaphorical Meaning in the Collocations of Chinese Classifiers." *Rhetoric Studies*, 4: 13-14.

Ma J (1898) *Ma's Grammar*. Beijing: The Commercial Press.

Meng F. 2009. The Emergence and Historical Evolution of Classifier Tiao." *Journal of Ningxia University (Humanities & Social Sciences Edition)*, 1: 35-40.

Rosch E. 1975. "Cognitive Representations of Semantic Categories." *Journal of Experimental Psychology*, 104: 192-233.

Rosch E. 1973. On the Internal Structure of Perceptual and Semantic Categories." In: Moore TE. (eds.) *Cognitive Development and the Acquisition of Language*. New York: Academic Press, pp.111-144.

Rosch E. 1978. "Principles of Categorization." In: Rosch E and Lloyd BB. (eds.) *Cognition and Categorization*. Hillsdale, N J: Erlbaum, pp.28-49.

Rosch E. and Mervis C.B. 1975. Family Resemblances: Studies in the Internal Structure of Categories." *Cognitive Psychology*, 7: 573-605.

Shao J. 1993. "The Study and Cognitive Explanation on the Mutual Selectivity of Classifier-Noun Combinations." *Studies of the Chinese Language*, 3: 28-32.

Shi Y. 2001. "The Cognitive Foundations of the Shape-Based Classifiers in Modern Chinese." *Language Teaching and Linguistic Studies*, 1: 34-41.

Tai J.H.Y. and Chao F. 1994. "A Semantic Study of the Classifier 'Zhang.'" *Journal of the Chinese Language Teachers Association*,

3: 67-78.

Tai J.H.Y and Wang L. 1990. "A Semantic Study of the Classifier 'Tiao.'" *Journal of the Chinese Language Teachers Association*, 1: 35-36.

Wang H., Qin X. and Yi X. 2022. An Empirical Comparative Study of the Intricate Categorization of 'X Shuang/Dui/Fu N' Classifier Constructions." *Journal of PLA University of Foreign Languages*, 4: 43-51.

Wang Y. 2007. *Cognitive Linguistics*, Shanghai: Shanghai Foreign Language Education Press.

Yasuhiro O. and Cui J. 1988. The Individualization Function of Classifiers." *Chinese Language Learning*, 6: 8-13.

Zhang C. 2012. *The Historical Evolution of Chinese Noun Classifiers in a Typological Perspective*, Beijing: Peking University Press.

Zhou S. 2006. "Explanation on Syntagmatic Regulations Research between Nouns and Classifiers." *Chinese Language Learning*, 1: 49-55.

Zhou S. and Shao J. 2014. "Dimensional Explanation and Combinational Mechanism of Classifiers 'Tiao(条), Gen(根), And Dao(道).'" *Language Teaching and Linguistic Studies*, 1: 81-88.

Zong S. 2008. On Semantic Choice Between Classifier and Adjunction in 'Num+Adj+Cl' Pattern. *Journal of Guangxi Normal University: Philosophy and Social Sciences Edition*, 5: 65-69.

Zong S. 2011. "The Path and Motivation of Classifiers' Categorization." *Journal of Shanghai Normal University (Philosophy & Social Sciences Edition)*, 3: 109-116.

Zong S. 2014. The Categorization Function and Its Hierarchical Sequence of Classifiers. *Journal of Shanghai Normal University (Philosophy & Social Sciences Edition)*, 1: 120-128.

Printed in the USA
CPSIA information can be obtained
at www.ICGtesting.com
LVHW062123170224
772039LV00039B/126